T0322393

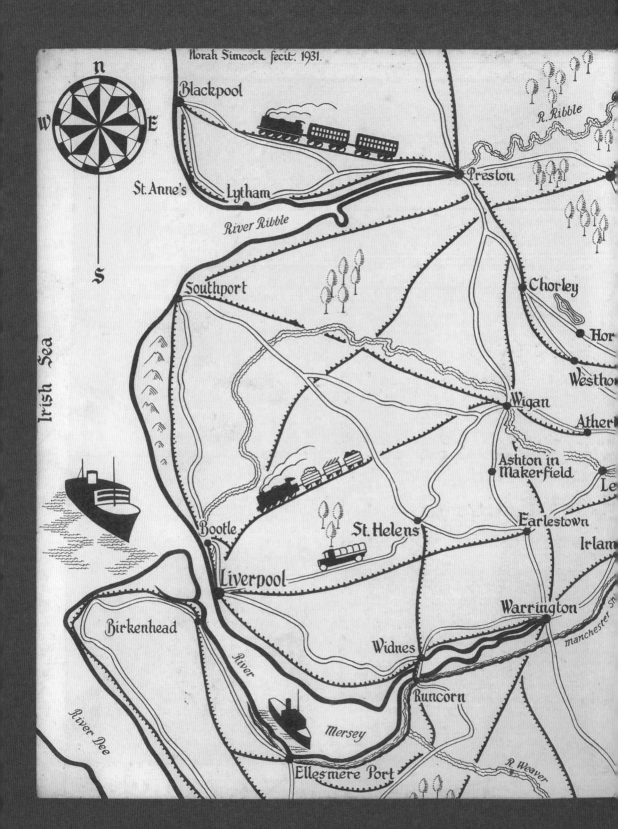

Industrial Towns Around Manchester, from the Manchester Chamber of *Commerce Handbook 1931–1932.* See p191.

Map of
Industrial Towns
around
Manchester

for Emma

First published Infang Publishing

This edition published 2022

The History Press
97 St George's Place, Cheltenham,
Gloucestershire, GL50 3QB
www.thehistorypress.co.uk

This book is set in Univers.
© Deodands Ltd, 2019, 2022.
Infang® and Infang Publishing® are registered trademarks
of Deodands Ltd, info@deodands.co.uk.

Despite diligent search It has been impossible to locate the copyright
owners of some material. The publishers will correct attribution errors in
future editions and at the supporting website for this book, which is:
www.manturing.net

British Library Cataloguing in Publication Data.
A catalogue record for this book is available from the British Library.

ISBN 978 0 7509 9994 6

Original print design by birthday: birthdaystudio.com
Printed in Turkey by İMAK

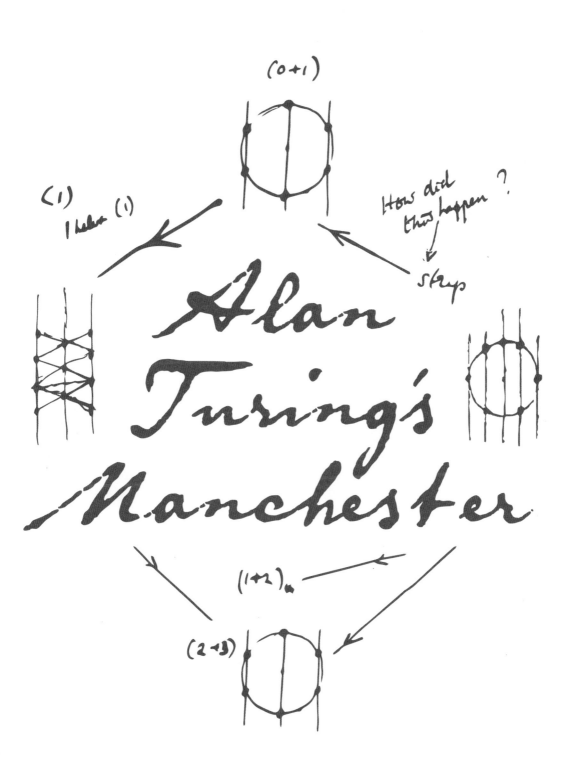

Jonathan Swinton

'Manchester is a good centre from which to watch the world'

The Guardian, on the day in 1959 it dropped the word *Manchester* from its title

'Manchester continues to attract the perverse gaze of the urban voyeur'

Peck and Ward, 2002

Contents

Foreword   5

Preface   7

Turing before Manchester   9

Manchester before Turing   13

Industrial Dismal   21

The Manchester Mindscape   31

Why Manchester?   53

The /////// at the Window   62

Manchester By the Sea   73

Is a Mathematician a Human?   79

The Festival of Manchester   97

Atoms and Whimsy   101

Is a Mathematician a Man?   115

On Growth and on Form   127

Playing, Learning and Working   145

Oxford Road Show   151

The Course of the Bee   163

Appendix: Turing's Biomathematics   170

Acknowledgements   172

Notes   173

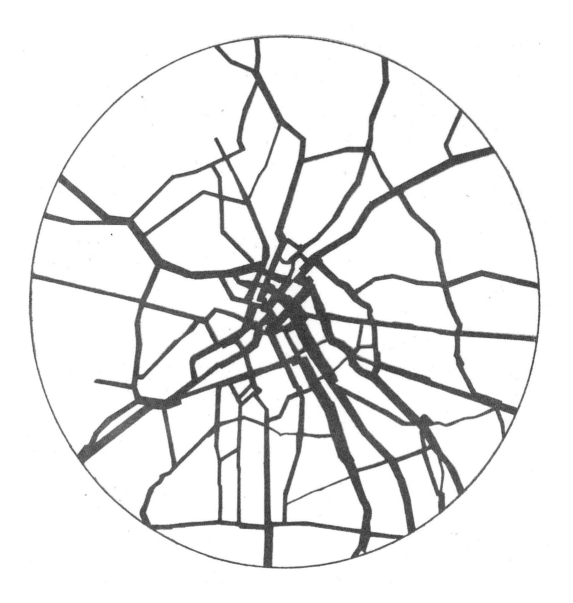

Figure 1. Central Manchester's road system from a 1947 plan.
Line thickness shows pre-war traffic density.

Cast

There are many names mentioned in this book; there's no need for the reader to keep track of most of them, but this is a list of those that recur. It gives the person's age during 1948, the year when Alan Turing arrived in Manchester aged 36, and the number of the page where they are **named in bold**. All except those marked NW have Wikipedia entries.

Bates, Audrey (age about 20) p119
Bernal, John Desmond (age 47) p105
Blackett, Costanza (NW, age 49) p32
Blackett, Patrick (age 51) p31
Bowden, Vivian (age 38) p145
Braithwaite, Richard (age 48) p94
Carlson, Kjell (NW, age unknown) p75
Cartwright, Mary (age 48) p46
Clarke, Joan (age 31) p46
Cunliffe, Mitzi (age 30) p110
Emmet, Dorothy (age 44) p87
Flowers, Tommy (age 43) p38
Hartree, Douglas (age 51) p50
Hush, Noel (age 24) p25
Irvine (Newman), Lyn (age 33) p43
Jefferson, Geoffrey (age 62) p80
Kermode, Frank (age 29) p28
Kilburn, Tom (age 27) p55
Lockspeiser, Ben (age 57) p57
Lovell, Bernard (age 35) p21
Megaw, Helen (age 41) p105
Newman, Max (age 51) p37

Nicolson, Phyllis (age 31) p118
Peierls, Rudolf (age 41) p24
Polanyi, John (age 19) p66
Polanyi, Michael (age 57) p87
Popplewell, Cicely (age 29) p119
Prinz, Dietrich (age 43) p148
Russell, Bertrand (age 66) p10
Rutherford, Ernest (died 1937) p31
Simon, Ernest (age 69) p18
Simon, Shena (age 61) p18
Strachey, Christopher (age 32) p146
Streat, Raymond (age 51) p57
Swirles, Bertha (age 45) p117
Thompson, D'Arcy (age 88) p127
Webb, Roy (NW, age about 36) p70
Wiener, Norbert (age 52) p79
Williams, Freddie (age 37) p53
Wittgenstein, Ludwig (age 59) p48
Woods, Mary Lee (age 24) p121
Wrinch, Dorothy (age 52) p130
Yule Bogue, James (NW, age 43) p18

Foreword

Alan Turing came to Manchester in 1948, 'stolen away' from the National Physical Laboratory by his lifelong mentor and friend M.H.A. (Max) Newman. Newman, who used that phrase, was perhaps being unfair about the process of recruiting Alan Turing into his nascent computing laboratory. The fact is that Alan Turing was frustrated at the NPL, by its bureaucracy, its lack of imagination, and above all by its inability to convert his design for a computer into an actual machine. Manchester, by contrast, was energetic, unconventional, and rather messy, just like Alan Turing himself. Manchester took Alan Turing by surprise. He fitted in.

Jonathan Swinton's book sets the scene into which Alan Turing arrived: crumbling in its heritage yet experiencing the massive transformation of the British economy which began at the end of the Second World War. The transformation was in part led by the technology being developed under Newman in what became the Royal Society Computing Machine Laboratory. It was no coincidence that Turing and Newman were, in turn, responsible for the two machine puzzle-solving projects which brought wartime codebreaking into era of computing. Now, in Manchester, the knowhow gained at Bletchley could be put to uses which everyone could discover and understand. Manchester was the home of the Electronic Brain.

But a codebreaking puzzle remained even after computers had become commonplace. Alan Turing's untimely death in 1954 meant that his last project, which was deciphering the mystery of how plants develop mathematical patterns, remained a work in progress. He drew the beautiful pictures to illustrate his forthcoming paper on the subject, but writing the paper was something he put off. The meaning of the Turing drawings remained one more of those coded secrets with which the final months of Alan Turing's life abound. Until, that is, the painstaking analysis by Jonathan Swinton brought their meaning into the light: it is through his research that we are able to understand and appreciate what Alan Turing was actually doing in his last years of research using the Manchester University computer as his collaborator.

Jonathan is highly qualified, as a mathematician working on problems in biology, to master this challenge and to describe what the Turing drawings mean. But, unlike the stereotypical maths professor, Jonathan has many interests and occupations beyond mathematics. His portrait of Manchester midway through the last century has a lightness of touch as well as wealth of incidental detail. I hope you will enjoy this book as much as I have.

Sir Dermot Turing, 2022

Preface

Alan Turing is a patron saint of Manchester, his face popping up in street art and heritage branding. Indeed, with the dignity of a civic celebrity, his name now marks the dual carriageway to the Velodrome. Turing was never quite forgotten after his tragic 1954 death, but only emerged as a public figure after 1983 when Andrew Hodges' passionate biography was published. There is a direct line from that book to a Hollywood film and more importantly to a change in English law, offering retrospective pardons to those convicted under now-obsolete sexual behaviour laws. But Hodges was a careful scholar and bears no responsibility for three myths also now in circulation: I exaggerate them, but not that far, if I say Turing is now remembered as the Mancunian who won the war, invented the computer, and was put to death for being gay. Each myth is related to a historical story. This not a book about the first story, of Turing at Bletchley Park. But it is about the second two, which each unfolded here in Manchester, of Turing's involvement in the world's first computer and of his refusal to be cowed about his sexuality. Turing provoked — intellectually and socially — and I was curious about how his chosen home rose to those provocations. Manchester can be proud of Turing, but can we be proud of the city he encountered?

So this is a book about the people one might have met in Turing's Manchester. It records the patronage of older men, triumphant from the successful prosecution of a scientific war, who could provide time to think and valves to think with; book-chats with a frustrated but sharply literary housewife and board-game sessions with young academic families; lunchtime speculations with the botanist hungry for a systematic biology and with the chemist refugee from totalitarianism who abhorred systematisation of science; the successful brain surgeon whose pomposity camouflaged unignorable fears; the proud inheritors of a local but world-class engineering tradition, still gruffly defensive about class; the younger men — and women — learning to become the first generation of hackers and futurists; the grammar schoolboy runner and, albeit on the margins of the historical record, the young working-class men of the Oxford Road cruising sites. There are marginal glimpses too of those one might not have met: the Special Branch bag searchers, the MI5 analysts, the GCHQ codebreakers.

This book leaves out some important parts of Turing's life, and indeed his most towering achievements, which were made away from Manchester. But what he did do in our city was enough in its own right to secure him, and us, a place in intellectual history. And Manchester was also where he was prosecuted for a sexual act which is today no crime. Twenty-seven months after his public guilt was pronounced, he was dead by his own hand.

Figure 2. Glazed tiling on the Palace Hotel, Oxford Road Manchester. The former Refuge Assurance building is close to where Alan Turing met Albert Murray in 1951.

Turing before Manchester

To understand Turing's time in Manchester, it is—unsurprisingly—essential to understand his class background. Alan Turing, son of a colonial civil servant, was conceived in India, born in London, and educated as a boarder at Sherborne School, a relatively prestigious public school in Dorset. He was securely part of an English upper middle-class culture that had no direct connection with northern or industrial Britain. One early sign of his departure from the norms of that culture was his preference at school for studying science, causing his teachers to regret: *'If he is to stay at a Public School, he must aim at becoming educated. If he is to be solely a Scientific Specialist, he is wasting his time at a Public School'.* [1]

Turing was already an able mathematician when he turned 18 in 1930. At that time, the University of Manchester was an institution which could well have made a first-rate scientific specialist out of him. In physics there was world-leading research taking place, and chemistry was not far behind. Manchester mathematics was thought less distinguished but the question did not arise: for the Turing family of Guildford it was geographically and socially obvious that Alan should go to Oxbridge. [2]

Alan indeed went as an undergraduate to King's College in Cambridge in 1931. [3] It was a time when the modernist cultural elite around the Cambridge Apostles and the Bloomsbury Group was—at least in hindsight—in an ascendancy, with what is now a famously relaxed attitude to the morals of wider society. His Cambridge was an institution where homosexuality, if kept obediently discreet, was not a bar to inclusion. [4] The subsequent involvement of some of the Apostles in Soviet espionage has drawn much wider attention to that particular tiny group. While the interwar Apostles now provide a convenient shorthand for a certain cultural moment, that secretive, all-male, society with no more than a handful of undergraduate members was perhaps not visibly significant at the time. Though Turing knew men who were Apostles and was considered for membership, he was not an Apostle and may not even have known of the group's existence. To Cambridge contemporaries, a much more visible arena was offered by the Heretics, a public debating society open to both sexes, partly born out of the atheist and pacifist debates at the end of the Great War, and which perhaps Turing and certainly a number of those around him attended.

After a slow start, Turing shone academically and quite soon after graduating he was appointed in 1935 to a prestigious Fellowship at King's, offering board, lodging and a comfortable stipend. It was as a graduate student that Turing attended the lectures of mathematician Max Newman, who would become the closest to a mentor that the independently minded Turing would ever have.

Figure 3. King's College Cambridge in a pre-war postcard.

It was from Newman that Turing heard about questions perplexing the more fundamentalist mathematicians of the time. In 1903 **Bertrand Russell** had published a book arguing that all of mathematics consisted only of making logical deductions from initial principles.[5] What are the limits of this mathematics? What does it mean to say we know how to find the answer to a question? A natural, if incomplete, modern response is to say that we can answer a mathematical question if we can program a computer to do it. But in the 1930s a computer was a woman who dutifully used a desk adding machine to multiply the numbers involved in ballistic trajectories. The modern response is unimaginable without the modern concept: the general-purpose computing machine. The computer is built of billions of logic gates made in silicon, which combine binary truths and falsehoods into new implications, with *ands* and *ors* and *exclusive-ors*. Russell, and the other logicians that Newman had learned from, already used the same logic gates, though built of mathematics, as the stuff from which human thought might emerge. But it took Turing's intuition to build a general *mechanism* for reasoning out of these parts. In 1935, Turing went away from Newman's lectures and, a full year later and without any further discussion, presented Newman with a paper that gives our best mathematical description of what a computer is: what we now call the Turing Machine. In later years, Newman described Turing as only averagely competent as a day-to-day mathematician — but that it was this idea in mathematical logic which propelled him into the international first rank of mathematicians.[6] It must have been a remarkable experience for Newman to be presented with this tour de force, and he remained Turing's champion for life.

Turing remained in Cambridge, apart from two years in Princeton, until the end of the decade. By 1939 he had been recruited for duty as a codebreaker at Bletchley Park.[7] After Turing's at first invisible and now famous war service helping to break the Enigma and other codes, he moved to the National Physical Laboratory in an abortive attempt to lead a computer project. The NPL in west London, together with the Universities in Manchester and Cambridge, emerged as three British centres, each separately competing with the Americans to build the world's first computer.[8] By 1947 it was obvious that the NPL would not finish in time to win that race, if at all. Amid bureaucratic fallout over the failure of the project, Turing retreated to Cambridge to take up a year of his King's Fellowship. Though he never lost his interest in practical electronics, back in Cambridge Turing concentrated on writing, thinking, and programming. In particular he took up the idea of the brain itself as a computer, perplexing contemporary neuroscientists with questions such as how many neurons the brain contained.[9] And it was during this year that Turing was offered a job, by Max Newman, who had preceded him to a Manchester whose industrial and scientific resources were ready to provide the next step.

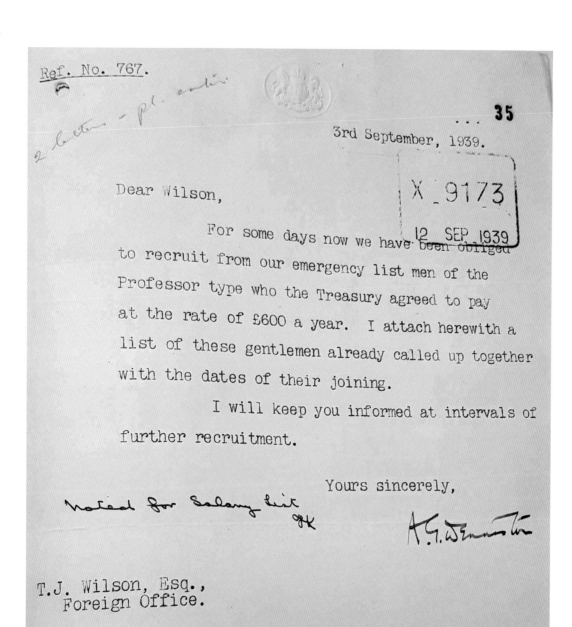

Ref. No. 767.

3rd September, 1939.

Dear Wilson,

X _ 9173

12 SEP 1939

For some days now we have been obliged to recruit from our emergency list men of the Professor type who the Treasury agreed to pay at the rate of £600 a year. I attach herewith a list of these gentlemen already called up together with the dates of their joining.

I will keep you informed at intervals of further recruitment.

Yours sincerely,

T.J. Wilson, Esq.,
    Foreign Office.

Figure 4. GCHQ requesting funds to pay the 'men of the Professor type', including Turing, it recruited for codebreaking duty at the outbreak of war.

Manchester before Turing

Manchester is irredeemably ugly...there are times when it seems...wrong-headed to call Manchester the centre of a civilisation. But it is.

AJP Taylor. [10]

You might think this was the end of the world, but we were very resilient. Manchester was the Athens of the North. 'What Manchester thinks today,' they said, 'London thinks tomorrow,' and it was indeed intellectually highly stimulating.

Noel Hush. [11]

Turing's Cambridge was a town dominated by its University, and dependent on education for the majority of its economic activity. By contrast, what was then the Victoria University of Manchester was a creation of its city, firmly under the control of local industrial wealth. It served to educate the sons and daughters of the local middle classes, and to provide a technical and managerial elite to the surrounding industry. But it also hosted fundamental physics, most extraordinarily Rutherford's 1917 splitting of the atom, and was much more than an institution for the provision of useful facts. Like the Central Reference Library and the Art Gallery, the University was a considerable source of civic pride, and world class research a visible fruit of the city's wealth. [12]

At the start of the Second World War, the majority of this wealth was still identified in the public mind with the cotton trade and the industrial engineering businesses that fed on it. Before the war foreign competition had significantly damaged trade and though war saw a temporary boost, cotton was in what is now evident as a terminal decline. But engineering had outgrown cotton, and the decades before the war had seen the development of relatively new, American-facing industries, symbolised by the vast Metropolitan Vickers plant at Trafford Park. [13] When war came, these sites had been well placed to move to production for the wartime economy — Metro-Vicks churned out a thousand Lancaster bombers over the course of the war — and Manchester's distance from German airbases had partially protected it from the destruction wreaked on other cities. War drove innovation in Manchester's industrial base. Radar, for example, created both new technical expertise and an industrial infrastructure for the mass production of electrical and electronic components.

Figure 5. ICI was primarily a bulk chemical company, whose Manchester branch diversified into pharmaceuticals in the 1930s. Along with Britain's other hi-tech companies, ICI advertised in the 1951 Festival of Britain Exhibition of Science programme.

NOW for reconstruction

FOR six long years the great factories and foundries of Metropolitan-Vickers were geared for war; their many thousands of workpeople laboured to produce "the tools to finish the job" and now that job is finished; but there is another battle to be waged—the great reconstruction of homes, of industries, of trade—both home and abroad, and the rehabilitation of millions of our men and women. In this enormous task, the same vast production capacity which made the 'tools to win the war' will make the 'tools to win the peace' . . . in the form of the finest Electrical Power Equipment in the world.

METROPOLITAN Vickers

ELECTRICAL   CO., LTD.
TRAFFORD PARK ··· MANCHESTER 17.

AX/A604

The British Trade Journal & Export World   *SEPTEMBER* 1946

Figure 6. Metropolitan Vickers was the largest of Manchester's engineering firms. Though in peacetime primarily an electrical company, in war it had produced the Manchester and Lancaster bombers in large numbers. This futuristic post-war landscape of 1946 recalls the imagery of the Manchester City Plan and other planning dreams of the time.

Figure 7. Metropolitan Vickers' actual home in 1947 was in low, red-brick factory
buildings set in the huge, partly developed and semi-planned industrial estate of
Trafford Park. The centre block was used in wartime for the assembly of Lancasters.
The site that ICI used for penicillin fermentation is on the far left, just above the
Bridgewater Canal.

Pre-war, the family-owned Ferranti firm had established a 'brown-goods' factory at Moston, producing consumer radios and electric clocks. The corporate history records that Ferranti had moved from London to Manchester in 1896 in search of lower land prices for its heavy industrial plant, making transformers nearby at Hollinwood. But the availability of a workforce disciplined by the experience of the cotton mills must also have played a factor. The Moston factory worked on a conveyor-belt system strictly segregated by gender, with lower-paid women carrying out the assembly tasks.[14] This factory was profitably turned over to war work assembling the radar receivers that those thousand Lancasters and more demanded.

Cotton engineering continued to create new sectors even as the trade itself declined. An important spin-out had long been the dye trade, a sector which drove great innovation in chemistry, although not always locally. The First World War forcibly demonstrated that the organic chemistry expertise essential for explosives and fertiliser was dominantly German. After that war, German patents were simply taken over, and the occupying British Army had moved through the Rhine Valley with a specialist chemical mission to *'pinch everything they've got'.*[15] Then domestic technology development was promoted: banning imports, creating the chemical giant ICI via merger, and for the first time, offering state support for University research.[16]

Figure 8. Ethel Gabain's *Cathode Ray Tubes*. Lawrence Haward, director of the City Art Gallery, set up a scheme by which local companies commissioned artists to document their war work and then donated the pictures to the Gallery. Ferranti's plant at Moston made cathode-ray tubes for radar purposes during the war. After the war they returned to producing them for televisions.

A large nineteenth-century dyestuff works in Blackley, founded by a German Jewish migrant to make magenta, evolved as this local leadership in organic chemistry developed into a home for the ICI Dyestuffs Division. In the pre-war years this expertise evolved further into pharmaceuticals, and during the war, this fledgling section of ICI was instructed to replace and then improve German anti-malarial drugs. Eventually it created Paludrine, which arrived in time for the British to use during postcolonial fighting in Malaysia in 1948. ICI's chemical experience was also used for the wartime mass production of penicillin at Trafford Park.[17]

Blackley, enfolded in the Irk Valley just north of the city, today is a typical piece of Manchester's post-industrial landscape, with networks of EU-funded cycle paths threading through housing built by the mass housebuilders, with gardens and drives if little social housing. It's now a pleasant, sheltered valley for lovers to stroll in. But when the dyeworks stood there, the shelter meant few winds to disperse the fumes. One of the lead developers of the anti-malarial drugs remembered that the air killed the lab animals before the malaria could: *'You couldn't open the window for black smuts. It was like a Lowry picture, but it was convenient for the textile industry'*. The work to make new drugs had to be done somewhere much cleaner than toxic Blackley, even though ICI used for its tests the canaries bred for unmetaphorical use in the coal mines, and it wasn't

Figure 9. Rupert Shephard, *A Penicillin Factory: Girls Filling Bottles*, 1945.
A fermentation plant was used at ICI's Trafford Park to develop the mass production of penicillin.

just canaries at risk: one of the human co-developers of Paludrine died in a rail accident caused by Manchester fog.[18] So ICI opened a research station amid the green and relatively clean fields of Fulshaw Hall in Wilmslow. The North West had little pharmaceutical infrastructure to provide trained staff or specialist supplies, and so when ICI recruited an Oxford professor, **James Yule Bogue**, to lead the post-war drug discovery effort, Bogue immediately and unsurprisingly recommended relocating the research laboratories to somewhere back down in the golden triangle of Oxford, London and Cambridge. But Bogue was overruled by the head of the board — a Mancunian — and ICI settled for a site near Fulshaw Hall. This became Alderley Park, for decades the region's most important pharmaceutical research centre.[19] Bogue himself settled in Bowdon, where he was to become a friend of Turing's mentor Max Newman.[20]

In the food industry, Robert McDougall had been the local patriarch of a national milling and chemical concern, whose most visible Manchester legacy today is the Rank Hovis (McDougall) grain elevator behind the Imperial War Museum North. There were multiple fortunes to be made: a German engineer, Henry Gustav Simon, came to Manchester as a penniless refugee in 1860 and developed a flour rolling mill for the McDougalls. The fortune that Simon made from this invention in turn funded the building of the Physics Laboratory at the University. It was in a building funded from Simon's wealth that the atom would be split and the world's first computer program run. The family money also enabled the public service of his son **Ernest Simon** and Ernest's wife **Shena Simon**, who would both long be linked with Manchester City Council and with the University.[21]

Post-war Manchester, then, had declining industries but also growing ones. In 1949 military contracts were declining and Manchester's firms were trying to resume consumer production, but Ferranti, for example, found it hard to sell radios from its reopened Moston line because of the lack of consumer credit.[22] It would still be the defence budget, and the personal connections of the science war, that caused the great post-war innovation of the electronic computer to appear in Manchester. Creating that new technology meant recruiting another new generation of incomers, and at first they did not like what they saw.

Figure 10. ICI's pharmaceutical division library bookplate showed its heritage in the dyestuffs trade, and a certain pride in its highly industrial Blackley birthplace, even as it moved to a new, greenfield site in Alderley Park.

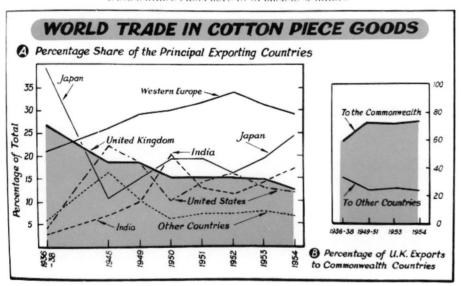

Figure 11. The war caused a temporary halt in the decline of the UK's cotton exports, but foreign competition rapidly recovered.

Industrial Dismal

There is a rich, coal-black seam of tales of arriving in Manchester. Today we read a blackened urban environment as a clear sign of economic decline, but around the time of the war, the recurrent first impression was not neglect but activity.

Civilian Manchester had not been untouched by the Second World War. As well as the death and injuries to family members directly engaged in fighting, and the privation of a war economy, bombing killed hundreds of people and left derelict sites in the centre of Manchester. [23] But as **Bernard Lovell**, later the creator of Jodrell Bank, almost lamented *'Manchester had been bombed* but by no means devastated. *In particular the dark grime-encrusted Victorian buildings of the University and the surrounding dreary slums had survived unscathed'*. [24] Independently of the Luftwaffe, Manchester's houses were simply falling down at the rate of two a day in 1944, a fifth of what still stood post-war was unfit for human habitation, and all was filthy. [25] A commuter from Altrincham arriving by train at Manchester Central, and seeking the University on the Oxford Road, would on their way pass slums intermingled with the municipal gas works and the coal-burning industry which penetrated into the centre of the city. Ernest Simon, a local cheerleader for post-war University expansion, frankly described it as in a *'blighted area, dirty and depressing'*. But we have to be careful not to jump too easily from the dirty into the dismal. The removal of soot from the London Road Fire Station was an annual ritual. The station had been built in 1906 by the Manchester Corporation with a façade of glazed terracotta specifically so that it could be cleaned in this way. A new arrival, as Turing was in 1949, emerging from Piccadilly Station, would see a modern building, sometimes dirty but proudly and expensively maintained. In 2017, the building was again filthy, this time as a consequence of a long period of private sector neglect; it took the combination of the public in the form of dogged legal action by the City Council and other private investment to clean it in that year. Today's visitor to Piccadilly can see a clean building too, but the implication of clean and dirty has changed. [26]

Sometimes the smut newcomers saw was vulgarity, such as when broadcaster Olive Shapley arrived at Piccadilly station in 1934 to *'a surprising number of advertisements for trusses'*. But much more often it is literal smut which is prominent in their memories: as in historian AJP Taylor's memoir of arriving in 1930 to a city *'very dirty, the buildings begrimed'*, or in Geoff Tootill's recollection of coming after the war to work on the computer, and noting the black marks settled on children's faces. Marcelle Kellermann, arriving in 1946 after a war spent working for the French Resistance, came to Manchester through

Figure 12. The University in a 1937 watercolour commissioned by the Chamber of Commerce for its promotional booklet *Manchester: Heart of the Industrial North*. Although the accompanying text frankly acknowledges that the city was undergoing a serious economic recession, the images show a bright, well-ordered city.

Figure 13. The cleaning of London Road Fire Station, an annual
event until stopped by union pressure in 1957.

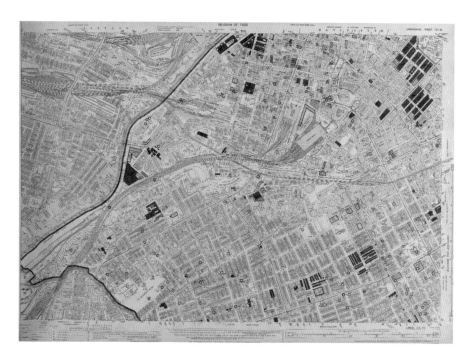

Figure 14. Bomb damage map of central Manchester, 1941. There had been small raids on Greater Manchester every few nights from July 1940 onwards; 'Manchester's Blitz', on two nights just before Christmas 1940, killed over 500 people. There were a dozen more small raids in 1941, and the last in 1942.

Figure 15. James Chettle's 1941 *War Memorial*, with the Grand Hotel on Aytoun Street visible through the bomb ruins around Piccadilly.

marriage to her physicist husband. At first she admired the resemblance to the quartz-black townscapes of the Auvergne; it was only when her husband stopped their taxi and used a penknife to cut through the grime on one building that she realised the stones were not granite. In 1933 the physicist Hans Bethe at least had the benefit of low expectations: *'Manchester is attractive well beyond my expectations. The city is not even anywhere near as dirty as I had remembered it'*. Another physicist, **Rudolf Peierls**, found the buildings both dirty and in a poor Victorian taste, aggravated by a fog, though one would think that would have helped. The *'soot-black'* place was nevertheless made pleasant by *'the warm and friendly nature of the local population'*, a trope which often recurs. When John Barbirolli arrived at Piccadilly in 1943 to discuss leading the Hallé Orchestra he was whisked straight to the Midland Hotel by taxi so that he should *'see as little as possible of the city'* but he too said that Manchester was good for those *'who can be oblivious to their surroundings provided they are content in their work'*. Physicist Bernard Lovell *'had spent my life in the West Country and all that I had*

Figure 16. Manchester & District Planning Exhibition 1945 was designed to show the public how planners would sweep away not just military damage but decades of poor housing.

MANCHESTER AND DISTRICT
PLANNING EXHIBITION - 1945
ART GALLERY - MOSLEY STREET - MANCHESTER
PRICE - TWOPENCE

ever heard about Manchester appalled me' but he saw *'attributes more valuable than the superficial rain and fogs that confronted us'*. When mathematician Mary Lee Woods arrived at Piccadilly and took a bus up the Oldham Road to the Ferranti factory, the view out of the bus window was so grim she resolved *'never, never, never will I live in this ugly place'*, but the interview, for the brand-new job of computer programmer, was so exciting that she changed her mind.

Chemist **Noel Hush**, coming from Australia, may too have found Manchester a new Athens, but nevertheless saw *'it was black with soot. Even the hedges were black with soot. It was freezing cold in the winter'*. Hush also recalled a side effect of bomb damage to the Free Trade Hall: the Hallé was having to play in a large tent alongside the zoo out at Belle Vue, and during the slow movements a lion's roar or hyena's scream would contribute. But the Hallé was nevertheless playing, in a symbol of Manchester's proud place in the world, and when the Hallé returned to the Free Trade Hall in 1951, Ferranti built an electronic tuning fork into the stage for it. Another chemist, John Polanyi, grew up

Figure 17. Manchester's increasing prosperity drove higher demand for water, and wartime interruption to infrastructure development meant that by 1945 dry periods saw regular official warnings of shortages and standpipes.

CITY OF MANCHESTER

Diagram
32

WATER SUPPLIED

1851

1871

1901

1921

1939

WAR
1945

1946

CITY OF MANCHESTER

KEY

Each symbol represents 6 million gallons of water supplied daily.
War year is indicated in red.

in the city rather than migrating to it, and remembers his family in a *'vigorous social-cum-intellectual life'* in a milieu of professors but also *'remarkable doctors, lawyers, factory and mill owners, people connected with the art galleries, the Northern Service of the BBC, the* Manchester Guardian *and the odd (really quite odd) aristocrat — a remarkable village community drawn together by a liveliness of mind through which they triumphed over the nastiness of their environment'.* [27]

The nastiness was supposed to be temporary. Much of the centre of Manchester was designated as the site of the nation's first 'smokeless zone' in 1946, although it was not to come into effect until 1952. [28] Slum clearance had been planned since at least 1935, and was a clear promise in 1945, inherent in the richly visual, if illusory, *Manchester City Plan,* though large-scale clearance didn't restart until a decade after that. [29] One of the largest pre-war schemes had been Wythenshawe, conceived in the 1930s as a new garden city, with considerable political and financial backing from Ernest and Shena Simon. As soon as war was over the Council restarted buying up land there but the immense need meant that the density of housing increased, the build quality decreased, and local amenities were endlessly postponed, so that the garden suburb started a long decline in reputation. [30]

Pre-war Manchester had a fast-growing thirst for clean water, and for all the rainfall jokes the Corporation had difficulty in bringing enough from the surrounding hills. Though there were ambitious plans to remedy this, they had been slowed by recession and then war, and 1947 saw threats that water would be cut-off for 12 hours a day. The great Victorian reservoir at Thirlmere in the Lake District had been supplemented with an even larger one at Haweswater in 1941, but the old aqueduct to Manchester had a very small capacity. It was not until 1948 that funding was secured to build a second route, and a further seven years to finish the work, culminating in the Heaton Park pumping station which was proudly decorated with a large mural designed by local sculptor Mitzi Cunliffe. But the funding *was* found, and all the smut in the air was not unrelated to the promise of economic power to support science and the humanities too, not to mention a deep pool of technological knowhow. [31]

The industrial basis of the city was continually generating possibilities for new science. There were a series of boosterish reports on how the region and the University had a mutually beneficial relationship, though occasionally a sardonic tone was smuggled in: *'The climate of Manchester provides special opportunities for research into the effects of damp and smoke on human psychology and physiology'.* The reports were created by a committee partly comprising University Professors like Blackett, Williams and Polanyi but in fact was largely the creation of the cotton trade administrator Raymond Streat, who recorded how Blackett had been *'snooty and difficult to a degree'.* They could have added Darwinism to the special opportunities too: the dark tint of the peppered moth in a polluted landscape is now a textbook example of evolution, and the first genetically blackened example ever caught was in Manchester. [32]

Figure 18. Age-related grime in St Peter's Square in 1961. The three-storey building on the right housed the Clarendon Club.

Figure 19. Mitzi Cunliffe's mural on the Heaton Park pumping station, 1955, the only post-war building in England listed solely for its sculpture.

Figure 20. Manchester's last tram ran in 1949. The removal of the service had been planned as early as 1929, and when it did occur represented a significant investment in new petrol motorbuses which were more comfortable and efficient.

So as the 1950s dawned, Manchester was still a dirty, slum-ridden city, short of water despite all the drizzle, but well-publicised improvement plans were in place and intellectual culture was not bowed. Literary critic **Frank Kermode** did not arrive until 1958; he still found it dirty but: *'the university had a kind of grim friendliness and a justified assurance of its own value, at a time when the metropolitan claims of Manchester were weakening but still pretty strong...the mood of the place was always to oppose the south, and the university had, or professed no inferiority feelings about the ancient universities; if bright people came to Manchester, sharpened their talents, and left for Oxbridge, that was their business and they might well come to repent their foolishness in leaving a serious place for institutions that devoted themselves to feasts and gaudies...But the city had more to give than the dense fogs, industrial filth and bronchitic sub-climate that depressed most newcomers'.*[33]

Although Kermode had arrived with southern prejudices he soon found he was wrong to think of Manchester as a place of scholarly deprivation. Kermode found, behind black walls on Deansgate, the John Rylands library to be a wonderfully lavish place, a product of Victorian cotton riches, as was the Hallé Orchestra, and found that 'fun' of a superior sort was guaranteed by the presence of *The Manchester Guardian*. But these three institutions were essentially nineteenth-century creations of the cotton trade and could also now be seen as leftovers struggling to find a new role. And despite living out in the Cheshire fringe and driving tediously into work each day, in the end Kermode left Manchester for the south after being advised his bronchitic children needed cleaner air.

There had been a sense in the University between the wars that it could not keep up with the pace at which Cambridge, Oxford and London were expanding research. Manchester University lost not just Rutherford and then his successor Bragg from its prized Physics department, but also what the University hierarchy was heard to call a whole *'first class waiting room for the career train south'.*[34] But every departure of an established Professor created an opportunity for a new and younger one: in Blackett as in his predecessors, the University had recruited a Nobel Prize winner *before* they had been recognised as such. And new state funding allowed the post-war University to make ambitious expansion plans which it started on as early as 1951, although completing them took decades.

Both pre- and post-war, then, Manchester was an ugly city, but one of promise, and two couples, the Blacketts and the Newmans, separately drawn to this opportunity, were to be crucial in the story of both the Manchester computer and of Turing.

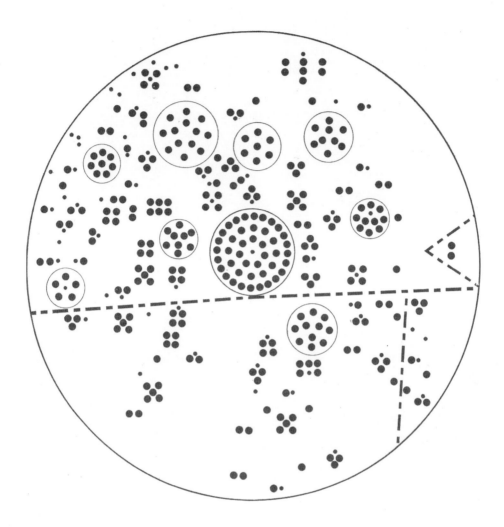

Figure 21. Post-war Manchester was the subject of multiple planning documents
with different agendas depending on their source. This 1947 illustration of planned
population density, with Manchester at the centre, is from a county-level plan that did
not want to see large-scale movement of people away from the industrial centres into
the surrounding land.

The Manchester Mindscape

The two Pat Blacketts

In 1937, **Patrick Blackett** arrived to cut a dash as Manchester's Professor of Physics. He came to chair what was perhaps the only part of the University with an international research reputation, and he and his wife would successfully deploy their charm to keep it that way. Pat and Pat Blackett were a glamorous and successful couple. Patrick was a Naval officer, a Nobel Prize-winner, and an ethical thorn in the paw of British defence policy even as he worked at the highest level of the state. It can't have hurt that Patrick was very handsome, his chiselled face evident in every photograph. His wife, often called Pat though her actual name was Costanza, also offered an educated, polyglot charm: to be invited into their home was to feel part of a community, not just of cosmopolitan intellectuals, but attractive ones at that. In the autobiographies of Patrick's scientific juniors, a sense comes through of a couple that shone in a dreary world: Bernard Lovell recalled his own wife saying Blackett was the only man she would have left him for. [35]

Blackett had been schooled at Naval College and saw action at sea in the First World War. He noted that German ships had much more accurate firing techniques than the Royal Navy, but when he found his own superiors intellectually uninterested in improving gunnery technique, he started to lose interest in a career under the men of action. In 1919, Britain's surviving elite young men were sent to belatedly catch up on their studies, and Blackett was accordingly despatched by the Navy to Cambridge. It was when he wandered into **Ernest Rutherford's** physics laboratory that his career in science was set. Rutherford had just moved down from splitting the atom in Manchester, and Blackett was one of his students in what was to be a golden period for Cambridge, Manchester and world physics. Blackett was an experimentalist more than a theorist, and would win his Nobel Prize for work in Cambridge developing apparatus to detect cosmic rays for the first time. There was a notorious clash in Cambridge with a younger student he was supervising, J. Robert Oppenheimer, later creator of the US atomic bomb as leader of the Manhattan Project. Oppenheimer was a theoretician and chafed under Blackett's insistence that he do experimental work. Oppenheimer was always a troubled soul, but his Cambridge years were his most unstable, and a story, told by Oppenheimer himself, was that at one stage in 1925 he had left an apple poisoned with cyanide on Blackett's desk. [36]

Figure 22. Lucia Moholy, *Patrick Maynard Stuart Blackett,* 1936, shows a relatively young Blackett in the year before he moved to Manchester. Moholy was an ex Bauhaus documentary photographer who fled from Berlin to London as a political refugee. Blackett tended to pick non-establishment portraitists. Even after he returned to London in 1953, by now a Nobel laureate, he chose Emmanuel Levy, a distinctly Mancunian painter of Jewish heritage, and art critic of *The Manchester Guardian*, for the oil portrait which now hangs in the National Portrait Gallery.

Whether it happened or not—and there is considerable doubt—it would have been possible for the tale to form part of the local physicist gossip, ready for a young mathematician Turing to hear a few years later. But this is wild speculation; in any case the story has a tragic resonance.

It was in Cambridge that Patrick Blackett met his Pat. **Costanza Bayon**, to use her birth name, or Pat by her choice, was a student at Newnham College, and had a respectable upbringing by an English couple in Florence. To Cambridge eyes there was perhaps an underlying intrigue in that these were not her birth parents and that, via her biological father, she brought an Italian heritage. The Blacketts were the *'handsomest, gayest, happiest pair in Cambridge'* and somewhat anti-establishment and unconventional.[37] Patrick was a Fellow at King's when Turing arrived as an undergraduate, but the Blacketts were no part of the set around the Apostles that valued science some way below the humanities. Pat and Pat did attend the Heretics, and were visitors to Cambridge's scandalously bohemian Half Moon Club, where sexual education and license were freely discussed.[38] If they were bohemians in Cambridge, there is little evidence that this survived to family life in Manchester, where Pat and Pat brought up two children in what seems to have been a happy and socially conventional marriage. One glimpse of the social standing they acquired in Manchester comes from the advice from the University to Blackett's peer, Michael Polanyi, the Professor of Chemistry. Polanyi, who was also married with two children, was advised in 1933 he should rent a five-bedroomed house in Didsbury, and to employ four maids and an au pair.[39] The Blacketts imported their salon to their Manchester house, and Bernard Lovell recalls a wide-eyed move from his West Country roots into a world where English was a rare language at the Blackett parties.[40] As Patrick acquired distinction he became increasingly patrician and perhaps more than a little arrogant, but Costanza remained more grounded: she saw to it that all of the staff of the Manchester Physics department, including the cleaners, were invited to the 1948 party for his Nobel Prize.

Despite the Blacketts' growing respectability, what did remain was a commitment to left-leaning politics. Unlike many of their Cambridge contemporaries, the Blacketts were never Communists, though their son and son-in-law were Party members. Their daughter Giovanna Blackett Bloor recalls the time when Picasso's *Guernica* came to Manchester as part of a Left fundraising tour during the Spanish Civil War and her mother helped nail it to the walls of a car showroom in Cateaton Street.[41] Before and during the Second World War, Blackett's military background, and unassailable scientific authority in nuclear physics, meant he was an inevitable member of government committees on air defence, radar, and atomic energy. His easy physical access to Bletchley Park alone suggests he must have known many of Britain's cryptographic secrets. He rarely joined public campaigns, preferring to remain an insider. But access did not mean success: inside government he unsuccessfully opposed mass civilian bombing of Germany and Britain's attempt to develop its own atomic weapons.

Figure 23. Costanza Blackett during the early 1930s, by Noel Teulon Porter, owner of the scandalous Half Moon Club in Cambridge.

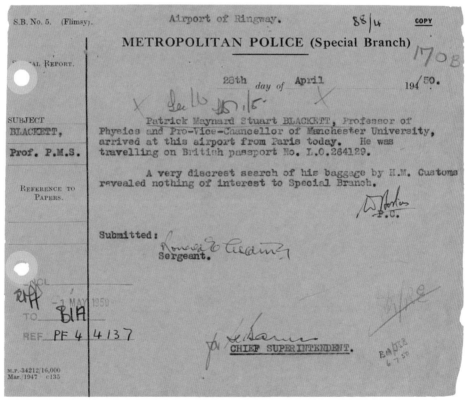

S.B. No. 5. (Flimsy). Airport of Ringway. 88/4 **COPY**

1708

METROPOLITAN POLICE (Special Branch)

...AL REPORT.

28th *day of* April 194 50.

SUBJECT BLACKETT, Prof. P.M.S.

Patrick Maynard Stuart BLACKETT, Professor of Physics and Pro-Vice-Chancellor of Manchester University, arrived at this airport from Paris today. He was travelling on British passport No. L.O.264129.

REFERENCE TO PAPERS.

A very discreet search of his baggage by H.M. Customs revealed nothing of interest to Special Branch.

P.C.

Submitted:

Sergeant.

TO

REF PF 4 4137

CHIEF SUPERINTENDENT.

M.P.-34212/16,000 Mar./1947 c135

Figure 24. Report of a secret bag search on PMS Blackett (whom Special Branch incorrectly thought was Vice Chancellor of the University) when he left Manchester Airport in 1950. The telephone in Blackett's Fallowfield house was also tapped.

He did join with many on the left in publicly, if not uncritically, supporting the Soviet Union, and Churchill increasingly mistrusted him and requested his loyalty be checked. A hot anti-Nazi war was being replaced by a cold anti-Communist one, and Blackett – who was anti-fascist but distinctly 'pinko' – caused perplexity to MI5, attested by his thick security file. [42] In the end they concluded that he *was* a patriot, but a rather arrogant one. The trouble with Blackett was that he *did* wish to defend national security, but insisted on making up his own mind about what this was. There is a distinct irony in the fact that this judgement was signed by Peter Wright, who later overrode MI5's secrecy judgments to publish his own *Spycatcher* revelations. Blackett was no longer allowed access to Britain's nuclear secrets but continued to speak out on defence-related science policy. Into the 1960s Blackett was a supporter of CND, although he kept this support private. On Blackett's account this was to retain internal influence with the British government, although AJP Taylor thought it was more to do with Blackett's desire to become Lord Blackett and President of the Royal Society. [43]

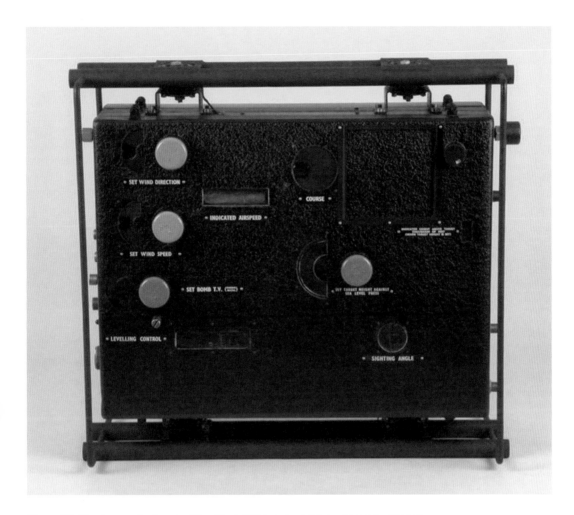

Figure 25. The 'computor' part of the Mark XIV bomb sight, invented by Patrick Blackett in 1940. It was a radical improvement over previous sights, using an analogue computer that could adjust for changes in height, and became the RAF's standard technology during the war.

Max Newman

The Blackett charms were at their most consequential in 1945 when the couple lured **Max Newman** to Manchester to set up the Computer Laboratory. The Blacketts had known Max for years, and Patrick had been best man at his 1934 wedding to Lyn Irvine. Max Newman was born with much less social capital than a Turing or a Blackett. His mother was a south London schoolteacher, and his father, Herman Neumann, was a German Jewish immigrant who was interned during the First World War and then abandoned Max and his mother by returning to Germany. Max's mathematical talent won him a scholarship to the City of London School, and then onto St John's College in Cambridge in 1916. He shone and set out on the career of the Cambridge mathematics don. By the time he was a young lecturer he was interested both in the kind of pure mathematics known as topology but also in more logical questions about the nature and limitations of mathematics: he exchanged ideas with Bertrand Russell.

Newman had none of the Blackett glamour and there's no record of him attending the Half Moon Club. He is instead vividly remembered in accounts of the time as a witty and entertaining but serious-minded man. He spent some time in Vienna in the 1920s with a college friend named Lionel Penrose. Penrose, who was an heir to Quaker banking wealth, went to learn the new science of Freudian analysis, but for Newman Vienna was important as the world centre of mathematical logic. Penrose and Newman were visibly clever young men: a young English friend, Margaret Gardiner, later recalled in awed tones the pair of them walking the streets of Vienna playing chess in their heads. When they each returned to Cambridge, Penrose recognised that his own quest for scientific Freudianism was a dead end and turned to genetics. But Newman's quest for the roots of reasoning had begun. It was these new, Austro-German, problems of mathematical logic that Newman passed on in that Cambridge lecture of 1931 with a young Alan Turing in the audience. [44]

At the outbreak of war in 1939 the 41-year-old Newman was an established mathematician and teacher. But unlike Turing, he was not on Bletchley Park's list of 'men of the Professor type' to be called up in the event of war, and at first remained teaching in a reduced Cambridge. Newman's name had actually appeared on a Bletchley list made in 1938, with the word 'No' against it. It's unclear whether it was Newman or GCHQ that objected. Newman may have been planning to go with his family to the US in the event of war, or thought the job to be too uninteresting to be any good at it; or GCHQ may have had security concerns about his German connections. In any event, Blackett was prime mover in encouraging Newman to work at Bletchley, going to some lengths to reassure Newman's doubts about finding work *'big enough to keep you interested and*

Figure 26. Max Newman, Alan Turing's mentor, co-creator of the Colossus, and head of the University of Manchester's mathematics department from 1945 to 1964.

usefully employed for the duration'. Blackett also deployed the Cambridge old boy network: he said, in the jocular teasing tone of a member of a rival college, that Newman would find Bletchley a *'hotbed of Kingsmen'*. Blackett got his way and in 1942 Newman moved to Bletchley Park. At first Newman's fears were realised and he felt intellectually inadequate to the task: it was only when he saw how to mechanise cryptography that he decided to stay.[45]

Turing's contribution at Bletchley Park to decoding the German Enigma code has been widely celebrated, and the role played by the electromechanical machines known as Bombes is also well known.[46] Max Newman was set to work on a different German code, which was vulnerable to attack only after large numbers of tedious letter counts had been made. Newman knew that Blackett's pre-war physics laboratory had used electronic valves to automate the counting of radioactive emissions and quickly devised an electromechanical machine to attack the codebreaking problem.[47] This machine worked, but too slowly, and an electrical engineer named **Tommy Flowers**, who had impressed Turing with his work on improving the Bombes, was asked to improve it. Flowers came up with a brilliant series of inventions that were to result in the Colossus, but it was Newman's specifications that drove two innovations of great significance: the Colossus could store data internally, and it had an automatic decision-making capacity. These combined to make Newman and Flowers the two creators of the world's first reprogrammable electronic computer. Although the Colossus had been designed for one specific cryptographic task, it was realised after construction that, by reprogramming, it could be used for a different one. As one of his staff, Jack Good, wrote, the new possibility was *'overlooked for a few months and was discovered by Michie with some help from me. The discovery multiplied the value of Colossus by a very large factor indeed'*.[48] The majority of the pioneers of early computing in Britain and America never knew of the Colossus,

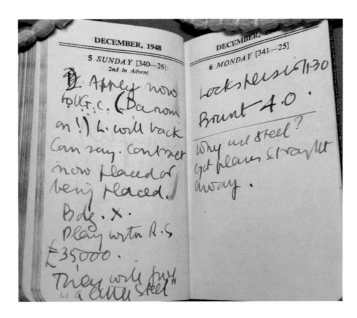

Figure 27. Max Newman's 1948 diary recorded the visit to Manchester of Ben Lockspeiser, government adviser responsible for all new military science. Lockspeiser saw the Baby in action and promised to find 'a little steel' for a new building to house the Manchester Mark I.

and so the direct, felt, influence of the astonishing power of the *general purpose* computer was limited. But, via Newman and Turing, it was to have profound implications for computing in general and Manchester in particular.

Newman decided he would set up a computing laboratory after the war had finished. His plan was not to develop computers, but to explore how computers could be used to do mathematical research. Newman, unlike Turing, had no mechanical bent and was uninterested in the practical electronics needed. But Newman and Turing, almost uniquely among computing pioneers of the time, knew of both the theoretical possibilities of general-purpose computing, thanks to Turing's own 1934 paper, and its achieved reality, thanks to Newman and Flowers' Colossus at Bletchley Park. Max Newman had also seen that these new machines were instruments of war of great interest to the state. The modern computer was called into being by defence need as much as by curiosity-driven research. Patrick Blackett arranged for Newman to come to Manchester after the war as the head of the Mathematics Department. Blackett and his wife visited Cambridge to persuade Max and his wife Lyn to come: Lyn recalled a weekend where the Blacketts campaigned by appealing to *that always sensitive place, pride in a husband's career'*. They targeted Max's career opportunities as a counterweight to the supposed disadvantages: *'At first I was utterly appalled to think of leaving [Cambridgeshire's] cold but wide skies for the perpetual gloom of Manchester...for Max the job is much more interesting...and for both of us in our post-war hopes and plans there will be more scope & encouragement than there could be in Cambridge. We can't of course live in the city itself & there are some not unattractive places in Cheshire where we might find a house'.* [49]

As well as persuading the Newmans to come, somebody leaned on the Vice Chancellor. He had been preparing to offer the job to Harold Davenport, a local, Accrington-born candidate. But by the time the committee met, which included Blackett and the computing expert Hartree, Newman had the job. Whatever happened, the Vice Chancellor took some flak; another Professor, an old friend of Davenport, later had to write to the VC to apologise for the violence of some outburst about the appointment. Davenport himself was exiled to Wales for a few years, but later, in 1958, beat Newman to a chair in Cambridge. [50]

There must have been intense interest from GCHQ and its patrons in making sure that the defence state did not lose control of development of future technology as its wartime staff dispersed. There's no documentary link between Newman's appointment and the government's knowledge that he was one of the Bletchley Park mathematicians with an invention of great power, but Blackett must have played a role. The combination of Blackett's access to state power and his position in Manchester, strongly suggest that his wooing of Newman was with at least the knowledge, if not the connivance, of high-level government defence science. And once Newman was in Manchester he was allowed to scavenge parts from GCHQ. The first rack of the computer was taken directly from a Colossus, though it was later replaced because its big feet kept tripping people up.[51] Another piece of circumstantial evidence is the funding that Newman acquired to build the new computer. The Treasury awarded him a grant of £35,000 on the basis of a recommendation from a Royal Society committee on which Blackett sat. This was enormous amount of money (about a hundred times a new lecturer's salary) for austerity Britain to invest in University technology, but it was not only cash that the state provided.[52] The money came through with what Newman called *record swiftness of action...due to urgent appeals by Blackett*.[53] Blackett provided space in his own Physics department for the new 'Calculating Machine Laboratory'[54] and even the chassis of the magnetic drum for the Mark I was a discarded cloud chamber of Blackett's.[55] By the time in 1948 that it was clear that the new computing machines would need a new purpose-built building, Newman was promised the necessary steel from the country's scarce stocks by the Chief Scientific Adviser himself.[56] Newman's own appointment and the funding and resources for the computer laboratory point to a deliberate strategy at the highest levels of government to have a computer built in Manchester.

The strategy paid off: among the first few computers that Ferranti sold were ones to the Atomic Weapons Research Establishment and, secretly, to GCHQ. The secrecy was so strict that Ferranti were instructed to place the machine on a lorry and to leave the lorry, keys in, in a layby outside Cheltenham for later collection.[57]

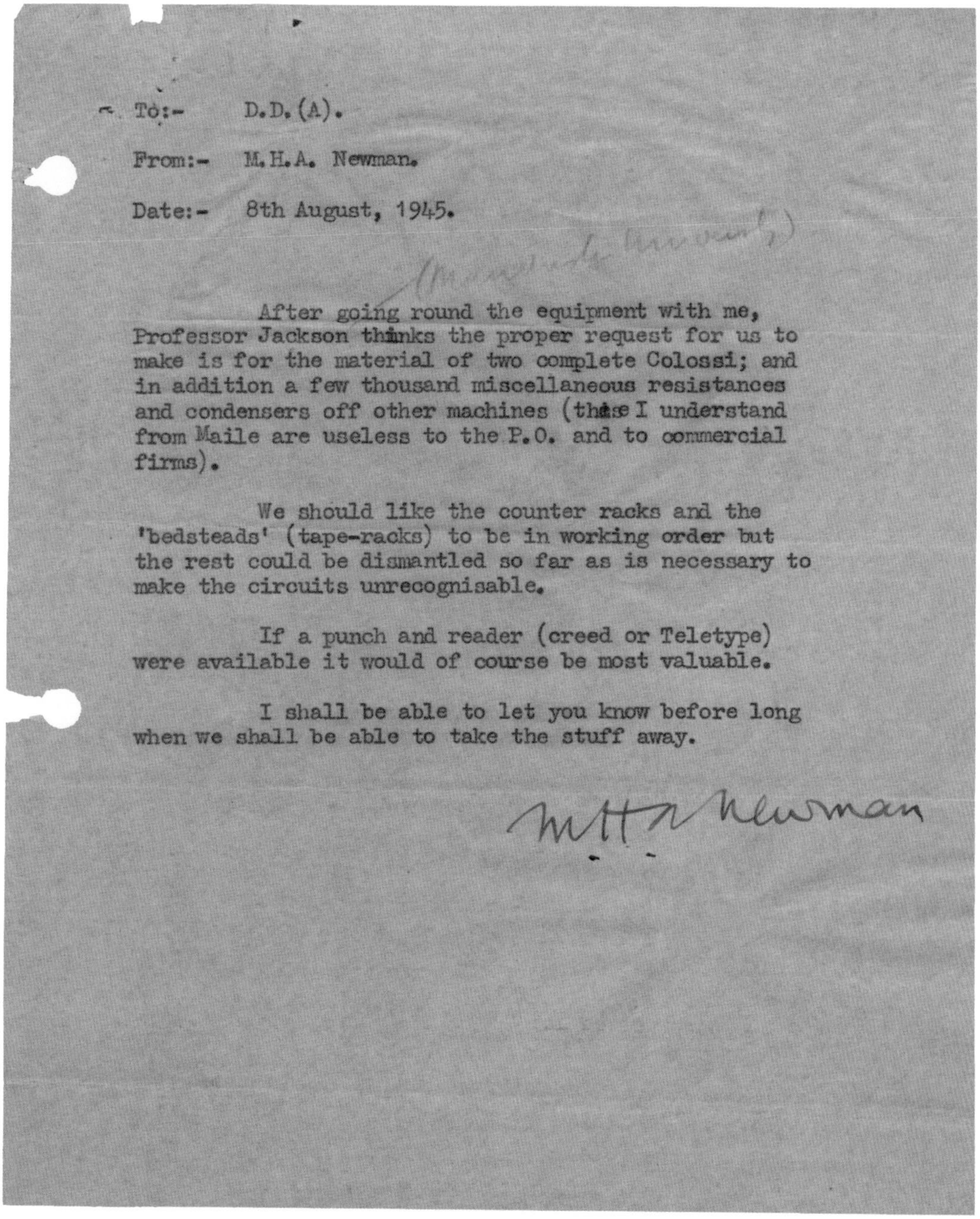

To:- D.D.(A).

From:- M.H.A. Newman.

Date:- 8th August, 1945.

After going round the equipment with me,
Professor Jackson thinks the proper request for us to
make is for the material of two complete Colossi; and
in addition a few thousand miscellaneous resistances
and condensers off other machines (these I understand
from Maile are useless to the P.O. and to commercial
firms).

We should like the counter racks and the
'bedsteads' (tape-racks) to be in working order but
the rest could be dismantled so far as is necessary to
make the circuits unrecognisable.

If a punch and reader (creed or Teletype)
were available it would of course be most valuable.

I shall be able to let you know before long
when we shall be able to take the stuff away.

M.H.A. Newman

Figure 28. Newman was permitted to take the contents of two Colossi from GCHQ.
Although he kept in one piece the 'bedsteads' that allowed high-speed tape operation,
they were not in the end used for this: the Baby would have no paper tape facility,
and only later would Turing discreetly reintroduce the Bletchley Park tape technology
to the Manchester engineers. Indeed, Newman was no engineer and most of the
components he chose were discarded. The racks that carried the electronics were
reused, at least at first, but even these had large feet that tripped people up and were
replaced by standard TRE ones. 'Jackson' is Willis Jackson, the outgoing Professor of
Electrotechnics that Williams would replace and who was evidently cleared at a high
security level.

THE MONOLOGUE

EDITED BY LYN IRVINE

Issued on the 1st and 15th of Every Month
No 24   February 1st 1935

CONTENTS

MODERN NOVELISTS   Page One
LETTERS FROM GEOFFREY SCOTT   Page Twelve

Lyn Lloyd Irvine's Northern Adventure

In 1934 Max had married **Lyn Lloyd Irvine**, whom he had met through mutual Cambridge connections. [58] Lyn was to keep up a large, well-preserved correspondence that give the most personal views we have of the birth of the computer age in Manchester, of her husband's 'complicated and angular' personality, and Turing's 'rare' genius and 'gentle' manner.

Theirs had been no undergraduate romance. When they married, Lyn was 33 and Max was 37: he was living a bachelor existence as a Fellow of an all-male Cambridge college and had a few romantic entanglements before but been in no long-term relationships. Lyn Irvine had been a serious young student of English at Aberdeen and then spent a few years as a research student in Cambridge. In the late 1920s, Irvine abandoned her thesis for life as a high-brow literary journalist on the fringes of the Bloomsbury Group. Literary London was at first welcoming to Irvine: she was dined and unsuccessfully courted by lothario critic Clive Bell, and she made a lifelong friendship, on more intellectual grounds, with Leonard Woolf. [59] Irvine's first book was *Ten Letter Writers*, published by Leonard, and she was always aware of the literary power of the letter. She had a mutually wary relationship with Leonard's wife Virginia Woolf, who was well known for her ambivalence about younger writers, and Lyn's letters sometimes rival Virginia's in their combination of stylish, considered judgment and telling, scornful comment. Irvine worked very hard, but in the end was unable to financially sustain a career as a critic and writer. Her friendship with Max blossomed on his trips to London: he had been entrusted by St John's with the task of buying their new piano. She seems to have been genuinely charmed by Max and to enjoy his intellect, but it was never the giddiest of emotional relationships. Her letters suggest that when they married, after an acquaintanceship of a year or so, it was for both of them a sensible before a romantic choice. After marriage, Irvine swiftly became pregnant with the first of her two sons and was not to restart her literary career until after her children had left home. It was in writing an obituary foreword, to Sara Turing's maternal biography of Alan, that Irvine rediscovered that *'it is when something hardly can be said & one has to rise & sleep & rise again trying to take the kink out of a sentence that writing becomes the most fascinating occupation in the world'.* [60]

Figure 29. Frontispiece of the final copy, February 1935, of *The Monologue*, Lyn Irvine's one-woman subscription magazine. For a year, Irvine wrote almost every word of every fortnightly issue, save for a few articles by Newman. She spent even more time typing the stencils for every page so they could be copied by the low-cost but labour-intensive Gestetner method. Despite the presence of high-profile Bloomsbury names on her subscriber list, Irvine was exhausted by the constant effort and decided to stop publication. Within a few weeks she was engaged to Newman.

Figure 30. Lyn Lloyd Irvine during her pre-war years as a London literary journalist. Irvine was for a while part of the Bloomsbury world, through her friendship with Virginia and Leonard Woolf. This photograph was taken at the Woolf's country cottage. Irvine sacrificed her writing ambitions to family life with Max Newman, only beginning to publish again when her children left home.

Figure 31. Altrincham Market in 1928. By the time the Newmans and Turing arrived, a cast-iron canopy had been erected on the adjacent open space. Today the Market hosts a premium 'food destination'; in the 1940s it was a source for hard-to-find off-ration fabric.

Figure 32. The Newmans' first Manchester house in Bowdon. It was in the back garden of this house that Lyn first heard Max and Alan discussing thinking machines and voiced her first doubts about the dawn of the computer age.

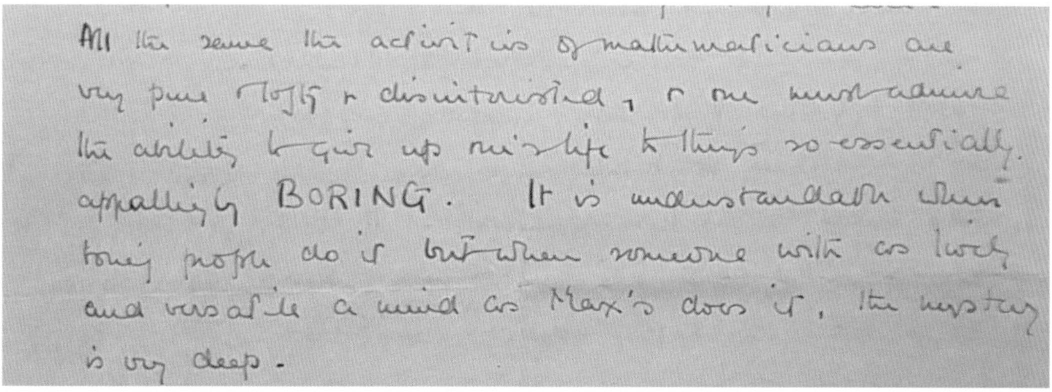

All the same the activity of mathematicians are very pure, lofty & disinterested, & one must admire the ability to give up ones life to things so essentially appallingly BORING. It is understandable when boring people do it but when someone with as lively and versatile a mind as Max's does it, the mystery is very deep.

Figure 33. Lyn watched the exploits of the mathematicians with occasional disquiet, but more often bemusement.

The Newmans moved to Bowdon in January 1946. Bowdon is ten miles south of the University, further out than the Blacketts and Polanyis in Didsbury, but with good transport links through nearby Altrincham and adjacent to green fields.[61] At their grandest, the villas of Bowdon are a little more substantial than most of Didsbury, and were the homes of the owners of manufacturing concerns rather than of their professional staff. Max and Lyn took a smaller, professional's house nestling below the great mansions on the Bowdon hill, small by cotton magnate standards but still substantial. From here Irvine vividly described her resentments of Manchester, perhaps less to do with the city as much as Max's lack of recognition for the life of domestic drudgery she led. They found themselves less well off than they had been in Cambridge, and Irvine struggled in the post-war world to recruit the servants that her new establishment needed: *'continental...girls prefer to stay at home, so now I'm back to [an] old Irishwoman with high blood pressure to wash and iron, a respectable Lancashire lady so deaf she can't hear the telephone bell to clean, & a girl who works in a factory by day to wash up at night & help at the weekends...I would like a household secretary who filed our thousands of possessions, & knew where every book, toy, garment, ball of string, nut & screw could be found instantly. The right kind of house would help, thousands of pigeonholes'.*[62]

The Newmans struggled — or at least Lyn struggled — to find the material needs of their middle-class family life. She kept chickens, and her letters record some difficulty in finding food, as well as fuel and fabric, and complaint about the oncoming water shortages, though also that the local Altrincham Market was full of 'export quality' products of the region's mills.[63] Though she was a little apprehensive about the accent her son might acquire when she sent him to the local state primary school, the urban and partly working class environment was less worrisome than the *'awful faux-genteel'* of Cheshire. Later, they were to be able to afford a pre-war Daimler and to find and pay for its fuel. Max seems to have sometimes used it for commuting into work, although its main value was in making the Manchester to Cambridge journey bearable.

Part of Lyn's role was to offer hospitality to visiting mathematicians. For the most part she found mathematicians good company, though she was a little puzzled by them: *'Mathematicians are very pure & lofty and disinterested and one must admire the ability to give up one's life to things so essentially BORING. It is understandable when boring people do it, but when someone with as lively and versatile a mind as Max's does it, the mystery is very deep'.*[64]

Lyn was particularly unimpressed with the Cambridge mathematician **Mary Cartwright**, the first female mathematician to be elected to the Royal Society and an early developer of what would later be called Chaos Theory. Cartwright, she thought, was rude not to offer to help with the washing up and treated the house as though it was a Cambridge college with invisible servants. Lyn still remembered the slight twenty years later. She would also have to regularly entertain the mathematicians of Max's department, all male, with their wives and 'cabbagey' babies. She struggled to find local friends: only just before they left for Cheadle Hulme[65] did she met a couple she really liked, the Bogues who lived nearby in Bowdon. James Yule Bogue was also a migrant, recruited to Manchester to set up the ICI pharmaceutical division, and his wife Charlotte Boettcher, a professional pianist, would duet with Max. The childless Bogues had a fifteen-room house, which they said was the only one large enough for both their pianos.[66] Although somewhat vague about the science — Lyn described the physiologist Bogue as a physicist — she was impressed by the fact that he had developed a treatment for epilepsy. There was not much going out, but Lyn did see and was thrilled by the Paul Nash exhibition, which came to Manchester in 1948.[67]

Lyn was constantly frustrated by domestic *'string and struggle'* from getting time to write and to maintain her literary connections. She kept her hand in by getting letters published in *The Times,* but this had its hazards. After one about the difficulties faced by the wives of academics, *'The Daily Mail were disgusting & when I refused to be interviewed on the telephone it rang up Max at Manchester University to his astonishment & disgust & asked him what kind of shirts he wore!'*[68] Once Costanza Blackett came to look after the household for a few days to let Lyn get away to Cambridge, but Lyn was suspicious that this was out of guilt at having lured her to Manchester in the first place, and the offer was not repeated. The only better option would have been an Oxbridge chair for Max; and though Max built a well-run and highly respected department in Manchester, he repeatedly lost out to others as these chairs came up. Perhaps, Lyn thought, he might be a good manager, but a poor colleague, and they worked out their exile. In December 1950 they had moved to an 'unloved' newer house. Although physically closer to their son's school and to the city centre, Cheadle Hulme was more modern and suburban than Victorian Altrincham. Lyn was delighted with the views across to woodland and open fields, but they discovered when they tried to get a mortgage that the rural area was zoned for what would become the A34 dual carriageway. Once the children were old enough Lyn returned to Cambridge, while Max lived in furnished rooms in Bowdon *'in one of those huge Victorian castles built by cotton kings & now converted into flats...the view to the north is quite startling — first a green expanse with the Bridgewater Canal winding through it, & then the factories of S. W. Manchester, a mile or two away, & beyond that the great smoky welter of Manchester itself, and beyond that when the air is clean enough (not often) the wall of the Pennines, remote and unbelievable'.*[69]

Up in another part of those Pennine walls there had, forty years earlier, lived a remarkable figure, as remote and unbelievable as any philosopher has ever been.

Ludwig Wittgenstein

The folds of the Pennines mean that the hilltop town of Glossop is not visible from Altrincham, even on the clearest day from the grandest cotton castle. But it was from there that the spare, intense-eyed figure of **Ludwig Wittgenstein** had descended onto Manchester; he now seems almost like an Old Testament prophet in the way he prefigures Turing's post-war age of uncertainty about the power and limits of logic and the machine.

The heir of a very wealthy Viennese steel family, Wittgenstein was as a young man obsessed by flying and had come to Manchester University in 1908 to learn how to design an aeroplane. He spent his experimental time flying kites in Glossop but needed to study mathematics too, and — probably with a push from Manchester philosopher Samuel Alexander — became passionately interested in the mathematical logic of Russell and his circle. [70]

Figure 34. Ludwig Wittgenstein (on the right) in front of the Grouse Inn, Glossop, in 1908. The wealthy Austrian, who would go on to be one of the most significant philosophers of the twentieth century, came to Manchester to learn how to make an aeroplane. He spent his time flying kites in Glossop and, on one possibly unreliable account, testing his rocket engines on a disused railway in Stockport.

Russell quickly recognised Wittgenstein as a genius suitable as his own protégé and as a consequence Wittgenstein held a fellowship in Cambridge from 1929 onwards. Wittgenstein first attempted to do for philosophy what Russell was doing for mathematics by expressing it as a series of linguistic propositions linked by logic, but then rejected his own approach as an utterly misleading description of thought. By the late 1930s Wittgenstein was surrounded by a small but intense circle of followers, and when he gave a series of Cambridge lectures on the foundations of mathematics Turing and Newman attended and on occasion argued with Wittgenstein, who told his class at one point that Newman *'should have been drowned at birth'*. The Wittgenstein/Turing discussions, recorded by those disciples, show minds with very different agendas, both thinking hard about the nature and purpose of mathematics and language, but perhaps so different that neither altered the thinking of the other. But the relationship of logic to language and intelligence, and indeed the seriousness of the questions, was a common preoccupation that would come to Manchester with Turing and Newman. [71]

It's notable that back in 1908 Wittgenstein *could* choose Manchester for that first engineering doctorate and could *not* have chosen Cambridge to do this. Although Cambridge had an engineering school of some achievement, there was no significant activity there in the new field of aeronautics, and the University did not then offer any formal PhD programme. But when Wittgenstein later wanted to study the pure rather than the applied, it was Cambridge that the great German logician Frege recommended. The Cambridge PhD was indeed later introduced out of a fear that it was losing good international students. As it happens, Lyn Irvine was one of the earliest students to register for a Cambridge PhD, although she never submitted a thesis. Wittgenstein did submit one, in mathematical logic: his examiner declared it not only a work of genius but, fortunately, also good enough for a Cambridge PhD. [72]

Apart from Turing, Wittgenstein is the only other figure in this book to be described as a genius by those remembering him in person, and he seems to have shared with Turing an air of suppressed irritability and dislike of being interrupted in things that mattered to him. [73] Manchester scientists found him an 'odd fish' and recalled him innocently betraying his immense wealth, whether in dressing expensively when going out to the Hallé from his Didsbury rooms, mentioning how very hot he liked his bath, or attempting to travel with one friend to Blackpool by hiring an entire special train. [74] Wittgenstein also shares with Turing that he has been historically labelled as a gay man, though his sexuality was even more obscure to his Manchester colleagues than Turing's would be.

Douglas Hartree and the Differential Analyser

Chubby-faced and prone to blushing, **Douglas Hartree** had no air of an Old Testament prophet about him at all, but his work in Manchester, leaving just as Turing arrived, also foreshadowed what would come after the war. Like his successors, he was a complicated mix of Cambridge and Manchester, built a Manchester computer with Blackett's support and in Blackett's space, provided essential secret computations to support the defence effort, and was profoundly important in post-war computing.[75] And like Max Newman, the best man at Hartree's wedding was, of course, Patrick Blackett.

Hartree's first mechanical computer was a low-cost prototype, built in 1933 of Meccano, and he needed funds to scale this to a production machine to be built by a local industrial giant, in this case Metropolitan Vickers. Like the Ferranti Mark I, Hartree's production Differential Analyser was funded externally, although in this case locally, through the McDougall grain milling family. The links to the Mark I are more than analogies: one of the young men Blackett helped recruit to pre-war Manchester to work on the Differential Analyser was the FC Williams who would so momentously return to the city after the war.[76]

The machine worked well enough, and three variants were installed in Cambridge and elsewhere: one was built at Macclesfield Grammar School. It's not clear by how much the Differential Analyser speeded up calculations: it was in fact quite labour intensive. During the war Hartree ran what was in essence a national consulting service for the numerical solution of mathematical problems vital to the war effort, ostensibly receiving requests with no indication of their source.[77] But once electronic computers were on the horizon, and promising a 1,000-fold speedup in calculation, the Differential Analyser was considered obsolete even before the new machines actually worked.[78] Hartree moved with the times after the war and became intimately involved in electronic computing in Cambridge, leaving Manchester with a slightly embarrassed search for what to do with the old machine. Blackett wanted it out of his Department, and in the end it was sent to NPL, where it limped on for a few years.[79]

Figure 35. A single integrator component of the Differential Analyser built by Metropolitan Vickers for Douglas Hartree in Manchester, and now housed in a store room at Manchester's Museum of Science and Industry.

Hartree has another, slightly unfair, claim to historical fame. He probably said some version of *'We have a computer here in Cambridge, one in Manchester and one [in London]. I suppose there ought to be one in Scotland, but that's about all'*. To a modern reader this seems an absurd judgement, but Hartree was thinking of the specific demand for numerical solutions of the equations arising in contemporary science and engineering, and for the next few years he was not so wrong.[80] But Hartree's conception of the computer as a much faster version of the slide rule, an idea shared by almost everyone else involved, does starkly show how different Turing and Newman were when they considered it as a thinking machine. Hartree may also have been unwilling to accept this vision of machine intelligence for more political reasons, perhaps influenced by his colleague Polanyi: Hartree said in 1947 that he thought any idea of substituting humans by computers was *'a path which leads straight to Nazism'*.[81]

At the end of a long and wearying war, a path away from Nazism, at least, looked to have been won with some help from Hartree. Turing, Blackett and Newman had also made nationally noted wartime contributions that secured them reputations among those who would oversee Britain's post-war defence needs. That credit would be spent in Manchester.

Figure 36. Manchester Victoria West signal box. Douglas Hartree was never happier than inside a Manchester signal box, spending a Saturday afternoon with a favoured son or nephew.

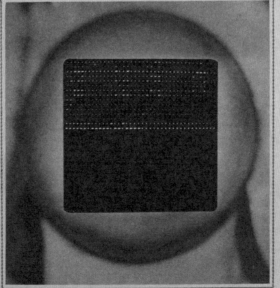

A CALCULATING MACHINE WITH A "MEMORY": THE CONTROL PANEL, AND A STORAGE TUBE IN USE.

(ABOVE.) THE CONTROL PANEL OF THE AUTOMATIC SEQUENCE-CONTROLLED CALCULATING MACHINE AT MANCHESTER UNIVERSITY ; SHOWING THE MONITOR CATHODE-RAY TUBE WITH DR. T. KILBURN (ON LEFT) AND PROFESSOR F. C. WILLIAMS, INVENTOR OF THE MEMORY-STORAGE SYSTEM EMPLOYED (ON RIGHT), FEEDING A PROBLEM INTO THE MACHINE. (LEFT) ONE OF THE CATHODE-RAY STORAGE TUBES, SHOWING THE POINTS OF LIGHT INDICATING A MATHEMATICAL PROBLEM IS BEING SOLVED.

WHEN Professor Geoffrey Jefferson delivered the Lister Oration at the Royal College of Surgeons of England on June 9, he disclosed that experiments were being conducted at Manchester University with a machine possessing a "memory." As a consequence, a number of misleading reports were published about the machine attributing to it almost human qualities. It is in fact similar to the American Electronic Numeral Integrater and Computor which we illustrated in our issue of November 9, 1946, but mainly differs from it in having a "memory," *i.e.*, it does not have to wait to be told what to do by a human operator when working out a problem, but, by the use of electronic circuits with a delay action, it is able to store a vast quantity of information which automatically takes its proper place in the calculation. This memory-storage system was invented by Professor F. C. Williams, who is seen in our photograph with Dr. Kilburn, feeding a mathematical problem into the machine for solution. The Manchester Automatic Sequence-Controlled Calculating Machine has been devised and constructed to undertake a wide variety of complex calculations which would take human [*Continued opposite.*

Continued.]

beings, using ordinary methods, possibly months to carry out, where the machine takes only an hour or so. The human controller has to decide how the Calculating Machine can perform the desired calculation, and draws up a list of "instructions" for it to obey. He breaks up the complex calculation into a series of simple basic operations and translates these from numbers into a specified code. For instance, the operation of subtracting one number from another is called operation No. 29 in the code. The list of "instructions" is fed into the machine, and the initial numbers (in code) on which it is to operate are then loaded into a special position. All the information having been fed into the Calculating Machine, its "memory" can be switched on to start operations. When the machine has worked out the whole problem, a red light switches on and it stops automatically. The final result can then be read off the monitor cathode-ray tube (shown in our photograph) in the form of light dots which are translated into figures by the human controller. A photograph of the complete apparatus appears elsewhere in this issue.

Why Manchester?

Newman was well placed to identify Turing as brilliantly able to explore the mathematical potential of the computer and it is no surprise that in May 1948, Newman offered him a position in Manchester University as Deputy Director of the Computing Laboratory. But why did Turing accept the offer? Turing's comfortable Cambridge Fellowship had another four years to run, and he was very greatly valued at the time by GCHQ: he told one friend he had been offered £5,000 a year to work for them.[82] Turing was also in international demand. In 1939 he had been offered a US job at the prestigious Institute for Advanced Studies and it's unclear why he had turned it down, though he had found his years in Princeton socially—and sexually—disappointing. Post-war there was another invitation from MIT, and suggestions that he might move to a renowned centre of mathematics in Nancy: he was not unaware of the comic potential to the English of being a gay man in such a job.[83]

But it was in Manchester that in June 1948 the Small Scale Experimental Machine, or Baby[84], was used to run the first computer program in the world.[85] Turing was not in the room, or even the city, when this happened. He and Newman *had* been central to making the mathematical possibility of a computer visible to engineers, and as we have seen, Newman was at first administratively responsible for the project. But after 1948 Newman had no, and Turing, little direct input into the immense challenges of building a working computer. Turing did not come to Manchester to build a computer: he came to use one. And the machine he came to use was built by Freddie Williams.

Freddie Williams and Tom Kilburn

The official start of the Manchester computer project had been the arrival of Max Newman in its Mathematics Department, and the original plan had been to recruit the necessary engineers into a laboratory under Newman's direction and funded by the grant he had obtained. But the arrangements evolved rapidly. Newman's first choice of engineer had been Tommy Flowers, the creator of the Colossus, but when Flowers made it clear he preferred to remain at the Post Office Research Station in Dollis Hill, the second choice was **FC, 'Freddie', Williams**.[86] Williams had no personal knowledge of the Bletchley Park developments, but like Flowers he had established himself as a brilliant radar engineer, and had taught in Manchester before the war, including working on the Differential Analyser. Williams was offered a job, but as

Figure 37. Williams and Kilburn, 1949. This is one of the earliest photographs of the Manchester computer, taken over a year after the Baby first ran. Although the mathematicians had given input into the logical design of the machine, both the memory tube it tested and every aspect of the electronics was a creation of Williams and his team.

chance had it the relevant Professorship came vacant just then, and with Blackett machinating in the background, the relatively young Williams was appointed to a chair too. [87]

Williams is one of the few men in this book to have been born locally. [88] He went to Stockport Grammar School and then on to Manchester University, where he graduated with a First in Engineering in 1932, and then briefly moved to work for Metropolitan Vickers before going to Oxford, sponsored by Ferranti, to study for a doctorate. Armed with this he returned to a university career in Manchester, and then at the outbreak of war was recruited to the work on radar that made his reputation. Blackett had been instrumental in both latter moves as well as his Professorial appointment. Williams was not the choice of the outgoing Professor; Blackett specifically insisted that Williams be shortlisted, and that the selection meeting be delayed so that both he and Newman could attend. Williams was far from being an anti-Oxbridge candidate: Hartree was on the committee too and had concerns about his narrowness, but was partly consoled by the fact that Williams *'was second choice for cox of the Oxford boat, which, I imagine, needs other qualities than just a light weight'*. Williams had already been approached to work on Turing's computer project in London but turned it down in favour of Manchester because, it's said, of unease about whether he could work with Turing. [89] There is no record of Williams' reaction when he later learned that Turing was coming to use the machine that Williams had successfully built where Turing had failed. Williams made little use of the components that Newman had scavenged, but used his own government contacts to get the

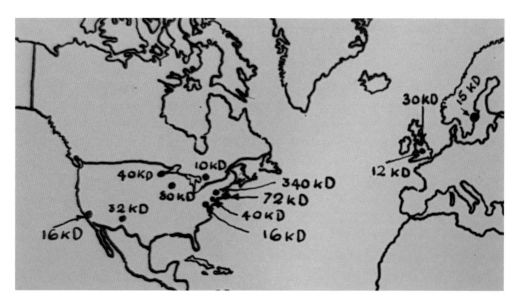

Figure 38. The Williams' Tube map of the world, around 1952, showing the thousands of binary digits of the world's first practical computer memory spreading from Manchester across the Atlantic. In the US, IBM's adoption of the technology dwarfed British efforts. Note the small installation apparently in Sweden.

specific parts that he needed. After the first prototypes, Williams largely moved on to other problems and the leadership of the Department, handing over all subsequent computing developments to Tom Kilburn. [90]

Williams later explained this by saying that 'one out of one' was an unimprovable success rate, but perhaps like Turing, the increasing corporatisation of the computer development process became less congenial to the brilliant wartime problem solver. Unlike Turing, though, he was remembered as an able administrator, keeping something of a distance: he was known as FC to his staff and as Freddie only to his old wartime colleagues and his close neighbours in suburbia. Williams settled to a domestic life in a Timperley mansion and his own take on the Manchester myth: *'The Manchester weather was terrible, but the pubs sold Boddingtons bitter beer, and in any case the North of England was God's own country'.* [91]

Williams' student **Tom Kilburn** was a Northerner too, but from the other side of the Pennines. Williams said, when explaining to a colleague how to handle Kilburn, that *'what you must always remember is that Tom is a Yorkshireman'* to explain (or perhaps justify) his stubbornness. He was the kind of Yorkshireman who was delighted to be a Manchester United season ticket holder, and he took care to spend every August on holiday in the North West not too far from Manchester. [92] He had worked for Williams in the TRE lab, but there was no post-war job for him there and so he accepted a secondment in a move that was to define Manchester computing for generations. Kilburn had wanted to be a chemist, not a mathematician, but his Dewsbury grammar school couldn't offer Cambridge entrance tuition in chemistry. [93] Kilburn went to Cambridge during the war and was taught by Max Newman, but he was squarely in the applied mathematics camp. [94] Kilburn's Cambridge was not Turing's: the actual membership list of the Apostles may be famously secret, but it has never disclosed any grammar school boys of engineering bent from Leeds. Kilburn was perhaps more formed by the five years he then spent on defence work, after which he thought of himself as *'more of an electronic engineer than a mathematician'.* [95] The idea was that he would return to TRE as soon as the problem of the memory store was solved, though he did register for a PhD. But when the Lockspeiser contract was signed with Ferranti, Kilburn moved to a permanent job at Manchester University, and here he stayed for his entire academic career. At first Kilburn was newly married with a young child, and to save money he commuted from his parents' house over the Pennines. It was literally on the back of an envelope, on the train from Dewsbury to Manchester, that Kilburn supposedly wrote the world's first computer program. [96]

Kilburn quickly emerged from under Williams' shadow as a natural leader, inspiring great loyalty with a somewhat dominating personality which allowed only a single vision of the computer to emerge. [97] Turing had been recruited as 'Deputy Director' of the Laboratory, but by 1951 Kilburn was describing himself as Director. [98]

The Baby and the Marks 1

The prime technical hurdle in creating a working computer in 1948 lay not in the logic circuits but in a workable memory to connect them to. And this is what Williams and his young assistant Kilburn achieved. The rival Cambridge project was using 'delay lines', long tubes filled with mercury, but they were hard to use with a digital computer, despite a serious suggestion from Turing that performance could be improved by filling them with gin instead. Williams and Kilburn instead took off the shelf cathode-ray tubes, which wartime radar developments had made increasingly reliable and standardised. [99]

When a phosphor dot on the screen of the tube is hit by the cathode ray it illuminates briefly and then decays. A dot which remains is a memory. If it is possible to detect the illumination, it can be refreshed, but there was no reliable way to do this. Static was generated when the ray hit the screen, and even before arriving in Manchester, Williams had brilliantly noticed that this static behaved surprisingly, in a then little-understood way, but one which could allow the signal to be refreshed indefinitely. Williams first designed and built a circuit that demonstrated the storage of a single bit. In Manchester, but with the resources of TRE to supply parts and skilled staff, he had within a year constructed the Williams Tube and Oxford Road became home to the world's first practical

Figure 39. The Baby, as reconstructed in the Museum of Science on Industry, seen on the 70th anniversary of 21st June 1948, the day its first program ran. Kilburn commented that the main difference between the original and the 1998 reconstruction was that the original had been much dirtier.

computer memory. [100] The Baby was built to test and show off this memory. It did need to do some calculations to be a convincing demonstration, and so the engineers took *'instructions from Newman as to what facilities needed to be provided'*, albeit ones that they remembered took *'only half an hour'* to deliver. [101] But by the time the Baby ran that first program on 21st June 1948, Williams and his team no longer needed to be told what to do by mathematicians, and they started a tradition of computer engineering in Manchester that was to continue for decades.

The mathematicians may have been largely out of the development process by 1948 but Newman was still central to the political one of marshalling further resources for the new computer. [102] In July it was Newman who reported to the University on the visit of a senior government scientist to see the machine. That was successful enough for Blackett to arrange for a second visitor to make the trip, this time the even more senior defence scientist **Ben Lockspeiser**. Further evidence of the close relationship between the City and the University comes from the fact that Blackett persuaded the cotton trade administrator Sir **Raymond Street** to host a party for Lockspeiser at the Clarendon Club, a businessman's club in what had once been the Duke of Bridgewater's own house on St Peter's Square. [103] The hospitality paid off when the city received a contract notable in its largesse and lack of specificity: Ferranti was offered almost £100,000 to construct a machine *'to the instructions of Professor FC Williams'.* [104] This milestone marks the point by which political and intellectual responsibility had moved decisively from Newman to Williams. But Blackett was, as before, still in the background.

Later, the City Council's consent was needed for a compulsory purchase order for the site of a new Dover Street building to house the machine, and it is another mark of the closeness of City and University that the Council immediately agreed. The owners of the garage occupying the site weren't so easily convinced and there had to be a Public Inquiry. The Deputy Bursar of the University was sent to say that *'In Manchester it had been possible to invent an electronic calculating machine, which had been attempted in many other countries without success…it is most important that we should start leading the world in this line of research. The Government has provided equipment and materials for this project'.* The Inquiry found for the Council. [105]

The landmark events of 1948 took place in a 1912 extension to the back of the Physics laboratory on Coupland Street. Turing's office was elsewhere; he and his assistants shared an office based in the Mathematics department on the top floor of the original, Victorian, University building. [106] The Baby was built in a room labelled the 'Magnetism' room after its former use in the Rutherford era, and still tiled with a glazed brick, originally a technical innovation to keep the laboratory clean just like the London Road Fire Station. [107] The engineers who had used the Magnetism room were fond of recalling this tiling, now lost, as 'late

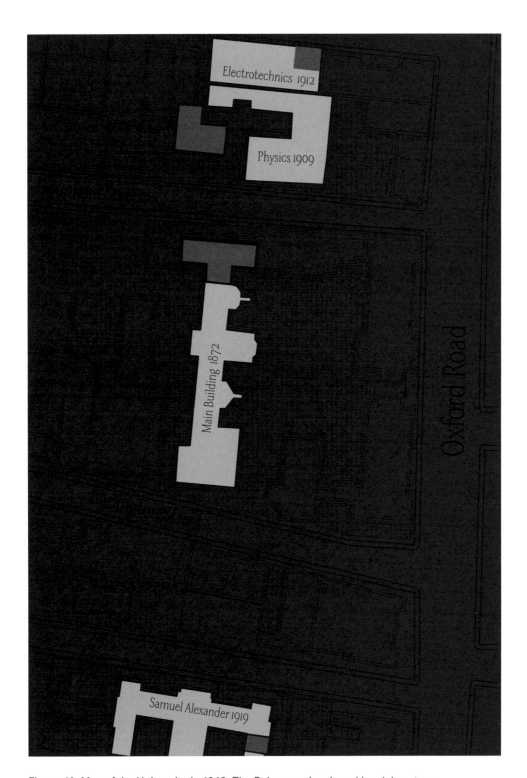

Figure 40. Map of the University in 1948. The Baby was developed in a laboratory space in the 1912 Electrotechnics building at the back of the then Physics department, while Turing and Newman remained in the main University building. When the new building designed specifically for the Ferranti Mark I was opened in 1951, Turing, but not Newman, joined the engineers there. The 1949 seminar took place in what is now the Samuel Alexander building.

Figure 41. When the institution that became Manchester University had moved to Oxford Road in 1873, it was on the rural edge of the city. By the 1940s it was surrounded by dense streets of terraced housing, sharing with the University a thick black coat of soot. In this 1957 photo the H-shaped Electrical Engineering building of 1954—with a Ferranti computer on its top floor—stands out for its cleanliness, though still hemmed in by pre-war housing.

lavatorial'.[108] The room had been built within one of the most highly advanced scientific spaces on earth, but thirty years later, perhaps it suited the anti-theoretical, string-and-struggle self-image of the engineers to forget this.

Over the following three years Williams and his team built further prototypes in the Magnetism room, but by 1951 the long-envisaged extra space had been built and Kilburn and Turing moved into offices facing each other in a 'temporary' two-storey building, that still stands, further up Coupland Street. It was into the ground floor of this building that the first Ferranti Mark I came when it arrived later in the year.[109] It wasn't until 1954 that a permanent building was finished on the other side of Oxford Road where the later Ferranti machines could be installed *'like an oracle surrounded by priests and acolytes'* in *'un-heard of luxury'*. The building was intended as the first in a new, open science precinct, but the rest of the plan was not erected until the 1960s and so it was initially hemmed in by Victorian terraced housing.[110]

Some of the government's huge payments to Ferranti came back to the individuals in the University. Relationships between the University and local industry had often had a financial component, and if a firm wanted a particular

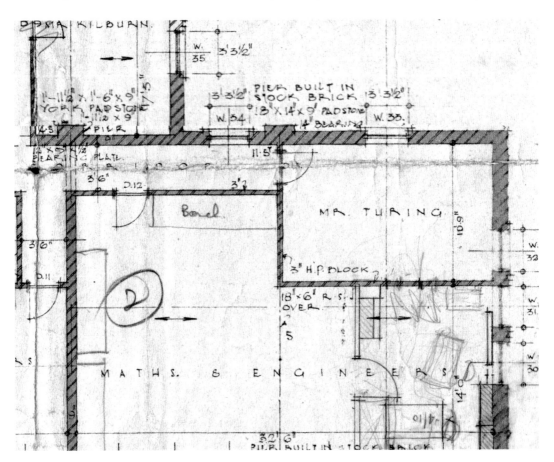

Figure 42. First-floor plan for the building that housed the Ferranti Mark I from 1951, with offices for both Kilburn and Turing.

piece of work done in the Engineering Department it had been common for them to fund a research assistant or student to carry the work out. It had been the clear policy of the pre-war Professor of Engineering that permanent University staff should not be paid for their role in projects, but his successor had no intention of being financially unrewarded as the inventor of the world's first computer memory. When Williams visited IBM in the US in 1949, to sell the Williams tube as a storage device, IBM offered him a $1,000 dollar fee for the visit. The UK government took a dim view of this and insisted that they should be the ones paying the $1,000, presumably to guarantee that Williams was on their side and not IBM's: characteristically, the problem was smoothed out over after-dinner drinks at the Blacketts. [111] Turing, Williams and Kilburn were all to sign consultancy agreements with Ferranti. [112] Kilburn's was to amount to a significant fraction of his salary, and separately Kilburn and Williams had income from their memory patents as well. These were not temporary arrangements: Turing was still being paid when he died in 1954, and Williams was still being paid under his until 1969, almost two decades after he had ceased to be personally researching technical innovation relevant to Ferranti's computer. The grammar school lad from Stockport in the end retired to the Cheshire town of Prestbury, famed for the affluence of its residents. [113]

Figure 43. As well as the initial advance for the Ferranti Mark 1, Ferranti sold most of its production run at a profit back to the Government through the National Research Development Corporation. This Ferranti sales forecast from 1954 is unique in the Ferranti archives for mentioning by name the normally hidden GCHQ as a customer. A further £100,000 of commercial sales was also predicted.

```
N.R.D.C.
4 + 1 Mk.I Computers
(5x55,000 less
£200,000 already
received)  £75,000

1 + 9 medium sized
computers  50,000
plus (9x22,000)
            £248,000

1 Mk.II
prototype .£75,000        £398,000

G.C.H.Q.                  £ 27,000

Uncommitted
manufacturing output     £ 51,000

Total over
3 years                  £576,000
```

The /////// at the Window

Turing's official role was to help users exploit the Mark I. He has been called ill-suited to the task; though he is remembered by some as intensely helpful and capable of enjoyable lectures, to others he was unapproachable and rude, *'not temperamentally suited to helping users who weren't fairly competent themselves'*. The difference seems to have been that he decided very rapidly who was 'tuned into a Turing wavelength' and did not give others a second chance.[114] Turing wrote the first programming manual, universally agreed to be incomprehensible, though one reader said it was an excellent tutorial text because all of the examples were wrong and by the time you had worked out how to make them right you had learned to program.[115]

    Most notorious was Turing's habit during explanation of using the machine's base-32 arithmetic, and assuming that everyone else like him had memorised the 32 different 'digits' of its code. The code used the slash, '/', for zero, which meant many output pages were covered in '//////////', an effect which, almost self-parodically of the South's view of the North, *'at Cambridge was said to resemble the Manchester rain lashing at the windows'*.[116] In 1948 the idea of

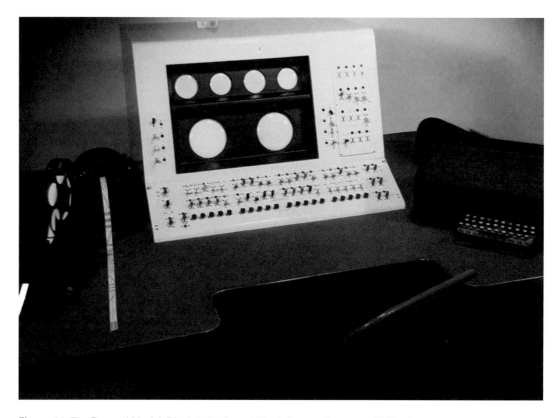

Figure 44. The Ferranti Mark I. Blackett had used his defence science credibility to steer resources towards William and Kilburn's prototype Manchester Mark I. He was then instrumental in ensuring that prototype was seen by the senior defence scientists, who could then lavishly fund Ferranti to commercialise it into the Ferranti machine.

counting in different bases was a well understood but obscure branch of pure mathematics with no practical application; few engineers or applied mathematicians would have encountered it in their prior education. When Turing gave one talk in 1949, the person most well placed to understand him recalled *'I do not think he was being funny or trying to score off us, it was simply that he could not appreciate a trivial matter of that kind could affect anybody's understanding one way or the other'*. [117]

Though Turing did contribute his own software to the Mark I until 1951, this work was uninfluential either in Manchester or elsewhere. Hodges described him, by the time of the Manchester computer's inaugural conference in July 1951, as a dull irrelevance, a *'shabby and eccentric survival from the Cambridge of the 1930s...against the classless stainless steel of the dawning 1950s'*. [118] Irrelevance may be an over-statement if his job was understood as to create demand for time on the Mark I, for demand there certainly was and several scientists recall helpful discussion with Turing. Turing had made important, but literally peripheral hardware contributions to the Manchester Mark I by showing the team how to use and source punched-tape technology, knowledge he had acquired at Bletchley Park. But for new designs, Turing was out of the inner loop, if not out of the program: a planning meeting on the shape of the Mark II in April 1951 went ahead without him, but he was minuted as to be consulted.

Figure 45. This Ferranti Mark 1, seen in a sales publicity shot from Ferranti's 1952 catalogue, was the first computer ever sold. The cabinets on either side enclose what had been bare valves in the University prototype, and their cosmetic function literally provides a reflection of Turing. The lab coats of the 1949 University engineers have been replaced by suits for the Ferranti engineers sitting at the console. Although Turing has been pushed to the side, his inclusion does reflect a commercial desire to emphasise the applicability of the new technology.

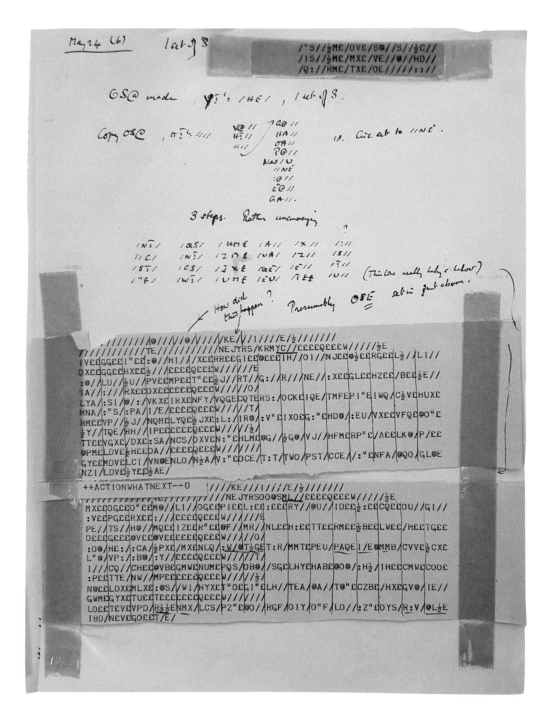

Figure 46. Alan Turing's programming note, probably from 1953–54. He has identified a bug with the words 'how did this happen' attached to unexplained data in the computer memory. This newly complex software was very hard to debug, even without the Mark I's notorious hardware breakdowns. The engineers believed that they had done their job because the machine worked at all: the mathematicians felt that they could not do theirs because it kept breaking down. The ////s were said in Cambridge to represent Manchester rain.

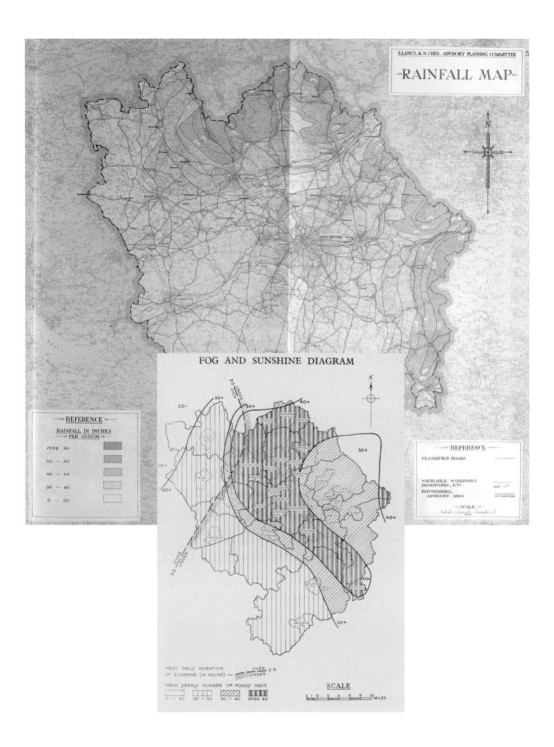

Figure 47. Manchester actually had a relatively low rainfall for a city in west Britain, and lower than the surrounding hills, as shown in the upper map, drawn in 1947. But grey skies were largely an issue of pollution, and the lower map, from the same source, shows how fog could cloak the industrial belt.

Turing did contribute one piece of design to the Ferranti Mark I. It was a random number generator. [119] At the time Turing was interested in the evolution of random biological noise into form and it is possible that he was intent on modifying the new computer for his own intellectual ends. But it's much more likely that the intended application was for cryptographic research, which would tend to support the argument that much of the Manchester development was driven by an intended GCHQ consumer. [120] In the end GCHQ did buy a machine, and continued working with Manchester on technical innovation for at least a few years more. A successor to Colossus was being developed internally at GCHQ from 1952, but they still worked closely with the Ferranti factory in Moston to develop the magnetic drum. Ferranti probably got technical knowhow from the contract that it would use in its general drum technology, but the secrecy surrounding the design of GCHQ machines meant there were few other spin-offs. [121]

The secrecy of the GCHQ work had implications for how Manchester thought about its achievement in public. The Mark I was about automating reasoning, but for the majority who did not know about the secret work, the only immediately visible and commercially viable application was just faster versions of adding up. By contrast the more-or-less contemporary development at Jodrell Bank (also with Blackett's finger-marks all over it), was, thanks to Sputnik, within a couple of years seized on as a symbol of the city's self-image, a process that the thinking machine would take fifty years to achieve. Newman's lost original vision had been for a machine for doing mathematics, the manipulation of logical facts through which thought could emerge. Instead the public promise was to calculate number sums quickly. Ferranti could have been a Manchester factory, manufacturing fact-making machines for Turing or any other man or woman: but no one could see it. [122]

The cold of Nursery Road

What did Turing make of Manchester? What was the social network for outsiders like him or Lyn? On arrival in 1948, Turing initially took lodgings in Nursery Road, not far from chemist Michael Polanyi. Polanyi recalled visiting Turing in his Hale lodgings to find him practising the violin, *'not bothering or not daring'* to ask his landlady for a fire. [123] The lodgings were also close to the Newmans, and Turing and would often walk or run to their house. There would be mathematical chats with Max, and later more literary ones with Lyn, and then board games with their boys; once Turing turned up very early in the morning to leave a message, without pen or paper, and impressed one of the boys by scratching it into a rhododendron leaf pushed through the door. [124] Turing become a family friend of the Polanyis too, with more puzzles and board games, and Michael's son **John Polanyi**, like the sons of the Newmans, would be treated to scientific encouragement. Perhaps Turing's encouragement made a difference: John followed his father Michael into chemistry, and while Michael Polanyi came close

Figure 48. Turing's first lodging, in Nursery Avenue Hale, near to the homes of Newman and Polanyi. Many University staff lived rather closer: Patrick Blackett was in a grand mansion in what is still a University enclave in Fallowfield. Altrincham and Hale are 10 miles south of the University, well served by train and bus, but with access to open countryside.

Figure 49. In 1950, Turing acquired his first home with the purchase of *Hollymeade,* a semi-detached house backing on to fields on the outskirts of Wilmslow. This plaque was unveiled there by Mancunian mathematician Kathleen Ollerenshaw in 2004.

ALAN TURING
1912 - 1954
Founder of computer science and cryptographer, whose work was key to breaking the wartime Enigma codes, lived and died here.

Figure 50. A letter explaining the game solitaire from Alan Turing to Maria Greenbaum, the 8-year-old daughter of his therapist, in the summer of 1953. In the later years of his Manchester life, the Greenbaums became one of Turing's closest social contacts.

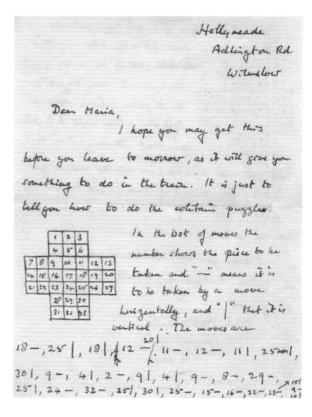

Figure 51. Turing was pleased to show off the marvel of the Bridgewater Canal bridge to visitors. A gated basin (in the distance) allows the Canal to cross over the much larger Manchester Ship Canal running below, but the basin rotates to allow tall ships to traverse the Ship Canal. The power station, on the Eccles side of the Ship Canal, has since been demolished.

to winning a Nobel Prize, John actually did. These friendships were in the early Manchester days; later on, when Turing was in therapy with Franz Greenbaum, he became a family friend of the Greenbaums too.

Out in the city, Turing of course noticed the dirt: *'I am getting used to this part of the world, but still find Manchester rather mucky. I avoid going there more than I can avoid'.* [125] But Turing took pride in taking one visitor to see the city's remarkable industrial heritage in the shape of the Bridgewater Canal aqueduct over the Manchester Ship Canal.

In his London years, Turing had taken up running long distances as a way of handling stress, and in Manchester he found Nursery Road within a minute's run of the open countryside of the Cheshire plain. A train into work was the very reason the Hale suburb existed, but Turing would more usually cycle, or sometimes run, the eight miles into the University, with all the associated runners' workplace comedy of shorts and wallets to sort out once he arrived. [126]

In the south, Turing's teammates had included public school runners like Chris Chataway, who moved easily into banking and the Conservative party after he had paced Roger Banister's four-minute mile, but long-distance running had perhaps a more democratic tinge to it than track-based athletics. [127] Manchester's club for elite runners, the Salford Harriers, had a significant working-class membership, and proudly remembers the complicit support it gave John Tarrant, the 'Ghost Runner'. Tarrant had once taken a £4 professional fee as a boxer and ever after had to duck out at the finishing line each time he won a race to avoid the whole event being disqualified under the Amateur Athletics Association's rules. Turing didn't join a club in Manchester, though he would have found himself among the few athletes who could have offered real competition. In 1947, the year before he arrived, the Salford Harriers had organised a marathon, from the city centre out to Hale. The winner came third in the British Olympic trials the following year, beating Turing down to fifth.

But it was not working-class boys that Turing ran with: he struck up a running partnership with Alan Garner, a Manchester Grammar School sixth-former, and they ran a thousand miles or more over the course of 1951 and 1952. They often ran through Alderley Edge, where Garner would later locate his well-known novel *The Weirdstone of Brisingamen*, adjacent to the site where ICI would later make Alderley Park. Garner remembered Turing as obsessed by mathematics and biology and as asking Garner's opinion, as a budding linguist, whether artificial intelligence was possible. [128]

Since 1948, Turing had been in a relationship with a younger Cambridge student, Neville Johnson, but maintaining this long-distance relationship under the eye of a suburban landlady may not have been easy. In addition, the friendly haven that was the Newmans' Hale household moved elsewhere, and Turing was by now earning a substantial salary as a Reader, together with significant consulting payments from Ferranti and GCHQ. [129] So in the summer of 1950 Turing bought a house, moving eight miles west from Hale to Wilmslow. Though built at a similar period as the suburban streets of Hale, Dean Row Road was a ribbon development backing on to fields and Hollymeade was, though semi-detached, much more private than Hale. In the end, the remoteness didn't help the dwindling intensity of the relationship with Johnson, but Turing was not isolated. The twin of the semi was owned by the family of **Roy Webb**, a Manchester solicitor who had been an almost exact contemporary of Turing's at Sherborne school. [130] The family became friendly with Turing: he would babysit their young son and they would often invite him for meals. Turing had a home.

Figure 52. Turing took up long-distance running after the war and was for a few years a prospect for selection for the English national team. After he moved to Manchester he retained an affiliation with his southern club.

CRICCIETH

THE OFFICIAL GUIDE

PRICE ONE SHILLING

Manchester By the Sea

We had built a network of railways and could travel about without passports and settle down anywhere without permit: a degree of civilization inconceivable today...it was one great united European culture in which I grew up and went to the university.

Michael Polanyi, recalling his student years in Budapest. [131]

Before the war, travel on the European mainland had been a feasible, almost essential, part of the formation of a young English intellectual as much as a Hungarian one. One of the things Lyn and Max discovered they had in common was their separate travels through Weimar Germany and Austria. For family holidays this was less of an option and the Blacketts and Polanyis had holidayed in North Wales. After 1945, a near bankrupt Britain imposed strict currency controls on its citizens, and international travel returned to being even more of an elite activity.

Manchester academics like the Newmans stayed in the UK for their family holidays. They often returned to Wales, and rarely followed Wittgenstein's footsteps to working-class Blackpool. Or Freud's, for that matter; astonishingly Sigmund Freud too had a day out in Blackpool in the same summer of 1908 that Wittgenstein started to explore the North West from Glossop. When in Blackpool, Freud sent his daughter a postcard prominently featuring the Blackpool Tower, a relatively recent local erection. Freud was visiting his half-brother Emanuel; he'd visited Manchester once before when Emanuel ran a trading business in what is now the Gay Village. [132]

Lyn first properly got to know Turing nine months after he arrived, not in Manchester, but in Wales, where Max invited him to holiday with them in the seaside resort of Criccieth at Easter 1949. Lyn recorded her first impressions of Alan: *'with his off-hand manners and his long silences — silences finally torn up by his shrill stammer and the crowing laugh which told upon the nerves even of his friends'.* [133]

Bertrand Russell came for Sunday lunch at Criccieth, having left serious philosophy behind — Max's friend Richard Braithwaite privately described Russell's latest book as 'senile' — but now a well-known public intellectual. Turing and Max Newman and Russell all had common backgrounds in logic and philosophy symbolised through their contact with Wittgenstein. Together with

Figure 53. Criccieth, post-war holiday destination for Manchester professionals with families. It was here, in 1949, that Lyn Irvine got to know Alan Turing, though he spent much of the time on long solitary runs around the bay.

the times that Polanyis and the Blacketts were all in North Wales, it made for high-brow holidays with what Lyn labelled the 'Manchester gang'; in later years the historian Eric Hobsbawm called the set-up nearly a Welsh Bloomsbury. For Lyn there was also the prospect of a freedom from domestic demands: *'Wet, wet, wet here, but always wonderful to be free of the household chores'.*[134]

In 1946 and 1947 the Newmans went to Borth-y-Gest, a holiday much improved the second year when they could go by car and *'cut out the unspeakable journey from Manchester to Porthmadog by train'*, though by 1952 Lyn was again having to do all the shopping and sandwich making. That year had some compensation: Patrick Blackett's 'Nobel Prize yacht', the 26-footer *Red Witch,* was anchored in the bay.[135] The unmarried could go further. Manchester University's Philosophy Professor Dorothy Emmet often holidayed abroad, always alone, from France to Norway. Wittgenstein had also spent time in Norway, most notably in 1936 and 1937 while he was writing *Philosophical Investigations,* and judging by the confessions he insisted on delivering to close friends at the time, romantic potential was not for him at the heart of the Norwegian experience.[136] Turing had once tasted all the joys of a romantic North Wales holiday, with his fiancée

Figure 54. A postcard sent by Sigmund Freud to his daughter in 1908, on his summer holidays in Blackpool with his brother Emanuel. Two years later, Wittgenstein followed in Freud's footsteps, and in the 1950s Turing visited too, accompanied by his (Jungian) psychoanalyst.

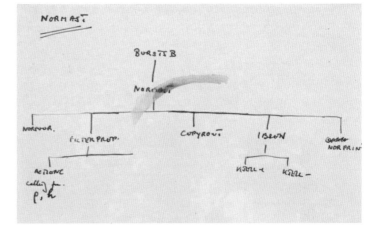

Figure 55. Turing's fascination with Norway persisted after his 'light kiss' with a man named Kjell. The tree he drew up of the subroutines of his code has includes named KJELL+ and KJELL-, each called by a routine named IBSEN. The master BURSTSB routine was part of an embryonic operating system.

Joan Clarke, in 1941. They went to Porthmadoc and found the booking mixed up and the rain recurrent, and they broke off their engagement soon afterwards. But as a single man with consultancy work, even without Nobel Prize money or a Professorial salary, Turing was able to holiday abroad. He went, alone, to France post-war, to Norway in 1952 and Corfu in 1953. These foreign trips carried heavy erotic memory and promise for Turing: he wrote a brief fragment of a story set in December 1951, with extremely close parallels with his own life, and his alter-ego in the story had not 'had' anyone since that *'soldier in Paris last summer'.* Turing had heard that Norway held men-only dances and invested in learning Norwegian grammar and then in a trip. Though his visit left him disappointed on the dancing front, he did acquire a photograph of one **Kjell Carlson**, with whom he had exchanged *'a light kiss beneath a foreign flag'.* [137] When Turing went to Corfu the next year he was after more than a holiday romance: *'There I expect to lie in the sun, talk French and modern Greek, and make love, though the sex and nationality of the favoured ones has yet to be decided: in fact it is quite possible that this item will be omitted. I want a permanent relationship and might reject anything which could not be permanent'.* [138]

Figure 56. Clipper Travel, the in-flight magazine of Pan-Am, from Kilburn's December 1951 trip to Philadelphia. Kilburn kept the magazine until he retired.

But a significant perk of being a defence-critical scientist was international travel on official business. After the war, there were conferences to attend and machines to inspect or to sell, and Williams and Kilburn joined Turing in the elite that travelled abroad for work. Turing said he had had enough of the US by 1953, refusing one trip to a prestigious and interesting conference on the grounds that 'I detest America': if he knew or feared by then he would not be allowed a visa he didn't tell his peers. By then it may have been more than just American travel that became infeasible: Turing mysteriously cancelled a 1953 trip to Germany well after it was all planned. [139]

Kilburn was much more excited about his 1951 trip to the US, probably his first out of the country: he kept the in-flight magazine all his life, complete with the notes he made of the pilot's announcements and the currency restrictions. The women for the most part stayed at home. But those with programming expertise to impart could travel internationally too: two of Turing's staff, Bates and Popplewell, made long working visits to Canada from 1952. [140]

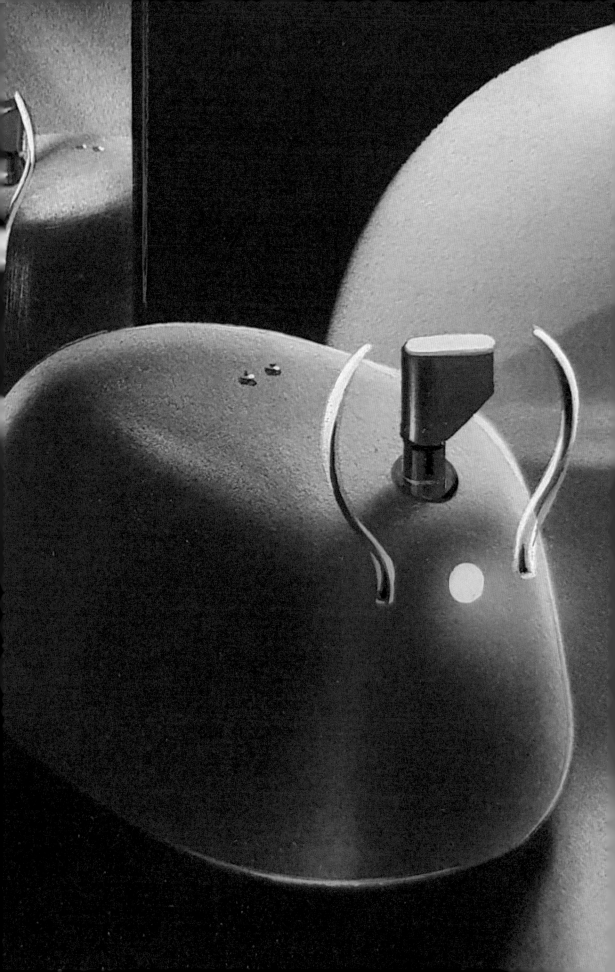

Is a Mathematician a Human?

Cybernetics comes to Manchester

In 1949 Lyn Irvine was witness to unsettling conversations between her husband and her new friend: *'To hear [Max] & Alan quietly chatting about the machine in our garden sometimes make me feel very queer & uncomfortable. Max hopes to teach it to see a joke. It will learn how to play chess probably in the Autumn & Max is to have the first game & a wager that he will win. That's all right...but when I heard Alan say of further possibilities "Wh-wh-what will happen at that stage is that we shan't understand how it does it, we'll have lost track", I did find it a most disturbing prospect. It was Professor Jefferson's Lister Oration which broke the peaceful silence & started first The Times & then all the tabloid papers on their stampede for stories & pictures'.* [141]

Although Lyn may have found talk of the new computer disturbing, she recognised its significance, and she was not alone. Plans for electronic computers were being dubbed 'electronic brains' by journalists as early as 1946. [142] An American press conference in June about the Princeton computer had led to a flurry of US articles heavy on 'brain' imagery, but in the UK it was a report by Hartree in the scientific journal *Nature* in October 1946 that was picked up and eventually reported in *The Times.* This had been a fairly sober report, but the hype really started in 1948 when the American **Norbert Wiener** published *Cybernetics,* the book that put the cyber into *Doctor Who*'s Cybermen. Wiener came to England during the writing of the book and spoke 'above all' to Turing, then in London, and noted *'Mr Williams' remarkable achievement'* in Manchester in making memory work. Wiener had worked during the war on automating anti-aircraft gunnery, where electronic advances started to allow the technology to make its own decisions by responding to feedback loops. Wiener inflated the mathematical technology involved into a hugely ambitious vision for how all human activity was part of a system whose feedback loops could be controlled.

It's hard now to see why the public were so interested in *Cybernetics*, which is mostly a dense technical mathematics text, dusted with references to the philosophical nature of time, and enlivened with few concrete examples. Simply the idea that scientists were discussing intelligent machines seems to have been enough to make it a best-seller. Wiener, on the *'art and science of control'*, caught the imagination of a population used to tales of wartime technological triumph.

Figure 57. Post-war fascination, and fear, about new ways of using machines to automate tasks was often labelled as 'cybernetics'. One of the most prominent British examples was the *Machina Speculatrix*, or mechanical tortoises, of W Grey Walter, which were constructed so as to explore their environment and then follow a light source back to their charging station before their battery failed. Grey Walter and Turing were both members of the Ratio Club, a group of young British scientists interested in intelligent mechanisms. These British cyberneticians looked down on the American Wiener's *Cybernetics* book as limited and self-publicising. Nevertheless, Grey Walter was happy to court press attention and to provide tortoises for the Festival of Britain's Science Exhibition.

The only other scientific book which sold as well that year was the *Kinsey Report*, with a new data-driven approach to talking about sex: both books would influence Turing's life but neither his thinking.[143]

Cybernetics reached the UK in 1949, and a reviewer noted that the cyberneticians hoped to make machines that ate *'equations as quickly as youngsters gobble peanuts'* but wondered about the possibility of *'an army of automata that will arise and take over'* and that cyberneticians could not *'hope to create a robot with a mechanism known in the terminology of another profession as the conscience'*.[144] Yet it was just these assumptions that Turing was prepared to challenge: *exactly* to create a robot with a conscience. It was Turing's bold claim that contemporary thinkers would have to grapple with, and the first considered British response to Wiener's techno-optimism came from Manchester.[145] It came not from a mathematician, engineer, philosopher or divine, but, as Lyn had noticed, from a brain surgeon.

Geoffrey Jefferson

Geoffrey Jefferson was a Manchester-made surgeon, but he had seen the world. The son of a Rochdale doctor, he'd been sent to Manchester Grammar School before studying medicine at the University and taking a junior post in the Manchester Royal Infirmary after graduation. Jefferson had met a young Canadian woman, Gertrude Flummerfelt, when she had been a Manchester medical student, and in 1913 he left to set up a new practice in British Columbia. With the onset of war, and the discovery that rural Canada did not provide the patient base for an ambitious young surgeon, Geoffrey and Gertrude eventually travelled to a military hospital in Petrograd.[146] They left Russia in the early days of the Bolshevik Revolution, and Jefferson spent the rest of the First World War in France before returning to Manchester. Jefferson was unusual for a surgeon of the time in valuing scientific research as means of medical progress, but struggled at first to establish a client base of patients that could pay adequate fees. However, Manchester possessed one of a network of specialist convalescent hospitals funded by the Ministry of Pensions to provide care to those maimed in combat, and the fees from the Grangethorpe Hospital in Fallowfield, together with the opportunities for research it provided, were crucial in giving Jefferson a platform to establish his reputation. By 1936, Jefferson was nationally prominent, and was made Professor of Surgery to prevent him moving to London. In 1949 Jefferson had, somewhat unusually for a doctor, been made a Fellow of the Royal Society in recognition of his scientific work. He was probably the highest paid figure in this book, earning over £3,500 a year, and his wife Gertrude was working part-time as a doctor too, running a family welfare service. She was until 1951 one of the three psychiatrists working at the Manchester Royal Infirmary. They ran two cars, though on one Lake District holiday they managed to leave their children behind as each thought the other had taken them.[147]

Figure 58. Grey Walter's day job was the developing science of the electroencephalograph. Here he is photographed (far left) alongside his Bristol colleague, neuropsychiatrist Frederick Golla (centre, standing). It was Golla who published the paper on hormone castration treatment that was to guide Turing's therapy.

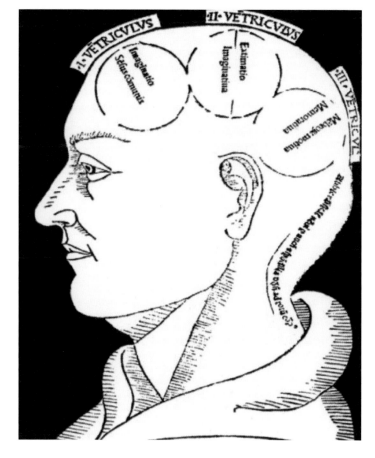

Figure 59. The idea of brain as a machine was hardly new in 1948. As Geoffrey Jefferson headed towards retirement as the dominant figure of Manchester neurology and neurosurgery, he expanded his amateur philosophical interest in the nature of mind, partly through discussion with Dorothy Emmet. Jefferson himself had published on *René Descartes on the Localisation of the Soul.* Jefferson was uniquely well-placed to raise intellectual challenges to Turing's claim that machines could think.

Jefferson was physically and professionally well placed to argue that the specialness of human consciousness meant there must be limits to what a computing machine could do. Physically, he was based a little further down Oxford Road at the Manchester Royal Infirmary but his teaching made him a part-time Professor in the University and member of its Senate, so he had probably been aware of the Manchester computing developments for some time. With a few years to go to retirement, his thoughts were tending to the philosophical too. When he was chosen to deliver the prestigious Lister Oration in June 1949 to the Royal College of Surgeons in London it was the Manchester Mark I that he chose as his subject, rather than the more normal surgical fare. [148]

Jefferson said that his understanding of the computer came from both his local colleague Williams and the US cybernetician Wiener but he was unimpressed by Wiener's glib analogies between the valve circuits of a computer and the neurons of the human brain. He reflected that the brain was believed to have about 10,000,000,000 neurons and compared this with the 20,000 valves in Princeton or the 1,000 in Manchester (though adding, loyally, that the Manchester machine was more efficient and most ingenious), and quoted an American estimate that a computer with wiring approaching the wiring of the human nervous system would require a *'building the size of the Empire State Building to house it and the complete electrical output of Niagara to power it'*. But Jefferson's lifelong career of literally sliding his hands into brain tissue had convinced him of the mysteriousness of where consciousness could possibly be located in the grey and bloody mess. He simply could not see how the brain could be a machine: *'not until a machine can write a sonnet or compose a concerto because of thoughts and emotions felt and not by the chance fall of symbols could we agree that machine equals brain'*. For Jefferson, his own felt emotions could not coexist with a chance fall of symbolic processing in his own brain. He went on *'No mechanism could...be warmed by flattery...be charmed by sex, be angry or depressed when it cannot get what it wants'*, and concluded that no achievement of machine competency could help us explore thinking.

When it comes to discussing cybernetic creations that act like humans, anxieties about sex and power have often surfaced, and Jefferson is an early example. What happens, he asked, if the machine can be charmed by sex? (Jefferson had his own ideas about the basis of gender. A few years later, his own doctor heard Jefferson joking *'I feel petulant, peevish and easily upset. I think they have transfused me with women's blood'*.[149]) But at the climax of the Oration he revealed the most alarming fear for a Fellow of the Royal Society: if machines can become FRSes, then what happens if *'the gracious premises of the Royal Society have to be turned into garages to house the new Fellows?'*

Jefferson's Lister Oration was to be quite significant for Manchester, not so much for any novelty, as the fact it didn't take place here at all. Instead it was delivered in London, and so in the presence of the national media. Over a year after the Baby had first run, *The Times* found a good story, combining

Figure 60. Geoffrey Jefferson, Manchester brain surgeon. As a young couple, Jefferson and his wife were present at the start of Bolshevik revolution in Moscow and later he worked in the military hospitals of the First World War. The science of surgery expanded rapidly under the brutal pressure of casualties, and Jefferson was part of a generation that adapted this new knowledge to peacetime. It was Jefferson who described Turing — with whom he profoundly disagreed about the nature of mind — as a *'sort of scientific Shelley'*.

Figure 61. Dorothy Emmet (right) on a Yosemite trail in 1929. Emmet went to the US specifically to study under the ex-Cambridge philosopher Alfred North Whitehead at Harvard. She found Whitehead inspirational, although concerned about sexual promiscuity among Harvard students. Whitehead's wife Evelyn told Emmet never to say she had 'experience' as it 'could only mean one thing'.

morality, anxiety, and British technological achievement. They rang Manchester and managed to get hold of Turing, who bit back at Jefferson: *'I do not think you can even draw the line about sonnets, though the comparison is perhaps a little bit unfair because a sonnet written by a machine will be better appreciated by another machine'*. [150] In short, Turing knew no reason why thought and emotion should not be a mechanical process and thus in principle be as accessible to a machine as to a human. Turing did not realise the media storm this would raise, as Lyn observed: *'[Turing] is wildly innocent about the ways of the press & has a bad stammer when he's nervous or puzzled. It was a great shock to him when he saw the Times & to Max...We had a wretched weekend starting at 12.30am... some paper rang up to get a story. By Sunday Max was getting a bit gruff & when he said "What do you want?" one reporter [said] "only to photograph your brain"'*. [151]

At the end of the wretched weekend Newman sent a letter to *The Times* giving a soberer description of the Manchester project: it's notable that neither of the men now remembered as creating the machine, Kilburn and Williams, were co-signatories on the letter. [152] Although Newman was concerned in public to play down the possibilities of the new machine for understanding the brain, in private he was more positive. When Lyn remarked how sometimes waiting overnight for a memory caused the 'good brownie' in one's brain to recall a fact, and asked Max if the new machine might explain this phenomenon, he said it might. [153]

Fortunately for marketing purposes, the attention came just as a significant software milestone had been reached by running a Mersenne prime program. The Baby of June 1948 had run only the barest of test programs and every bit had to be entered and retrieved by hand; the Manchester Mark I that followed had a little more memory but was still without very useful input/output, so it remained extremely hard to program. Newman made a canny choice of first problem by setting the task of calculating whether a particular kind of large number known as a Mersenne number was prime. As a demonstration application it was simple to code, not completely inexplicable to the layperson but nevertheless a visibly significant breakthrough to the scientist.

The Mersenne program was created by Kilburn and later substantially speeded up by Turing. [154] The London media started sniffing for a follow-up story, and the *Illustrated London News* printed what is now a classic image of the Manchester computer, still in the semi-lavatorial Magnetism room. A BBC film unit arrived too, and by then the engineers were able to show a machine running so that *'anyone who urgently wants to know whether $2^{127}-1$ is a prime number or not can be given the answer by an electronic brain in 25 minutes instead of by a human brain in six months'*.

All the publicity drew attention to Turing's much broader claims about the possibility of a mechanical nature for thought. These clearly polarised academic opinion, and so in October 1949 there assembled a cast of some distinction

Figure 62. The 1937 St Michael and All the Angels, Wythenshawe, designed by Nugent Cachemaille-Day. Emmet was a regular attender at services at this church, which she thought one of the most beautiful she had ever seen.

PROFESSOR IN THE KITCHEN

She cooks for relaxation

News Chronicle Reporter

MISS Dorothy Emmet, M.A. (Oxford) whose appointment as Professor of Philosophy at Manchester University was announced yesterday, believes

Figure 63. Newspaper interview marking Dorothy Emmet's appointment as Professor of Philosophy in 1947. Emmet's first Lectureship, at Newcastle University, had been welcomed by Wittgenstein solely on the grounds it would prevent one of his own protégés from taking up professional philosophy.

Figure 64. Jacob Epstein's bust of Samuel Alexander in the hallway of his eponymous University building. Alexander, born in Australia, was the first Jewish Fellow of an Oxbridge college and moved to Manchester to become Professor of Philosophy from 1893 to 1924. He created, almost single-handedly, an intellectually nurturing salon for students of the humanities during the pre-war years when vocational training dominated the University. He was probably the first professional philosopher to guide the young Wittgenstein, and his benevolent interest in Dorothy Emmet probably helped her to later take his place in the Chair. Anthony Burgess remembered the bust as a meeting point for assignations.

in the Philosophy department. *Can machines think?* It wasn't the first or last such discussion for philosophers, and nor was it the first time that machines were being thought of as brains. But for the first time there were the voices of logicians who had made machines that they believed could think, and it is very telling of the Manchester environment to look at the participants and their responses.

Emmet & Polanyi

The seminar was chaired by **Dorothy Emmet**, the Professor of Philosophy.[155] Emmet had been teaching in Manchester since before the war, although only just promoted to Professor. She had studied philosophy in a serious-minded Oxford of the 1920s, prominent in the Christian Union and once literally having Gandhi in the back of her car. But much of her political outlook was formed in the General Strike of 1926, when Emmet, unlike most Oxford undergraduates, found she did not wish to strike break.[156] By contrast, Hartree had been innocently delighted with the strike as an opportunity to scab in a railway signal box, and schoolboy Turing was cycling sixty miles cross-country to get back in time for the start of the Sherborne term. On the Left, Patrick Blackett spent 1926 ferrying copies of the pro-strike *British Worker* by car from London to Cambridge, though the effect on the Cambridge labour movement is unrecorded. Emmet never lost her leftish instincts, but a couple of subsequent summers tutoring in mining districts and meeting actual working-class people left her much further away from Marxism than Blackett's High Table version. Her faith, lifelong but undogmatic, was Christianity, and hers was the only avowedly Christian voice at the seminar.[157] Emmet's philosophical enthusiasm was for Russell's one-time Cambridge collaborator, Alfred North Whitehead, who had moved to Harvard. Whitehead was not a Christian (probably: his works are notoriously unreadable) but he was interested in thinking about God and religion in ways that the logicians of Cambridge were quite indifferent to. As a young woman Emmet raised the funds for a transatlantic trip and studied under Whitehead for a year: she kept a photograph of him in her home for decades.[158]

Emmet had known Samuel Alexander, who had been greatly loved as a previous Manchester Professor of Philosophy and now gives his name, and an Epstein bust, to the Arts Building, and perhaps for it was this reason she came to Manchester in 1938. It was the book she wrote during her wartime nights fire-watching on the roofs of the University, *The Nature of Metaphysical Thinking*, that established her as a serious philosopher and secured her Chair. Blackett, at least, thought well enough of Emmet to recruit her to a scheme in 1947 for humanities lectures to 'civilise the scientists'.[159] Emmet was certainly interested in 'the scientists': while we know little about how Emmet and Turing interacted, she made an effort to know Newman socially and intellectually.[160] One of the civilised scientists that Emmet met in the University was **Michael Polanyi**, who imported to Manchester a cosmopolitan, Hungarian intellectualism, voraciously interested in multiple subjects. By the end of the 1930s Polanyi had lost interest in the theoretical chemistry that had made his international reputation and of which he was the Professor. Before the war, he had, among other things, enlisted the Chemistry department's glassblower to build a water-filled model of the flow of money through an economy, with variants including conveyor belts with coloured balls and a machine with 'lots of wheels' inspired by Hartree's computer. He even made a film of his ideas, which debuted at the Manchester Statistical Society in 1936.[161] The University coped with Polanyi's change of interest by offering him a chair in 'Social Studies' instead, a title they made up to ensure that it would be sufficiently broad to cover whatever it was that Polanyi would do next, without including the unfundable word 'Philosophy'.[162] Whatever it was, Polanyi and Emmet ran a weekly afternoon seminar on Social Science for some years.[163]

Most professional philosophers thought Polanyi's philosophy technically weak—one called him *'a Higher obscurantist'*—and Dorothy Emmet shared this opinion and may have warned the Vice Chancellor that Polanyi would face harsh judgement from the discipline.[164] But she admired his grounding in the importance of religious faith, and, in particular, his idea of 'tacit knowledge', the *'penumbra surrounding whatever it is we hold in focal awareness'*.[165] Polanyi was, Emmet wrote, *'a very dear personal friend'*, and she cooked for him and shared her meat ration with him during the war: his wife seems to have been elsewhere. But though no doubt Emmet gently educated Polanyi about more than Plato, their relationship seems to have been entirely platonic.[166] Emmet was a member of a small religious group known as the Blue Pilgrims, to whom she was known as 'Eager-heart', but if Emmet's heart was ever eager to know anyone as more than a 'very dear' friend, there's no record of it.[167] Her autobiography provides not a hint of romance, perhaps not an unreasonable reticence for a woman in a male world. Emmet was far from the only woman working at the University, but when in 1946 she was promoted to Professor, at the second attempt, she was the only woman to hold a Chair for decades in either direction, coming in between Mildred Pope for a few months in 1934 and Violet Cane a quarter of a century later in 1972.[168] The *News Chronicle* covered Emmet's appointment and noted she was the only woman professor of philosophy in Britain, but its tone of surprise was reserved for her hobbies: the headline was *'Professor in the kitchen: she cooks for relaxation'*. Much later in 1968 another journalist was equally unsurprised by Emmet's gender but wanted to know about how she came to live in Wythenshawe, *'not exactly a hive of highbrows'*. Emmet said buying her house there in 1939 was her 'best purchase' and mentioned the *'most beautiful'* local church of St Michael, built in 1937.[169]

Polanyi's outsiderness was that he was a Hungarian, secular, Jew. He came to Manchester in 1933 from a Germany in which the Nazis had taken power, not so much as a helpless refugee, but in part because he was wanted here and in part as an active protest against Nazism. Before the war Manchester accepted about eight thousand refugees from Fascist Europe. Most were Jews, and the attitudes to these refugees were a mixture of the suspicious and the generous that can be recognised in today's city. A tiny fraction were academics, a very particular class of migrant. British and American universities were picking the talent they wanted out of the wreckage of intellectual life in Germany, with no place for the *'un-tenured or mediocre'*. It was the same filtering of talent — by the hand of Blackett's predecessor Bragg — that had brought the German physicist Peierls to Manchester in 1933 to find it so dirty: Peierls then found a permanent job at the University of Birmingham where, in 1940, he co-authored with his fellow refugee Frisch a memorandum that was the first description of a feasible atom bomb and which gave the British a crucial leverage on their later relationship with the Americans. But when Polanyi was appointed, the national press mounted a violent attack on the University for preferring foreigners over native candidates and it was afterwards cautious in the numbers it would appoint and lobby for citizenship for. And though Polanyi would be granted citizenship, his lab technician, who came over as part of the deal, was only allowed to stay in Britain for two years and then had to emigrate to Israel. [170]

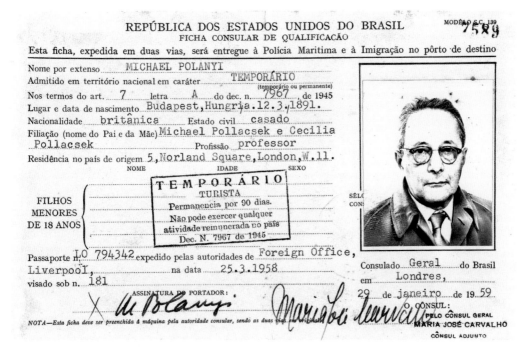

Figure 65. Michael Polanyi, chemist and libertarian philosopher, as registered by the Brazilian state on a visit. Despite, or perhaps because of, his lack of training in philosophy, Polanyi's has a significant philosophical legacy, providing ballast to those theologians attempting to come to terms with the need to acknowledge the reach of science into their field.

Despite this welcome, Polanyi had been reluctant to leave Germany, in part out of gratitude to the Weimar Republic that had already accepted him as a political refugee. He had fled to there from a first encounter with political interference that had come from the Left. In 1919, when he was an assistant in a Budapest university, Hungary had briefly become a Soviet Republic. The Communists applied pressure on the supposedly free University and Polanyi found himself unable to perform experiments. It was Polanyi's theoretical break-throughs of the 1920s, partly developed during this enforced solitude, that led to his appointment as a Professor at the centre of world chemistry in Berlin. Michael Polanyi had a lifelong marriage to Magda Kemény Polanyi, who had studied chemistry and registered for a PhD when Michael was in Berlin, but did not complete it. There are hints, though no more, that it was not complete plain sailing in being married to a defender of personal freedom. In 1946, not long after the time when Emmet was cooking for the apparently single Michael Polanyi, his wife Magda applied, in her own name, to rent a University house, and one of Lyn's acquaintances from the '51 Society later wrote of Michael Polanyi in a tone distinctly reminiscent of a discarded mistress. In any case, the Polanyis moved together after the war to a more modest semi in Hale, which would be a short walk from both Turing and the Newmans.[171]

Polanyi and Blackett

Blackett was not at the seminar, and perhaps that was for the best; for he and Polanyi had long been carrying on a committed, if respectful and affectionate, intellectual battle on other grounds. Unlike many with a well-founded fear of a Fascist threat to liberty, Polanyi's experience meant he was never blind to the same threat from Communism.[172] For Polanyi, the common danger was in the threat to individual liberty, which was for him the liberty to pursue scientific enqui-ry on one's own terms.[173] His colleague Blackett supported a rational, planned science for the benefit of society as a whole, and was happy to endorse, from a distance, the Soviet attempt to construct a scientific sector obeying the will of the Party. A senior University administrator found both of their positions somewhat ironic: *'Blackett the great theoretical planner had a genius for improvisation and getting things done. Polanyi the exponent of freedom and the critic of planning was most meticulous and cautious in action'.*[174] Despite their differences, at the height of Cold War paranoia both Blackett and Polanyi were separately banned as subversives from entering the US.

Polanyi and Blackett managed to remain friends even as Polanyi emerged as an ever more vocal critic of the Left and of any attempts to make science a depersonalised activity—that is, as a critic of Blackett's entire sup-port for science planned by the Party.[175] Perhaps this was because, as MI5 had concluded, Blackett himself never showed the slightest hint of doing what any party planned for him.

Mind and the Computing Machine

Emmet was much better prepared than Jefferson to analyse the philosophical issues arising from the computer. But it may well have been Polanyi who was most exercised by the emerging claims from Turing that human thought processes could be automated. Between Polanyi and Emmet, a seminar was put together to test these claims, with Newman, Turing and Jefferson invited. Polanyi put together a set of notes asserting that humans could solve problems that machines could not, which he circulated to Newman and Turing in advance of the seminar; Jefferson wrote something too. Newman seems to have agreed only to turn up to the seminar and was somewhat taken aback to discover he was expected to do rather more. In his notes, Polanyi set a hare running by claiming support from Gödel's results in mathematical logic about the limits of automated reasoning, but the professional mathematicians shot the hare with an effortless disciplinary putdown pointing out Polanyi's misinterpretations of Gödel. Nevertheless, claiming that Manchester possessed a machine that would, in time, think, was a strong claim that was not hard to challenge in other ways.[176]

Figure 66. Brass light fitting in the University's Samuel Alexander Building, constructed as the 1919 Arts Building in the neoclassical prestige style of the time, and though then hemmed in by working-class terraces at front and rear, showing a considerable, Mancunian, confidence in the future expansion of the University. It was the seminar room in this building that hosted Dorothy Emmet's seminar on *Mind and the Computing Machine*.

s a result, there is then a mechanism
hich led to the contradiction

ut this is an argument against the mac
his kind of thing?

- mathematicians.
- are mathematicians human beings?)
going back' process asked for).

ted that this kind of thing was mo

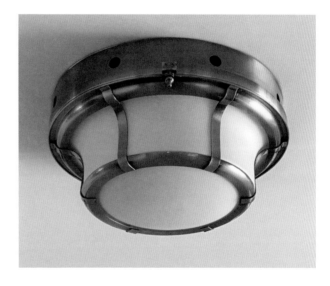

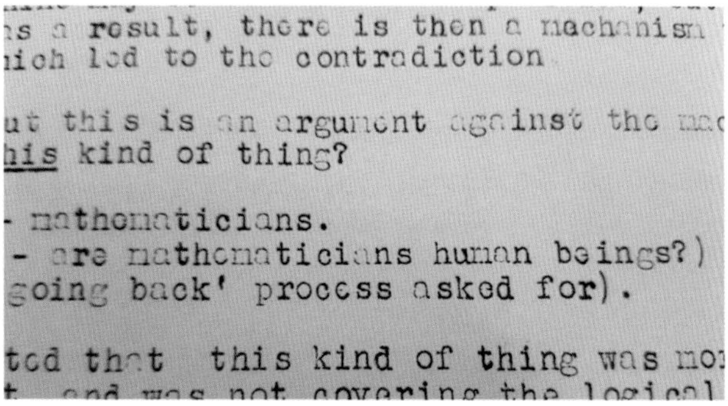

Figure 67. The mathematicians said machines could think like humans. One support for the position that machines couldn't was rooted in the feeling that mathematicians couldn't think like humans either.

And so, on the afternoon of 27th October 1949 there assembled a cast of some distinction in the Philosophy department. Turing and Newman and Polanyi seem to have started in the afternoon by reading prepared remarks; then they took a break, and in the evening the discussion proper started. Emmet outlined the problems to be discussed, though most of the discussants subsequently ignored her. Jefferson was there and was not afraid to weigh in. Manchester's industrial muscle was represented too, but not in the form of any representative of the electrical engineering companies. The sole non-academic voice was that of a representative of ICI, trying to make sense of the electrical signals from the mind embedded in the electro-encephalogram. As far as we know, all the faces there were white, but there was at least one foreigner in the person of Richard L Meier, an American Fulbright Scholar later to become a planning theorist and futurist. Meier wrote his own response to the discussion: *'it is very probable... that most cybernetic theory will be worked out in the next couple of decades. This is a breakthrough...of utmost significance. The imperfect performance of robots however will plague us from this day forward'.*[177]

In the seminar Turing was challenged about how a thinking machine would cope with a contradiction, and said that it would backtrack until it found the error: Jefferson said this wasn't how humans thought, and Turing responded that it was exactly how mathematicians thought. It was at this point that the murmur 'but is a mathematician human?' was heard in the room.

The Turing Test

The younger philosophers at the seminar are remembered as engaged with, if rather unimpressed by, Turing's ideas. They were struggling to understand consciousness and thought Turing merely sidestepped their questions (which was perhaps his intention). Nobody's mind was changed by the seminar, but Turing and Polanyi both drew on its criticisms when they developed their arguments into later, written work. Though Polanyi had started with a technical mathematical objection, his final comment was that *'acceptance as a person implies the existence of unspecified function'*, once again seeing the political dangers in reducing humans to rule-followers. Turing more than most at the discussion had his anti-Fascist credentials, but he was quite uninterested in this political implication: for him the question was how you could teach a machine to think, not what it meant to be human. And Turing had by now a maturing idea about the relationship between learning and doing: purpose, he said, is the *'use of previous combinations plus trial and error'*. Turing would remain interested in learning and in October 1952 he attended a series of lectures in Manchester — once again facilitated by Polanyi — by Jean Piaget, the world's leading thinker on human intellectual development at the time.[178]

Turing wrote up his remarks the following year in the philosophers' academic journal, *Mind*, as the article *Computing Machinery and Intelligence*. It is this paper that has created our most apparently graspable — if actually somewhat slippery — test of whether a machine can think. Turing invited the reader to imagine sitting at a teleprinter, of the kind that had brought so many hard-to-decode-looking signals to Bletchley Park, and typing questions at a man, a woman, or a machine sitting out of sight at the other end of the teleprinter line. Turing said that asking whether a machine could think should be replaced by asking how to create a machine that could not be distinguished from a human on the basis of the answers that the teleprinter pounded out. This, now called the Turing Test, has stubbornly refused to go away as a tool in thinking about machine intelligence, and it was Jefferson's obtuseness that provoked Turing into developing this vivid image. [179]

The Philosophy seminar and the *Mind* paper were for academics, but within another year a wider but still serious audience in the North West was hearing about the possibilities, doubts and fears of machine intelligence. Jefferson gave a series of extra-mural lectures on *The Working of the Human Mind* that finished with the thought that *'the soul is the very last mechanically unexplainably thing that will remain'*. [180] *The Manchester Guardian* started to cover the machine in July 1951, probably with prompting by Ferranti's commercial team. At the official opening of the Ferranti Mark I the reporter found it 'alarming' and commented that nobody knew what it would be able to do, though the reporter felt that whatever it could do, it would do for Turing; but later in the year they reported Dietrich Prinz's chess program without alarm. [181] During the summer of 1951 the BBC's Third Programme carried a series of talks by the most significant British computing pioneers: Hartree and Newman giving explanations from the mathematician's perspective of what a digital computer was, Turing defending his view that *'it is not altogether unreasonable to describe digital computers as brains'*, Williams giving a talk on the engineering issues, and a Cambridge speaker taking about scientific issues. The only distinctively Northern voice of the series, that of Williams, was the most practical. [182]

The local radio discussion series The '51 Society may have picked up on this local story in a talk Turing is said to have drafted for them. He argued not only that *'machines can be constructed which will simulate the behaviour of the human mind very closely'* but giving examples of a teaching process that would enlist a *'highly competent schoolmaster'* and a *'mechanic'* to do this. [183] It was the job of the schoolmaster to bring the world's knowledge to the machine, but he was to be kept ignorant of the way in which it worked. It was the job of the mechanic to supervise the smooth running of the learning process. The acolytes tending the Mark I called themselves engineers, not mechanics, and any painful suspicions they had about Turing's attitude to them were not likely to be assuaged by this language.

There would have to be both pleasure and pain involved for the machine as well. Turing had no qualms about that: the schoolmaster would be armed with a cane and need to use it, though in time the machine might learn to recognise anger on the face of the schoolmaster as ominous enough that the cane would not be needed. As a consequence of this teaching, he predicted, computers could pass through an education and that *'One day ladies will take their computers for walks in the park and tell each other "My little computer said such a funny thing this morning'"*.[184]

There was one more media outing for Turing in January of 1952, when the Third Programme paid them all to come to London for a pre-rehearsed discussion reuniting Turing and Jefferson, with Newman present along with his and Emmet's old Cambridge philosopher friend **Richard Braithwaite**. Turing listened when it was broadcast, finding his own voice *'less trying to listen to'* than before, but when Lyn listened it was Max's voice she noticed as rather unlike his normal speaking voice.[185] The programme was repeated a week later, on 23rd January 1952, but Turing had other things on his mind that day. He had returned from work to discover that his house had been burgled. But in 1951 that was all in the future, and there was life to be made sense of.

Figure 68. Jean Piaget stands in the Oxford Road smog in October 1952. Piaget was in the first rank of child developmental psychologists and it was a considerable coup for Michael Polanyi to get him to speak in Manchester. Turing, grappling with how to make an infant machine intelligence mature, attended the lectures.

The Festival of Manchester

Making sense of life

Lyn Newman was disappointed in the cultural resources she found in Manchester. She had writing projects she wanted to complete but found it difficult: *'there are no good bookshops in Manchester & libraries there are food only for reference & study...but nearly all my reading is aloud, to the children'*. Turing at first confirmed Lyn's prejudices about the literary taste she was amidst, when she found he read Trollope and Austen as unchallenging entertainment, but their friendship moved to a different level when she pushed Tolstoy into his hands and found Turing a morally sensitive reader of the kind she had been missing. What Lyn didn't know — or thought too heavy a hint to drop when she wrote in 1959 — was that Turing had other literary friendships outside Manchester, and with one friend discussed Stendhal, and with another a series of contemporary novels, each containing portraits of a male homosexual character of varying degrees of sympathy. Turing's time with Greenbaum had put Jung on his shelves and EM Forster's books were there too. Forster had been an Apostle and retired to King's College Cambridge in 1947, where he was close to Turing's friend Nick Furbank, so it's likely that there was some connection between Forster and Turing, both Fellows of King's even though they had little else in common. Forster might have shared a copy of *Maurice*, the novel of male love he had completed in 1912 and which remained unpublished — but known to a discreet circle — until 1971. Lyn certainly knew Forster: in 1927, *'when he launched round a book for us to sign & the undergraduate next to me passed it innocently to me, EMF snatched it up from me saying "Oh NO! only the men". I think it very forbearing of me when a few years later at lunch at the Woolf's I didn't remind him of this; Virginia would have been merciless'.* [186]

Turing's own writing is that of someone who has read deeply but not that widely: ambitious, and playful, and in most places in need of considerable sub-editing. Lyn never did this for him — although it would have done both of them some good — but she did heavily edit his mother's 1959 obituary volume of her son, helping the bereaved Sara Turing, who was *'without any gifts as a writer — in fact she writes quite abominably'*, to produce what she acknowledged as an *'extraordinary achievement of maternal devotion from an old and delicate woman'.* [187]

Figure 69. Manchester's Literary and Philosophical Society, the Lit&Phil, was bombed out of its George Street building in 1940, and in the post-war period it lodged with the Portico Library on Mosley Street, illustrated here.

If books were a somewhat compartmentalised form of culture, there was a thriving climate of debate, and Lyn and Max attended a variety of venues. The Literary and Philosophical Society was, by the 1940s, a century and a half old Manchester institution. In the 19th century, membership had been primarily social, with a steep entrance fee, and formed of a network of self-confident and self-improving merchants and professional men. With the rise of the University the 'Lit & Phil' had a small but increasing component of a southern professoriat: Hartree, Newman, Emmet and Blackett but neither Williams nor Kilburn were members. As Emmet attests, it was open to women on equal terms, and Magda Polanyi and Gertrude Jefferson joined their husbands as full members. The Lit & Phil did hear about computers from Williams, and about chemistry, and increasingly philosophy, from Polanyi. Turing was not a natural joiner of debate clubs any more than he was of the Salford Harriers, but when he was identified as a provocative new thinker he found himself in demand as a speaker. Turing finally become a member of the Lit & Phil in the last year of his life; he was referred to by name in a talk of Jefferson of 1954, and the Council noted his death in their Annual Report. [188]

Bombed out of its George Street premises in 1940, the Lit & Phil at this period was lodging with the Portico Library on Mosley Street. The Portico, though founded through a very similar social network and for similar reasons, had taken a different path. By the 1940s, membership was small, with few University members, and the Library's eponymous Greek Revival architecture was a front for little more than a lending-library for popular fiction. There were other elite social groups with a heavier representation of industrial leaders: 'The Luncheon Club', meeting at the Midland Hotel, was the venue where cotton administrator Raymond Streat and engineering tycoon Ernest Simon came together to discuss the filth of the University precincts. [189]

The new media of the time also offered space for thinking. Max became a regular discussant on the '51 Society. This distinctly high-brow BBC radio discussion programme was based in Manchester. The BBC North Talks division had consciously decided to draw on the northern tradition of the literary and debating society exemplified by the Lit & Phil for programmes to illuminate *'life in general and Northern life in particular'*. This tradition had the advantage that participants could be asked to take part for expenses only, and even this expense was limited by defining Northern as no further away than Leeds or Liverpool. [190] In November 1951 the first debate took place in the Grand Hotel on Aytoun Street. In the tradition of the Lit & Phil, most of the Manchester members were not academics, although many of those who were not had strong links to education. Newman, Blackett and Polanyi were members from the beginning, though only the latter two were well known enough to the public to be mentioned by name in *The Manchester Guardian*'s coverage. The programme was normally broadcast on the BBC's Northern transmitters and only occasionally rebroadcast in the south, the only episodes that would get more than a terse listing in the *Radio Times*.

There were few women who were officially one of the '51, but they included sculptor Mitzi Cunliffe, the wealthy but progressive educationalist Shena Simon, and Halifax novelist Phyllis Bentley; Lyn Newman was not and would attend and *'think a lot but say nowt'*.[191] In 1955 Lyn was present when *'Max took me as his guest to the 100th meeting of the Fifty-One Society. There was a birthday cake with 100 candles, much too hot, the icing melted & the candle wax tasted bitter; but it looked lovely. A charming & sincere French poet, Prince Emmanuel, opened the discussion…But the society is losing its brilliant chairman Norman Fisher & I think it will soon decline & cease to be'*. In fact, her friend Niel Pearson became quite a successful new chair and the '51 Society ran into the 1960s.

Figure 70. The Grand Hotel, Aytoun Street. When BBC North established the '51 Society as a debating group to provide cheap but distinctive Northern and Reithian content for its radio service, they tried to suggest a misleading degree of independence from the BBC by having the recording made at the Grand Hotel. Outside broadcast technology proved too unreliable and subsequent recordings were made at the BBC's Manchester studios in Piccadilly.

Stay at the Grand

Situated in the heart of the city, yet secluded from the noise of traffic, the GRAND HOTEL offers not only luxurious comfort and a splendid cuisine, but caters in an exceptional manner for the business man . . . . There are thirty well-lit stockrooms for the display of samples, etc., an electric passenger and goods lift, and close at hand is an all-night garage. Hot and cold water in 150 bedrooms. Spacious lounges, dining, smoke and billiards rooms. Within easy reach of theatres, business and shopping centres and all stations ● *Special weekly and week-end terms*

Telegrams : "Grand Hotel Manchester"
Telephone : Central 2493, 2494 and 2495

GRAND HOTEL
AYTOUN STREET, MANCHESTER

Atoms and Whimsy

As 1951 dawned, Turing could finally hope for a computer to help him with some thinking, but first there was a distraction for him and indeed the whole nation. The Festival of Britain showcased Britain to itself as what Christopher Frayling memorably described as a place of 'atoms and whimsy', and the way Manchester appears in that picture is worth examining. [192]

The prototype Manchester computer had been disassembled in 1950 to make way for the Ferranti version. Turing had been remarkably productive on the earlier machine, but that work had amounted to two projects at most. Now the replacement computer finally started arriving, into the new building, perhaps framed with Lockspeiser's steel. By 1951, Turing was ready for serious work. The first problem he faced was one that would become familiar in the decades to come: the computer did not arrive on time and when it did it did not work. It was promised in February 1951: the University engineers got their hands on the machine in May, and though it was shown off at the inaugural conference in July, the logbooks don't show users running programs until August. [193] By then Turing was spending the summer, as by now usual, in Cambridge. It was the optimistic summer of the Festival of Britain, and Turing went to London for the day, full of expectation for what British technology would offer him in the autumn.

The 1951 Festival of Britain was said by the organisers to be both for and about the whole of the country, but it was London's project. The Festival relied heavily on contemporary design for its symbolic messages, and Manchester had little to offer. The mid-century architects, designers, and typographers who established their reputations in the Festival on London's South Bank were overwhelmingly London-based. When it came to showcasing British art, the only area where the south was not dominant was in sculpture. Here Yorkshire roots were ascendant, with Henry Moores and Barbara Hepworths dotted about. There was just one Manchester-associated sculptor visible: Mitzi Cunliffe. [194]

The aim of the Festival was to show the British people to themselves, both in terms of character and material production. Defining the national character caused the organisers some head-scratching, and they concluded it was something about lions (for strength) and unicorns (for quirkiness). This section was in part the responsibility of *Cider with Rosie* author Laurie Lee, and there is a certain quirkily recursive quirkiness in his official civil service title 'Curator of Eccentricity'. [195] More solid ground came from the arm of the Festival designed to showcase British science and manufacturing, and here Manchester did get to play some role.

Figure 71. Screen near the Diamond Pavilion at the 1951 Festival of Britain on London's South Bank.

Nimrod

Science was already a strong theme on the South Bank, but in addition the Science Museum in South Kensington put on its own exhibition, co-branded with the Festival. In July 1949, with Turing's brave claims about machine intelligence fresh in the mind of broadsheet readers, the Festival planners asked Ferranti to contribute an electronic computing machine as an exhibit. Ferranti probably believed they would have a Ferranti Mark I ready for buyers in exactly the summer of 1951. As the Festival opening date of May 1951 got closer, and even the Manchester University installation was not functional, it became apparent that there would be not much more to show of the Ferranti Mark I than the on-trend curved metal that it was to be clad in. In its place, they rapidly put together an electronic machine to play the game Nim. [196] Nimrod was no general-purpose computer, but this was glossed over in the accompanying explanations. It didn't really matter as *'most of the public were quite happy to gawk at the flashing lights and be impressed'*: then as now the public loved pressing the buttons in the Science Museum and neglected to read the captions. Nimrod was a huge success and even Turing had a go, beating the machine, crashing it, and eyeing up the young stand attendants all in the same session.

Figure 72. A contemporary artist's impression of Nimrod, with the F of the Ferranti branding carefully highlighted, that appeared in *Discovery*, a popular science magazine.

Figure 73. Wanda Altar and Rae Berry play the Ferranti Nimrod machine in the Science Museum in 1951. The public loved two aspects of the Exhibition of Science: Grey Walter's tortoises and this Nim playing machine. The tortoises kept breaking down ('dying') but the only person known to have broken the Nimrod was Alan Turing. Although the Festival aimed at a family-friendly offer, Altar and Berry provided publicity value because they performed at the Windmill Theatre's 'revudeville' in which the climax of the act was censor-mandatedly motionless female nudity.

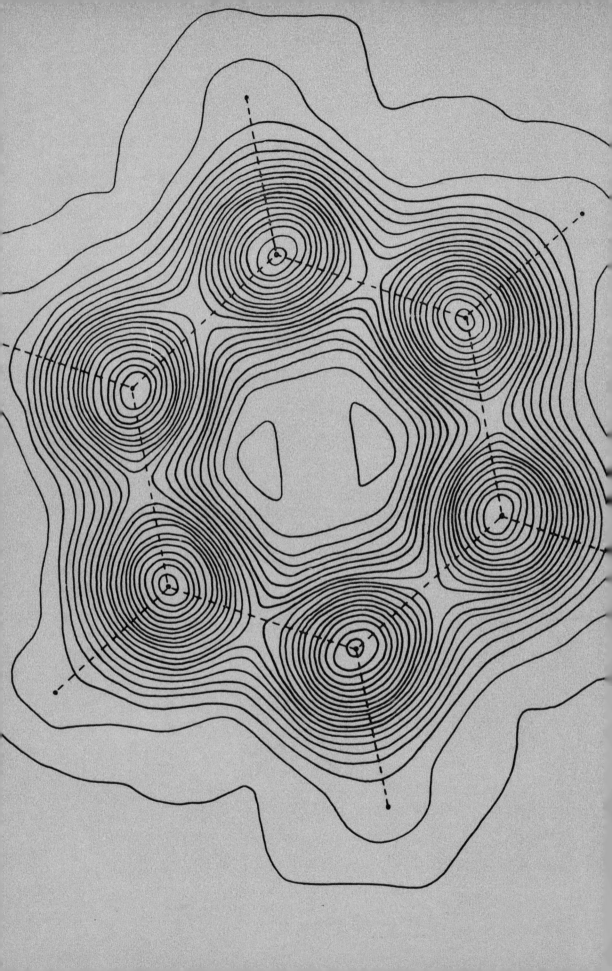

Patterns and drugs

Another Manchester contribution was literally sat on. One of the more unusual visual innovations of the Festival came not from a designer, but from **Helen Megaw**, a scientist at University College London, who used her connections to source new images from the very new science of crystallography. She was a member of a world-leading cluster of expertise in Cambridge, London, and Oxford that would soon deliver the structure of DNA. Manchester had before the war dominated crystallography through Bragg, Blackett's predecessor in the Physics chair, but after he departed the University's lead was lost, particularly when Bragg's protégé **JD Bernal**, in London and Cambridge, began to introduce the mathematics of group theory into the experimental but computationally intensive subject. Away from the South, there was one contributor to Megaw's project in Glasgow and Leeds apiece, and just one of the network was an industrial scientist from ICI, but even he had moved from Northwich down to London in 1946. The Manchester Mark I would later be used by the Leeds crystallographer Farid Ahmed, the only non-white face known to watch its console, but the cross-Pennine distance must have made for difficulty and Britain later lost Ahmed's skills altogether when he emigrated to Canada to use the FERUT computer. [197]

Megaw had been trying to interest industrial designers in crystallographic images for some time, and the Festival made it possible to make the connections she was seeking. The Festival asked three dozen different companies to use the images as inspiration for new product design and to exhibit designs at the Festival. There was one classic North West cotton firm on the list, the Bolton based Barlow & Jones, who made a short run of fabric, but chose not to devote their scarce production allocation to commercialising it. [198] But there was also newer Manchester technology represented. One ray of hope for the declining cloth trade was the British lead in artificial fibres, and ICI had acquired a Hyde firm with a method of making imitation leather reckoned good enough for the red benches of the House of Lords (though George Orwell inspected the upholstery and found it 'tatty'). The ICI Leathercloth Division were making an effort to move away from block pattern and enthusiastically took up Megaw's challenge. They printed four different patterns, used among other things to upholster the seats of one of the Festival restaurants.

Figure 74. A representation of the molecular structure of benzene as computed by Farid Ahmed on the Manchester Ferranti computer.

Figure 75. Farid Ahmed (left), with his Leeds PhD supervisor. Ahmed wrote programs for the Manchester computer to carry out extensive calculations involved in crystallography. Before electronic computers, punched cards had been used and Ahmed estimated that the Mark I could do the calculations 50 times faster. While that could make previously intractable problems possible, the frequent downtimes of the Mark I and the difficulty of software development probably meant that punched cards remained a better choice for some years.

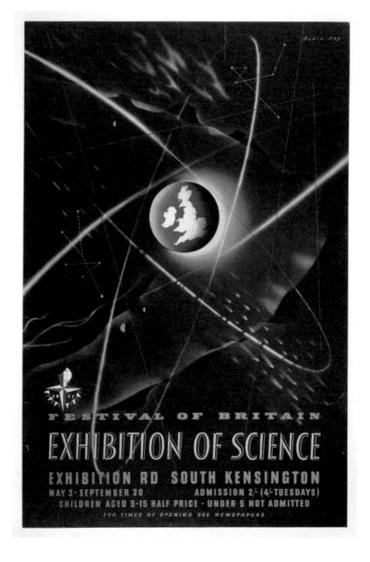

Figure 76. Robin Day's poster for the Science Museum's Festival of Britain Exhibition of Science, 1951. Day's design contributions across the Festival were important in establishing his successful post-war career. Although probably designed in the same spirit of optimism as the other science-led imagery of the Festival, in hindsight the poster's dark background foreshadows the fears about atomic power that quickly emerged.

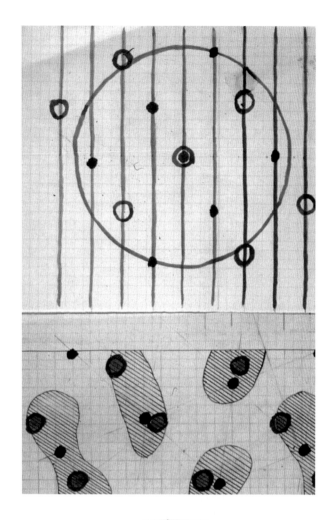

Figure 77. A figure prepared by Turing for a paper he never completed on the evolution of biological pattern. This is not crystallographic work, such as the Mark I was expected to do, but draws on similar mathematics, and through this bears a visual resemblance to the Midwinter plate.

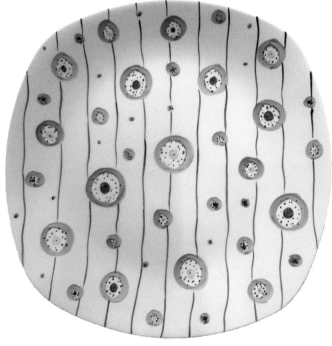

Figure 78. During the 1950s, Stoke-based Midwinter Pottery employed leading British designers. Jessie Tait's 'Festival' of 1955 is strongly influenced by the designs of the Festival Pattern Group and in turn by crystallography. By that time Midwinter's marketing material cautiously avoided mentioning atoms, preferring 'streamers' and 'confetti'.

Few of the collaborations led to profitable products, but the atomic look was for a time more widely fashionable, such as in the Festival design of the Stoke-based Midwinter Pottery. Within a few years, public concerns about atomic weapons had grown—with help from Patrick Blackett and Bertrand Russell among others—and the visual fashion faded. Turing's later work on mathematical biology led him to use a similar mathematical language as the crystallographers did. When Turing's drawings from this period were used to decorate the set of the 2014 film *The Imitation Game*, the spot and line images could recall the on-trend pottery of the 1950s, and for these mathematical reasons.

Britain's silver bullet

Another one of the Mancunian scientific stars of the Festival of Britain was penicillin, heralding the significant post-war pharmaceutical success that can now be seen to have peaked at Alderley Park. The national story of penicillin also sheds interesting light on how Manchester came to see its computer. In 1939 the strategic potential of penicillin for keeping a soldier on his feet was clear, but there was no process to make it in the millions of doses an army would need. There were two paths being taken to make penicillin in bulk: an engineering approach of fermentation that scaled up the existing approaches of farming the drug from parent microbes, and a more scientific one of identifying the chemical structure of penicillin, and using that knowledge to build penicillin chemically from scratch. The former looked to the scientists like a brute-force approach, wasteful both of resources and their hard-won elite knowledge: the latter looked to the process engineers like an entirely untried method with no guarantee of success. Wartime Britain had, in its crystallographers, exactly the elite to use for the scientific approach, and so it was that Quaker pacifist Dorothy Hodgkin spent her time in Oxford on this vital war work. But the structure determination was slow, partly because the numerical calculations were so laborious, and by the time she and her colleagues solved the structure in 1945, ICI based in Trafford Park had been using an American fermentation process to produce war-scale quantities of penicillin for years. Nevertheless, during the war ICI had invested heavily in public information films about penicillin that emphasised the British origins of the drug, and correspondingly distracting from the commercially disappointing fact that industrial scale-up had not been perfected in Britain. By the time of the Festival of Britain, a version of this history became one of the founding elements of an idea that the British were good at inventing but not good at exploiting, and that the country was entering a New Elizabethan era where it was the nation's intellectual leadership that would contribute more to the world than its woven cotton. There is an echo here of the distinction between 'thinking' and 'doing' that would bedevil Manchester's Computing Machine Laboratory.[199]

Figure 79. Mitzi Cunliffe in Didsbury. Cunliffe is supervising the transport of Man Made Fibres from her back garden studio to its present position on the Clothworkers' South Building of the University of Leeds. American Mitzi Solomon came to Manchester after her marriage to Marcus Cunliffe, an academic historian. She became a member of the '51 Society and an acquaintance of Lyn Newman, sending Lyn unsolicited advice about childcare. Cunliffe ran a successful practice in architectural sculpture well into the 1970s. The choice of subject is not purely aesthetic: man-made fibres were a significant compensatory development against the decline of the natural fibre trade. One such was Terylene, discovered in a laboratory just opposite the Oxford Road Gaumont Cinema.

Figure 80. Mitzi Cunliffe's *Root Bodied Forth* on site at the Festival of Britain. During design, the Festival's Director had to be despatched to Didsbury to reassure the Deputy Prime Minister over a suggestion that the sculpture represented sodomy. He reported this to be *'anatomically impossible'*. The sculpture's whereabouts today is unknown.

Penicillin promised protection against more than shrapnel infections. The marketing of penicillin in 1951 was clearly targeting heterosexual fear of physical corruption via sexually transmitted infections (STIs). By contrast the medical submissions on homosexuality to the Wolfenden report, say, are instead entirely about the potential for moral corruption. There was simply no contemporary version of the medical discourse about the physical risks of a non-heterosexual lifestyle that would so mark the HIV era. Turing's doctors may have had concerns about the consequences of his sexual choices, but STIs were not one of them.

No whiff of sexual diversity appeared in the family-friendly Festival, although the organisers were careful not to be too normative about lifestyle choices — a pavilion specifically celebrating the 'family' was rejected when the organising committee reflected on the nation's divorce statistics. But still a Sunday paper got a whiff of scandal out of **Mitzi Cunliffe**, who was beavering away in her Didsbury studio on a sculpture for the Festival site. The *Sunday Pictorial* alleged that the unfinished sculpture would be promoting sodomy, and the Festival's director was hurriedly despatched on the Manchester train. Solemnly he reported back to the Deputy Prime Minister that, although summoning up *'the dirtiest mind'* he could, the sculpture was such that any *'malpractice'* would be anatomically impossible. Indeed, though Turing and his friends went around the Festival in part with an erotic eye open, they didn't recall pausing at Cunliffe's sculpture. It is, in truth, a sexy piece.

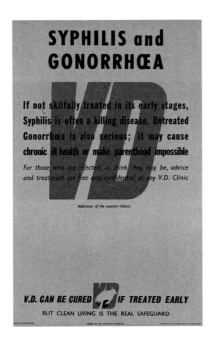

Figure 81. UK public health poster around 1950, emphasising the availability of effective treatment for syphilis.

Figure 82. US poster from a wartime drive to increase industrial productivity, emphasising instead the individual financial cost of lost work.

Magnificent but not home

It wasn't just the middle classes who went. The young Arnold Murray, who Turing would meet on the Oxford Road a year later, had hitchhiked down to London to see it, but those who could not visit London were not forgotten as consumers of the Festival. There was a Land Travelling Exhibition, 'the largest ever', that spent a few weeks in what was later the Air and Space hall of the Museum of Science and Industry.[200] The Victorian glass and ironwork frontage, now so proudly presented to Liverpool Road, was hidden under a temporary, modernist façade, and at night twenty-one red, white and blue ex-navy searchlights marked the sky above Deansgate.[201] *The Manchester Guardian* sent Norman Shrapnel, who responded in a characteristic Mancunian tone, both appreciating the cosmopolitan elegance and being perversely unwilling to be bowed by it: *'It is informative, imaginative, and always — excessively, some people may feel — elegant. Much of this show could call itself a Festival of Stockholm or of New York and the Manchester visitor may excusably decide that it is magnificent but it is not home. It is the cosmopolitan poker face that tires in the end. The bite of what is characteristically national (let alone regional) is to be found only here and there; one becomes exasperated and insular, hugging one's vices and wanting to look through the draped false roof at the surge of dirty glass above, or to gaze affectionately at the Albert Square statues. But this is perverse; the huge sculpture by Fiore de Henriquez in the foyer, is (in all senses) a cut above Gladstone or John Bright'.*[202]

Figure 83. Fashion models in the Travelling Exhibition of the Festival of Britain outside the former Air and Space Hall of the now-closed Museum of Science and Industry. The façade behind was a temporary one, topped by twenty-one red, white and blue lights sent vertically up into the Manchester night.

Figure 84. The centre hall of the Festival of Britain as seen by Manchester attendees to Lower Campfield Market. de Henriquez's sculpture group, *The Skill of the British People*, dominates the entrance.

Fortunately the *Sunday Pictorial* weren't paying attention to the huge de Henriquez piece.De Henriquez had been brought up and lived largely as a woman, but considered herself a hermaphrodite (actually, she thought everyone was a hermaphrodite, but that in her own case it was particularly visible) and later would have to put up with the press insisting she be photographed smoking cigars, but the 1951 Festival-goer was innocent of all this. In the 1960s de Henriquez underwent castration by radiotherapy, although unlike Turing's trea-tment a decade earlier, this was a voluntary decision. [203]

The Manchester Guardian acknowledged that the best of contemporary world culture, like de Henriquez's un-perverse sculpture, was accessible enough to be appreciated and admired but was sceptical about whether visitors could connect it with their own more mundane lives. It was only when the rough edges peeped through that Shrapnel felt engaged. He went on press day, which meant that *'nothing was finished. Men with brooms, like lost souls, were plodding up and down the Corridor of Time—an exciting dream-like construction with great pendulums swinging overhead. You pass from there into a section which shows something of what two centuries of science have done for us all, and into that devoted to People ("some people," might be the wryly justifiable comment) At Home. Plainly, it would all be charming when it was finished. Meanwhile queer notices lay about the place. "Do not mislay Adam stove handle," said one. Realism was caught here in the period of British Hortatory'.*

And that was that. Manchester's response was relatively subdued and ticket sales were disappointing. After a few weeks, the sixty-foot pantechnicons moved on to Birmingham. There wasn't much else save some sporting events that would probably have happened anyway. As well as a match against Red Star Yugoslavia, Manchester United also travelled to Stretford Gas Social Club to play a Festival of Britain Grand Football Match against a team from Sale. To my knowledge, there are now no physical relics of the Festival left in Manchester, save at Hyde Town Hall where there is a large and overconfident mural *'painted for the Festival of Britain'* but surely not with the consent of the Festival Design Group. [204]

Figure 85. Manchester United match programme from 1951.

MANCHESTER
UNITED

RED STAR
YUGOSLAVIA

SATURDAY MAY 12TH 1951 • KICK-OFF 7 P.M.
OLD TRAFFORD • MANCHESTER • LANCASHIRE

THIS SOUVENIR PROGRAMME IS PUBLISHED BY MANCHESTER UNITED FOOTBALL CLUB • OLD TRAFFORD • ENGLAND

Is a Mathematician a Man?

Where did the women go? The original premise of the Royal Society's Calculating Machine Laboratory was that engineers would build the machine and mathematicians work out how to use it. In 1948 almost nobody walking into the Magnetism room could have known any female research engineers, but they would all have seen women doing mathematics. Given a perceived shortage of men with mathematical skills and the gender identification of women with computation, it's unsurprising that the assistants Newman recruited for Turing were women. Women were planned to be part of the very beginning of computing, yet there are no female names on Manchester computing's blue plaques. [205]

It's not that female engineers were impossible, despite the observation of the Manchester suffragette Emmeline Pankhurst that engineering was not a suitable occupation for *'a lady'*. Many in 1948 would have been aware of Hertha Ayrton, a widely recognised electrical engineer. Although she had died a quarter of a century earlier, a Fellowship in Ayrton's name at Girton College supported generations of scientists including mathematician Dorothy Wrinch. And Ayrton's name had another notoriety. Her nomination to the Royal Society in 1902 had caused the Society some difficulty: it was obvious to the men of the Society that it was a society only for men, but on examination their own statutes neglected to say this. In the end legal advice was procured to explain that married women were not persons in the eyes of the law and so could not be members of the Society. There *is* a single memory of a woman carrying out engineering tasks on the Manchester Mark I: Geoff Tootill recalled, precisely because of her uniqueness, the female 'wireman' Ida Fitzgerald: testing every hand-wired connection in the prototype by hand. But it was as mathematicians that women could and did make their mark. [206]

Like any hub of commerce, the city of Manchester had been using machines for calculating for many years. A training in the use of mechanical adders was the starting point of a career that promised wages of up to £7 a week (comparable to a starting lecturer's salary) to women working in industrial and commercial offices. And Douglas Hartree's differential analyser service offered roles that evolved that into a new, highly specialised, but less repetitive job, still valuing precision and accuracy. Manchester hosted two pioneering women into these roles, both under Hartree's patronage. [207]

Figure 86. In 1952, Vivian Bowden was charged with creating a brochure explaining what the Ferranti Mark I was. He commissioned a series of publicity shots taken in the University installation. These staged photographs are unusual, not because they show operators doing the stereotypical female tasks of knitting and embroidery, but because they showed these 'leisure' activities at all, to underline that the computer 'requires very little attention'. This was not in practice true of the Mark I, which often failed because of hardware problems and software bugs.

Hartree is unique among the male scientists in this book through having attended a mixed-sex school, Bedales.[208] Indeed his wife, Elaine, had been a fellow pupil there, albeit five years below him, and they married almost as soon as she had left school. But Hartree would nevertheless blush in mixed company and his passion, apart from a musical house with two pianos, was for steam trains. He would spend free Saturday afternoons in the signal box at Piccadilly Station or the LNER locomotive works at Gorton, taking his young sons and any visiting boys, but his wife seems not to have been required to come along.[209] But for all this male stereotype, he is remembered as notably supportive of junior female researchers.[210] [211]

Figure 87. An unidentified worker on the Ferranti Mark 1 in 1955. Almost all of the hardware engineers on the Manchester prototype had been men, though there had been a sole female 'wireman', Ida Fitzgerald. checking connections. The male dominance of computer engineering in the University would also be challenged at Ferranti as market need created the new role of software engineer.

Bertha Swirles

One woman to finesse a talent for repetitive numerical work into a more satisfying research career was **Bertha Swirles**. She had met Hartree in Cambridge when they were both research students and she — impressed by his household's two pianos — accepted his suggestion to work on a problem in atomic theory.[212] She had already moved to Manchester in 1928 before Hartree followed as a Professor. In 1939 Swirles returned to Cambridge, where she continued to publish many papers on quantum theory. She went on to marry applied mathematician Harold Jeffreys. Bertha and Harold shared a long, childless, and seemingly happy marriage despite, or because of, Harold's enthusiasm for Freudian psychoanalysis in the 1920s. Harold is said to have turned to analysis after being rejected by mathematician Dorothy Wrinch, but in any case he was part of a circle of Cambridge scientists centred on St John's who briefly saw Freudianism as the opening of a new science; Jeffreys' other poor bet was a lifelong opposition to the idea of continental drift.[213] Swirles' primary legacy was the monumental textbook *Methods of Mathematical Physics*, published with her husband and under her married name and so known to generations as *Jeffreys and Jeffreys*. In recent years Cambridge University have memorialised Swirles by marking a building with her maiden name, so Bertha now has monuments under both of her second names.[214]

$$A_0 = \frac{1}{2\pi} \int_0^{2\pi} f(x)\, dx = \frac{1}{\pi} \int_0^{\pi} f(x)\, dx,$$

$$A_n = \frac{1}{\pi} \int_0^{2\pi} f(x) \cos nx\, dx = \frac{2}{\pi} \int_0^{\pi} f(x) \cos nx\, dx,$$

$$B_n = \frac{1}{\pi} \int_0^{2\pi} f(x) \sin nx\, dx = 0.$$

Figure 88. Bertha and Harold's compendious textbook includes definitions of Fourier coefficients, an important tool in many applied mathematical problems.

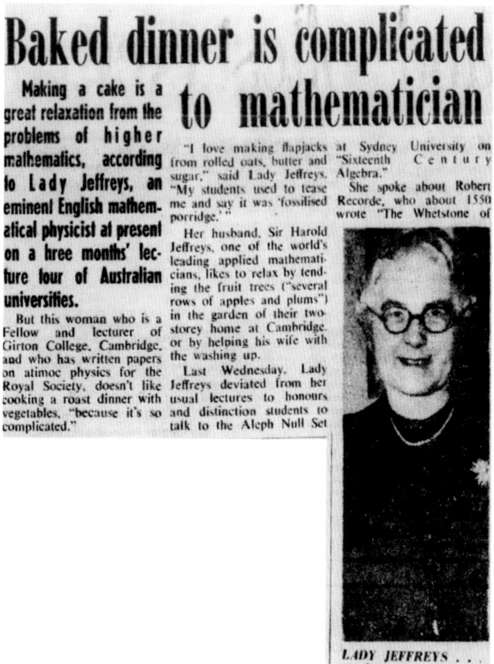

Baked dinner is complicated to mathematician

Making a cake is a great relaxation from the problems of higher mathematics, according to Lady Jeffreys, an eminent English mathematical physicist at present on a three months' lecture tour of Australian universities.

But this woman who is a Fellow and lecturer of Girton College, Cambridge, and who has written papers on atimoc physics for the Royal Society, doesn't like cooking a roast dinner with vegetables, "because it's so complicated."

"I love making flapjacks from rolled oats, butter and sugar," said Lady Jeffreys. "My students used to tease me and say it was 'fossilised porridge.'"

Her husband, Sir Harold Jeffreys, one of the world's leading applied mathematicians, likes to relax by tending the fruit trees ("several rows of apples and plums") in the garden of their two storey home at Cambridge, or by helping his wife with the washing up.

Last Wednesday, Lady Jeffreys deviated from her usual lectures to honours and distinction students to talk to the Aleph Null Set at Sydney University on "Sixteenth Century Algebra."

She spoke about Robert Recorde, who about 1550 wrote "The Whetstone of

LADY JEFFREYS . . .
mathematical physicist.

Figure 89. Bertha Swirles, by now Lady Jeffreys, in 1959 when the eminent mathematical physicist toured Australia.

Phyllis Nicolson

Another notable figure at the cranks of the differential analyser was a local woman, **Phyllis Nicolson**. Nicolson was born Phyllis Lockett and went to school at Stockport High before graduating in mathematics from Manchester, and then becoming a significant member of the Hartree's wartime consulting team. One of Hartree's major wartime projects was on the magnetron, the basic generator of radar signals. But *'calculations could not be done on the Differential Analyser so the 3 team members acted themselves as CPUs using mechanical desk calculators...Phyllis Lockett was always the fastest'*. A well-trained human — and perhaps not coincidentally a woman — provided the overarching skill, but it had been the capital donation made to the University by McDougall for Metropolitan Vickers to build a Differential Analyser that was publicly celebrated, not the craft of a woman computer. In later decades, human programming effort would emerge as a significant recurrent cost of electronic computation, but this was invisible in 1948. Because the difficulty of programming was not understood, the women who did the programming were not valued; or perhaps the logic went the other way. [215]

Phyllis married a fellow Manchester mathematician and they both did postgraduate work in Cambridge before moving to Leeds in 1950 when he got a lectureship there. She only found an academic post when he died in a level-crossing accident, leaving her with two young children, and she was appointed as her late husband's replacement. Sadly Nicolson died of breast cancer at the age of 51, but as the coinventor of the pleasingly named Crank-Nicolson algorithm she will be commemorated as long as mathematicians solve differential equations.

Figure 90. Phyllis Nicolson, working with Douglas Hartree (upper right) on the Differential Analyser in the basement of the Physics building in about 1942. The machine was in the basement because the room had been left too radioactive from the Rutherford era to be used for physics experiments. Jack Howlett, on the lower left, recalled that using the machine was 'what one can fairly call man's work' on the grounds that the protection of a boiler suit against machine oil was needed when changing the set-up.

The assistants in the room: Popplewell & Bates

As Manchester computing took post-war shape, Turing had two assistants, both women, who shared his office. Turing also had a female secretary, SJ Wagstaff, but she left no more than her initials on any of the letters she typed for Turing. His two assistants, Cicely Popplewell and Audrey Bates, both made careers out of computing, through rather different routes from the academic or industrial leadership roles that many of the men went on to. [216]

Cicely Popplewell was recruited as a staff member to assist Turing. She too was a mathematician, another Cambridge graduate, and she and Audrey shared Turing's office. She recalled Turing as an unsupportive boss to them, *'not really recognizing their right to exist'*, and that she and Audrey were glad when, as often happened, he worked at home. [217] Among those with memories of the Mark I, Popplewell's stand out for emphasising the physical work of interacting with the machine, pulling levers and running up and down stairs in the sweltering summer of 1950, as well as the emotional work of smoothing the feathers that Turing ruffled on the engineer, who had to be constantly present to manually switch the disk drive on and off every time it was used. Popplewell had no sense of being considered as an individual by Turing until later, when Turing prefaced his announcement of his prosecution with the words *'Are you shockable?'*: she wasn't particularly, but by then it was too late, she felt, to be sympathetic. [218] Popplewell was to write workhorse mathematical subroutines, help rewrite the programming manual, and become a figure within the University Computing Service: her role seems to have been a mixture of the advisory and the administrative. She was remembered as a 'universally liked' mother figure at the Computing Service, always reliable and 'helpful and efficient', and was sent to Argentina in the 1960s to teach users how to use a new Ferranti machine. Popplewell had no children of her own but married a widower when she was fifty and is remembered fondly by her stepchildren. Popplewell seems to have left the Service in the late 1960s shortly before this marriage but there is no other record of why. [219]

Audrey Bates took a similar initial path, but remained in technology well into her sixties. She was a Mathematics student at Manchester, and graduated with a First in July 1949. She was taken on as a research student, and in October 1950 she duly submitted an MSc thesis that represented exactly the direction that Newman hoped Turing would adopt in Manchester: she investigated how to mechanise the very framework of mathematical logic. A sign that Newman's hopes were optimistic is that this early thesis has never been published or made available online: it was at the time a dead end. But not a career-ending one for Bates. She moved immediately to Ferranti to work as a programmer and technical marketer. When Ferranti's Vivian Bowden produced his book *Faster than Thought* introducing electronic computers to the public she was a (partially uncredited) co-author.

Figure 91. Audrey Bates was a Manchester undergraduate who was attached to Turing as an MSc student, and successfully completed a thesis on using the computer for mathematical logic. Bates followed the second production Ferranti Mark I, named FERUT, to Canada, where she built a career as a computer scientist. Programming the early machines required a mixture of intellectual and physical dexterity, especially in handling the high-speed paper tape. Here Bates is overlooked by male colleagues as she deploys both of these skills in 1955. The photograph commemorates what the Canadians can claim as the first automated remote access to a computer, when a teletype linked to Saskatchewan produced paper tape fed directly into the Toronto FERUT.

Figure 92. Cicely Popplewell in 1939 and around 1970, before and after her many years running the University of Manchester's Computer Service. Popplewell was recruited to Manchester as Turing's assistant and, apart from a year in Toronto, remained part of the Service until her retirement in the late 1960s. As well as helping to rewrite Turing's incomprehensible programming manual, she wrote the first versions of many of the basic mathematical subroutines.

Just as Bates joined Ferranti, the computer division, so reliant on defence spending, nearly had a cash-flow disaster. When the austerity Conservative government was elected in the autumn of 1951 it cancelled all large projects. Ferranti resourcefully managed to sell the machine instead to the Canadian government, perhaps by appealing again to a national security need. An existing Toronto project was cancelled to pay for the Ferranti machine, but the project leader was transferred and came over to Manchester for several months in 1952. When he returned to Toronto, he invited Bates to join him and she went there to help run (but never direct) what became FERUT, the second machine off the Ferranti production line. [220] The following year Popplewell joined her for a year's lecturing. [221] Bates stayed in Canada, and spent a long career in computers, describing herself as a systems analyst as early as 1957, and being recorded in 1979 as a 'futurist' at a US military think tank. [222]

Bates was not the only woman who had been recruited to Ferranti. The University had no formal sexual segregation of roles, and does not appear to have deliberately paid women less as women, but that was exactly the formula that Ferranti management in Moston were used to. One of the other women recruited into the new profession of programmer was **Mary Lee Woods**, She discovered that she was paid less than her male peers and, helped by the section manager Bernard Swann, and against the disapproval of the (female) supervisor of women's work, fought and won an equal pay argument. [223]

Woods found the machine would always break down on her long program runs, causing tension between the engineers who said she should program to avoid such runs and the mathematicians who knew this was impossibly difficult. When Woods tried to put her case to Kilburn he simply refused to debate with her because, she thought, she was a woman, a resentment she carried for years. When she summoned the courage to mention this to him 50 years later, he conceded that she had been right all along; she somewhat generously chose to interpret this with amusement. [224]

There is at least one woman whose history suggests that being female did not intrinsically bar someone from being on Turing's wavelength. Never formally employed by Manchester, Beatrix 'Trixie' Worsley had learned her electronic computing down in Cambridge, and started working on an unknown project in Manchester well before the Ferranti Mark I arrived. She returned home to Canada for health reasons and so was able to take a job in the new FERUT installation, which developed into her career as one of Canada's first computer scientists. A record survives suggesting that Worsley and Turing interacted productively intellectually both personally and on paper; but in this she was the exception among the Manchester women. [225]

Figure 93. Mary Lee Woods and her husband Conway Berners-Lee. Mathematician Woods nearly turned down a job with Ferranti because of the dreary surroundings on the bus ride out from Piccadilly. But she was won over by the interest of the job. Even after she married her fellow Ferranti programmer, had children, and moved to London, Woods went on working as a freelance programmer well into the 1960s.

Figure 94. Beatrice 'Trixie' Worsley was a native Canadian who did a PhD with Douglas Hartree in the Cambridge computing project. She later returned to Canada and worked alongside Bates on FERUT. Although she never had a formal position in Manchester, she did make use of the Mark I and a productive correspondence survives between her and Turing, who had some role in her PhD. Worsley became a leading Canadian computer academic, although she was never made a full Professor.

Happening to float past: sex in the workplace

In Turing's school days, no textbook—no respectable non-medical book at all —talked about the mechanics of human reproduction. Turing learned biology from Edwin Brewster's *Natural Wonders Every Child Should Know.* It's told how Turing recalled this as a 'seminal' text but actually the book contains no mention of human sperm. The word 'sperm' does appear, just the once: plants have pollen, and sea urchins have *'milt, or sperm. If one grain of this happens to float against an egg, the egg at once begins to change to a young animal'.*[226] This 'happens to float' is an elegant example of the craft of saying the unsayable, and later on in the same book, Brewster pulls off a similar trick when he reveals the undeniable fact of evolution without mentioning Darwin. On human gender roles, though, Brewster does not seem to be trying to slip anything at all past convention: *'Mama stays at home and takes care of the little children...spanks them when they are naughty and kisses them when they are good...Suppose there were only just Daddies. Half would have to stay home from the office to take care of the little boys of the other half, and then their work wouldn't get done, and there would be no end of trouble. It would be almost worse if there were only Mamas. For then all the Mamas would have to go out to work'.*[227]

Post-war Manchester was, of course, full of women going out to work —the Ferranti Mark I was assembled in a Ferranti factory shared with the 'radio band', the conveyor belt on which an exclusively female workforce assembled components under the eye of male technical staff—but amongst the professional middle classes, the idea of the domestically vulnerable male was prevalent. Lyn Newman had no illusions at all about Max's domestic competence but when she had the mumps in 1950 it was a revelation to her husband to discover, after 15 years of marriage, that mashed potato was made by boiling a potato.[228] One of Max's mathematicians, the tricky but productive Kurt Mahler, was a solitary type who had to find his own lodgings when Donner House, the University hostel, closed down. His colleague Lederman claimed that Mahler put an advert in the paper saying that he was an unmarried academic and received a suitcase full of applications, but the woman Mahler chose turned out so domineering that he had to emigrate to Canberra. Turing inhabited the role of hapless male to some extent, accepting meals from his Wilmslow neighbours the Webbs and engaging a local, Mrs Clayton, to come four days a week for shopping and cleaning, but he often cooked for his guests and got Mrs Webb to teach him how to bake a cake.[229]

Woods had scandalised the Ferranti women's supervisor, not only by discussing pay, but also by her indifference to the moral risks of spending all night working on the University Ferranti Mark I with only a male engineer for company. The company's rule against this meant Woods was seriously discriminated against as the male Ferranti programmers had extra access time. But Woods' male manager, John Bennett, remembers the problem as quite different and arising from the request to buy camp beds for the programmers waiting their turn overnight. [230] Through her entry into a mixed professional workforce at Ferranti, Woods met Conway Berners-Lee, the man she would marry, and there were at least two other marriages formed in the Moston 'tin hut' where versions of the Ferranti computer were programmed. [231] The men around at the time remembered that *'Ferranti's first programmers were all very attractive young ladies recruited to the group by Dr Prinz. Many of those young ladies married members of the programming team or engineers'.* [232]

This sense of workplace pairing-off was a profoundly different atmosphere to that of the students of pre-war Cambridge. There, mathematics lectures and philosophy seminars had their quota of young women, taking the notes if not leading the discussions. Young men and women in the city of Cambridge of course pursued heterosexual romances as they happened to float past each other, but for women students (and especially their teachers) the long fight to be in the lecture hall at all meant they were particularly anxious to avoid the idea that they were husband hunting. But the access there to new intellectual worlds was remembered — by Lyn among others — as thrilling.

Figure 95. The Men's and Women's Staff Common Rooms in 1944, with four and two windows respectively. Staff House was built in 1937 on a site now occupied by the Alan Gilbert Learning Commons. The standing, balding man to the right is the Bursar, GW Kaye, who is holding a copy of *Vogue*. The separation of the common rooms was abandoned when it was discovered that most users preferred a mixed environment.

Though Dorothy Emmet was the sole female Professor in post-war Manchester, about a fifth of the University's teachers were women, and there was no sexually segregated College system. In the 1930s, the University had built three staff common rooms: one for men, one for women and one mixed. It was assumed that the male room would be the most in demand and was the largest, but *'very soon it was deserted and the distinctions had to be abandoned'.*[233] By contrast the men's Students' Union was more conservative, refusing to share with the women until the mid-1950s, although there was a (usually) locked door that joined the two, and writer Anthony Burgess remembered a pre-war *'Joint Common Room, where members of both Unions lolled on couches, were served tea and crumpets, and, in the dark during dances, made love'* although it should be borne in mind with Burgess' written recollections that he described at least three distinct occasions on which he had lost his own virginity, one of which was with the participation of a woman offering assistance with the card catalogues in the Central Reference Library.[234]

Among Manchester's women, memories of the thrill of entering into a new intellectual world are thin on the ground, though it certainly comes over in Woods' memories of Ferranti. But on the other hand, there's also none of the cant that heterosexual Cambridge produced when it came to that other educational dynamic: of sleeping with the Professor. The catastrophic nineteenth-century trial and imprisonment of Oscar Wilde had driven early twentieth-century intellectuals of male homosexual desire into hiding behind a classical Greek model of an erotic connection between male teacher and male student. In the 1920s and 1930s this was a language of male–male desire in Cambridge, drawn on by those who needed it in the Apostles and the Bloomsbury Group. Extending this model to heterosexual desire was no problem for Russell and Bernal, British architects of mathematical logic and crystallography respectively, each surrounded by a sequence of clever young women. In 1918 Russell lost his job for pacifism; today a Bernal could lose his for sleeping with his graduate student. But there is no record in post-war Manchester of any culture of sleeping with the students. Whether it was provincial morality or a lack of engagement with Classical ideals that protected young women from what would now be seen as abusive relationships is hard to say, as is quantifying their loss of the thrill of male Professorial attention.[235]

Essays on form in plants

C W Wardlaw

On Growth and on Form

Turing's main mathematical contribution in the Manchester years was to develop a mathematics of form. Where did this interest come from? The question is one that arises just after that moment when milt and egg happened to pass. How could shapes emerge in the developing, more-or-less spherical, more-or-less featureless, fertilised egg? Contemporary science was alive with possibilities for exploring this, although they didn't make it into the Land Travelling Exhibition as more than the wallpaper. But in London's more expansive Festival, there were exhibits that could show Turing, and everyone else, the modern scientific understanding of developmental biology, and at least one of these he is known to have seen. For the Science Museum exhibition, as well as offering Nimrod and his glamorous assistants, also included two small displays on animal and plant form. The exhibition catalogue explains that plants develop from growing points which influence the structure of the whole stem, and comments that much scientific research is being devoted to understanding the chemicals being made by the active cells there. In the next few years, Turing would develop theories of biological form that drew on exactly this tradition of seeing patterns as the result of concentrations of chemicals moving over a characterless, smooth surface. [236]

Fifteen minutes' walk away from South Kensington, there was even more of an appeal to the mathematical imagination at the Institute of Contemporary Art in Dover Street. This new institution did its bit for the Festival of Britain by commissioning the very young Richard Hamilton, who would go on to make a name as a founder of British Pop Art, to put on an exhibition named 'Growth and Form'. This title was a reference to the inspiration that a generation of Slade art school students had taken from **D'Arcy Thompson's** book, *On Growth and Form*. It is a readable and well-illustrated text that had been permanently in print since 1917, and which Turing cited in his own paper in 1951, but to a scientist it is now more a gallery of opportunity for exploration than a manifesto for a mathematics of biology. The 1951 exhibition was no slavish reproduction of a thirty-year-old book, but contained contemporary scientific images, with a huge blow-up of a crystallographer's X-ray and a film of the development of the sea urchin, after the moment when milt and egg happened to pass. For Hamilton, it was the variety and inspiration that the curated forms offered, rather than any connection to mathematics, that was important. It would be a highly influential show for British art, one of the strands leading to the formation of the Independent Group, but its influence on British mathematics is harder to detect.

Figure 96. Essays on morphogenesis by Manchester's Professor of botany.

The show included, for example, a glass three-dimensional model of just the *Radiolaria* structures that Turing was later to ask Bernard Richards to recreate mathematically using Turing's own theory. The variety of forms taken by these zooplankton had been collated by the German Haeckel in a widely known 1887 book. D'Arcy Thompson's 1917 book had pointed out how these forms could be imagined as the shapes taken by soap bubbles suspended inside wire frames and proposed that a similar form of surface tension applied to the creation of these planktonic forms. Did Turing himself attend the show? Probably not on the day of the Nimrod Festival trip, but conceivably another day: the ICA was ten minutes from the Royal Society he had been elected to in March of that year.[237]

Natural Wonders Every Child Should Know

In pre-war Manchester, Polanyi's Chemistry department had started to rival Blackett's Physics as a centre of intellectual excitement, but they both missed out on the growth of crystallography, one of the most significant of the twentieth century's new sciences. When X-rays are passed through crystals of a molecule, they are diffracted into a pattern of spots that can be captured on film. Blackett's predecessor, Lawrence Bragg, had made Manchester the pre-war leader in this field, using more and more complicated mathematics to analyse more and more complicated molecules. By the time Bragg moved his centre to Cambridge in 1938, it was realistic to study the structure of the large molecules like haemoglobin that cells use to do their work, and the science of molecular biology was being born. This was an international effort and within the UK it was primarily the Cambridge–London–Oxford triangle that made the running. But there was more to molecular biology than the laboratory skills to crystallise a protein. Opening up the molecules of the cell to scientific enquiry made it possible to conceive a new set of theoretical questions: how did the form and function of the cell emerge from the interactions of these proteins? D'Arcy Thompson's book created a huge catalogue of things to be explained, but for all his mathematical breadth, he had no training in the important tool of differential equations, and what he did know about this he had learned from a pure mathematician.[238] It would take a new breed of applied mathematician to attempt progress.

Figure 97. *A fern develops at its growing point*, an illustration from the 1951 South Kensington Festival catalogue showing a contemporary understanding of how form is created in plants. The individual fronds have each made a commitment to bud off, the youngest ones being those closest to the centre, and the morphogenetic process is whatever is controlling when, and at what angle around the centre, this decision happens. The fern is depicted as a smooth tissue that might see the interplay of chemicals — or in Turing's words, morphogens.

Figure 98. Another view of the 1951 *Growth and Form* exhibition from a 2014 reconstruction. On the left-hand side a large crystallographic image is visible: it was the intensity of the spots on these X-ray photographs that could, after intense calculation, yield the molecular structure of increasingly complex compounds. There were also models of marine plankton, believed by mathematicians to have a variety of geometric forms. Turing would ask his MSc student to model these forms using Turing's biological theory.

Dorothy Wrinch

There were many theoretical biology influences being felt in Manchester, although not always by the biologists. **Dorothy Wrinch**, another Cambridge-trained mind, provides a useful example in her pre-war attempts towards a mathematical theory of biological shape. One hopeful starting point for mathematicians was topology, which in the 1930s was grappling with the concepts of curve and dimension and offered the possibility of a new thinking about form. Dorothy Wrinch had followed Max Newman's path as much as a woman of the time could: she had achieved a good Cambridge First in mathematics, hung out at the Heretics club, became a close associate of Bertrand Russell, and learned mathematical logic and topology. She and Max also had in common not sleeping with Russell, which was more remarkable in her case given Russell's track record with his clever female acquaintances. Wrinch also trekked to Vienna to learn topology, but unlike Newman, when she got there she did sleep (unsatisfyingly) with her Professor. [239] Red-headed Wrinch was very attractive to intellectual men: she had already had to send her burly father on her behalf to turn down an offer of marriage from her Cambridge tutor, and she married her graduate supervisor.

Whatever else, Wrinch's mind appealed to mentors and funders alike and through the 1930s she picked up the sparse institutional financial support that a female mathematician could find: even the spurned tutor later recommended her for a job. Dorothy Wrinch had heard D'Arcy Thompson speak in 1918 and from then they became lifelong correspondents, but it was not until after her return in 1931 from the topologists of Vienna that she started to actively work in mathematical biology. She became a member of a set of left-leaning scientists that called themselves the Theoretical Biology group, and through this group, she started to discuss problems of biological form. [240] The group itself fizzled out after a few meetings but the individuals involved would be profoundly influential in British biology for decades; it is a mark of the conservatism of pre-war Manchester biology that none of them would be recruited here. But when Turing arrived later, the influence of the group was nevertheless detectable, and it had been transmitted via Dorothy Wrinch and Michael Polanyi. In 1935, she had come North to give a talk 'On the Molecular Structure of Chromosomes', when she proposed a model for how DNA was structured like a fabric, with proteins forming the warp and nucleic acids the weft. The model is of course wrong, but all models are wrong. Though it was elegant and testable, its fate was not to be disproved but to be neglected, because it paid less attention to detailed chemical complications than mathematical thoughts about how a large complex molecule might encode genetic information. In hindsight this 1935 paper was the first to suggest a mechanism for a central dogma of modern molecular biology: that genes were linearly encoded by physical sequence in chromosomes. But Wrinch got her chemistry wrong, and because of that and perhaps much more because she did not seem to care, this insight was ignored and had to be rediscovered by Crick and Watson fifteen years later.

Polanyi had been sceptical of the belief in reductionist theory that Wrinch embodied, just as he was sceptical of the analogous fellow-traveller political views of her Theoretical Biology group, but Wrinch was remembered by him, and even by the enemies she accumulated, as a provokingly unignorable thinker. Polanyi later wrote to her: *'You and I have much in common in the manner we managed to make our scientific careers less dull than usual'.*[241]

Wrinch was at the time also thinking about whether vein networks could be thought of as arising from electrostatics through roughly the same processes that cause the forks in lightning. Unlikely as it sounds, this was, in intent and formalism, one of the closer mathematical precursors to Turing's post-war mathematical biology. But it's unlikely there was any direct connection: by the time Turing came to work in Manchester, Wrinch had moved to other problems and they never corresponded. Nevertheless Wrinch's ideas were in the background of Polanyi's and thus of Turing's world.[242]

Figure 99. Biomathematician Dorothy Wrinch, who as a young woman in Cambridge frequently appeared in Harold Jeffreys' photo albums. Wrinch was friendly with both D'Arcy Thompson and Michael Polanyi, and visited Manchester in 1935. By the 1940s she had left the UK and was embroiled in a bitter dispute about protein structure with the dominant figure in the field, Linus Pauling. Wrinch's reputation never recovered from Pauling's crushing and somewhat misplaced dismissals.

Figure 100. The daisy typically has 13 green bracts visible on the underside of the flowerhead. On the upper side, the individual florets are tightly packed and the packing structure can be hard to see.

The Turing Instability and the Fibonacci Question

By 1951, Turing was well aware from his scientific contemporaries, through published work, personal contact, and popularisation, of the current questions about the generation of biological form. Remarkably, in the next few years he came up with *two* ideas of lasting value. The first was a mathematical mechanism, much later called the Turing Instability, for generating waves of pattern, and the second was a specific explanation of why Fibonacci numbers recurred in plants. We don't know when developing the first became a goal, but the second problem had been in Turing's head for a decade and probably more, and we know this because of his fiancée.

Joan Clarke, though possibly one of Britain's best post-war cryptanalysts, is primarily in the public record as a woman who was, for a few months at Bletchley Park, engaged to Alan Turing. Clarke knew Turing before Bletchley: her brother Martin had been a few years above Turing as a student at King's and the two men overlapped as Fellows, for Martin Clarke was a classicist and perhaps on the longlist of 'men of the Professor type' to recruit to Bletchley Park. In 1940 it was not Martin, but Joan, who was recruited, by cryptographer Gordon Welchman, after the experience of teaching her the higher geometry in Cambridge. She spoke frankly to Andrew Hodges for his biography of Turing, and on his pages her most vivid memory, apart perhaps from that terrible holiday in Wales, is when she recalled herself lying with Turing on the grass in front of Bletchley, talking about Fibonacci daisies. It was Clarke who knew about the way that botanists had for centuries classified plants by how many different leaf spirals could be found on their stems. From this classification certain numbers kept recurring: 1s and 2s of course, but 3s and 5s, and sometimes 8s and 13s.

Figure 101. Sunflowers are of the same family as the daisy but have larger heads, which makes it easier to see other Fibonacci patterns. This head, where the yellow florets have already developed into seeds, has had some of the seeds removed to show the apparent spirals. There are 55 of the steep spirals and 34 of the shallower ones. This (34,55) pattern, or its (55,89) cousin, are particularly common in sunflowers. 34, 55, and 89 are successive Fibonacci numbers, and other members of the sequence can also sometimes be seen.

By 1835, German scientists had noticed that if you knew how to look just right, you would find 89 or 144 spirals in the head of the sunflower, and that this is curious because these numbers have previous mathematical form. [243] The numbers 0, 1, 1, 2, 3, 5, 8, 13, 21, 34, 55, 89, 144 in fact form the first dozen Fibonacci numbers, each the sum of the preceding two. They emerge almost from nothing, or to be specific, from nothing, unity, addition and repetition, and as such are an easily comprehensible pattern arising from a simple system. In the 1930s Fibonacci numbers were simply part of the attic of mathematics, just like base 32 arithmetic, and their appearance in botanical structure was quite mysterious. [244]

In those geopolitically and emotionally uncertain times, on the grass in front of Bletchley Manor, the courtship of Clarke and Turing had included, in a precious break, a conversation about the daisy. [245] Whether picked in 1941 or today, a daisy, turned over to see the tiny finger-like green bracts, will show 13 bracts to count. We know from Clarke that the appearance of that Fibonacci number, and the others, in the spirals of the tiny florets is something that Turing thought needed explaining. But, frustratingly, that is all we know about Turing's thinking on form in the years before Manchester. And yet he once more made an innovative leap as he had done 16 years earlier: by 1951, he had finished a hugely influential paper, sprung apparently from nowhere, starting from a well-known if previously fluid problem, and without any collaboration, to help crystallise the problem into a specific form that could be solved. [246] But it was the pattern generation Instability that he was to attack in this published paper, and not the Fibonacci problem.

What was Turing's path to this remarkable paper, published the following year in 1952? [247] In a way it did start from that fascination with Fibonacci numbers. To a mathematician these are a strong signal of pattern: they cry out to be used as a key to understanding the processes that put plants together. To decode the pattern, Turing needed a model of where spots should be put on a diagram of plant tissue, and then made a jump to thinking about what made spots. Did he see the hand-drawn crystallographic diagrams of the 1940s? He must have done by the time crystallographers were looking to the as-yet unfinished computers, bringing handmade sketches: he definitely saw these visually reinforced, literally in the fabric of the Festival of Britain. The X-ray images that Richard Hamilton exhibited in 1951 are not straightforward microscope pictures of crystals: each dot is not an atom, but a superposition of many traces of waves of light, each perturbed by an interaction with the crystal as a whole. This dot made from waves is understood with a mathematical tool known as Fourier modes: the same tool used by quantum mechanics, or indeed the electronic theory needed to build radar sets. In a brain well-stocked with Fourier mathematics,

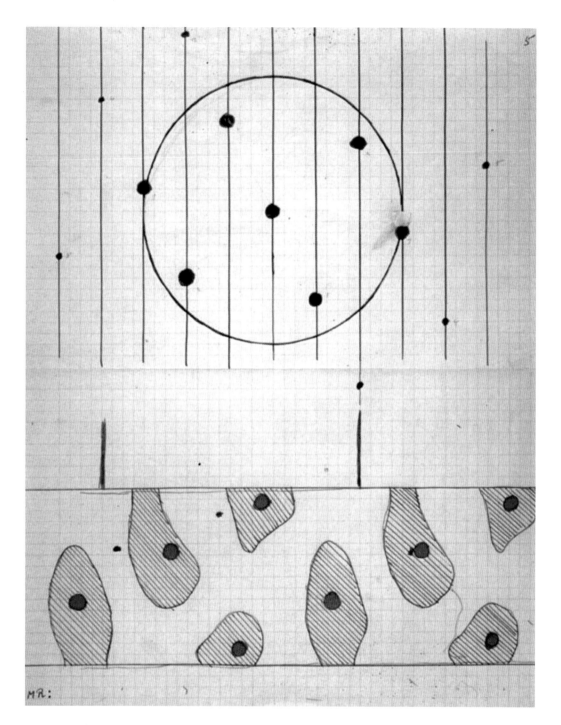

Figure 102. One of a series of pen-and-ink sketches that Turing was making for publication. The upper part is a pattern in Fourier space, similar to a crystallographic analysis. The lower part has probably been drawn by printing out the Ferranti Mark I's solutions of Turing's equations as a large array of base-32 digits, and then contouring the array by hand between high and low levels of morphogen.

the idea dawned on Turing, somehow, that a small model, pitting two chemicals against each other in the cells of an embryonic organism, could have the property that the natural outcome was not a bland mixing but a mutual separation—spots and stripes of pattern characterised by a typical length-scale. And this was the Turing Instability. [248]

Spending too much time on the computer

Finally, finally, the Ferranti Mark I was ready in 1951, and soon after returing from holiday Turing started to collect on the promise that had lured him to Manchester. First he finished off the final calculations needed before posting off the paper that would define the Turing Instability. What was next? The paper only introduced his general theory, and there was more work of an old-fashioned mathematical kind to be done in fleshing it out. Turing did indeed put much effort into creating a typescript that developed the theory further. But although he had used his new computer to illustrate his theory for the paper, there is no survival of any more numerical attacks on the general problem. For the next four years in Manchester, as time on the Ferranti Mark I was increasingly contested, Turing used his precious allocation—the opportunity that had brought him here—to work on one problem only: the Fibonacci problem.

Figure 103. Output from the Ferranti Mark 1 used by Turing to create contour maps of the spots emerging from what is now called the Turing instability. In the teletype code, V, X and £ stand for the largest possible single base-32 numbers. The output at each pixel is a 64-bit number, written as a pair of two base-32 digits, with the most significant digit in each pair appearing second.

It astonished and amused the Ferranti engineers to find that the precious new resource of CPU time was being used to study flowers, but for Turing this was a natural outcome of his characteristically grand project. It was work of great originality, and it was, fundamentally, on the correct path, but unlike the Turing Instability, he never got his work on Fibonacci structures to a convincing conclusion, and it remained unpublished at his death.

Turing thought by 1951 that he could *'account for the appearance of Fibonacci numbers in connection with fir-cones'*.[249] He told plenty of people *what* he was doing, but nobody recalls any idea *how*. One Ferranti programmer, John Bennett, recalled that *'At the time Turing was seeking a mathematical explanation for the role of Fibonacci numbers...The differential equations describing growth were slightly nonlinear, and with a random starting disturbance, the final configuration was displayed on the Mk I's monitors. It was always of interest to those of us who were watching to see what Fibonacci configurations would result. I remember spotting a cactus with 12 segments (rather than the expected Fibonacci 13) in my father-in-law's greenhouse — probably the result of some injury at an early stage of growth. I told Turing about it over coffee the next time we met. His immediate reaction was to propose the existence of a similar series that would include 12 and to ask whether there was a sufficient number of cacti in the greenhouse to provide relevant statistics!'*[250]

Claude Wardlaw, Manchester Professor of Botany, collected a lifetime of thinking about plant morphology in his 1968 set of essays: the name of his colleague Turing is the one most frequently indexed. Yet Turing never submitted a paper making good on his claim to 'account' for Fibonacci numbers. At his death he left a mass of unpublished material, and Max Newman agreed with Turing's logician friends that these were incomprehensible: he wrote to Lyn *'I doubt if anyone will be able to make any further progress with his biological theory'.*[251]

When I first saw the papers, in King's College Library in 1984, I agreed they were too confused to make sense of. But though there is no single coherent story, clues are there for the person with the right background. As it happened, life away from King's had made me a person with the right background. By the time I revisited them in 1999, I was a trained mathematical biologist and, with the aid of a trip to Manchester to see a few crucial pages in the University library, it was possible for me to reconstruct some of Turing's thinking, which I describe briefly in the Appendix. Under quite general conditions, when patiently packing discs onto cylinders, and smoothly and slowly changing the diameter of those discs, it turns out that Fibonacci patterns naturally emerge as mathematical consequences of packing rules that also make some biological sense.[252]

Why didn't Turing finish the problem he posed himself? He may have been too enamoured of his other developments. Subsequent mathematicians proved the Fibonacci property by simplifying the problem to the point where no computer is needed for a solution; but Turing's work was always wedded to the over-complicated reaction–diffusion equations that he had used to demonstrate the Turing Instability. And because they were so complicated, they had to be solved on the computer, and in 1951 no one more than Turing believed in solving problems on the computer. But the equations couldn't be solved well enough, not because of mathematical theorems about computability, or Polanyiesque ethical worries about totalitarianism, but because computers do what you tell them to do, not what you want them to do. The discussions about machine intelligence had foreseen that hardware would need to deal with noise and uncertainty and blown valves; but no one had worried about software bugs. Computer programming turned out much harder and slower than anyone, including Turing, thought it would be.

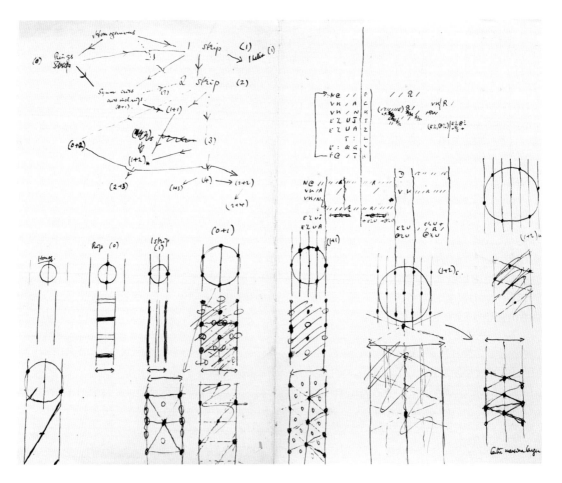

Figure 104. A note from what Newman thought were Turing's indecipherable notes. The top left-hand section shows the routes by which the patterns at the bottom move from simple (on the left) to complicated. There is a fragment of code (upper right) written in the Ferranti Mark 1 machine language.

Manchester Receptions

The lack of progress was not due to any lack of interest from Turing's peers. He discussed the broad theory of his work at a conference in 1952, just days after his arrest. [253] The trouble there was that these were inter-disciplinary discussions, prone to collapse into sterile debates or an illusion of progress from the mere translation of problems from one field into the language of another. Turing's mathematics can be seen as a striving towards what is known to mathematicians as dynamical systems theory (the 'chaos theory' of *Jurassic Park*). One of the early papers in that field, based on a wartime radar problem, came from Max's friend Mary Cartwright, who might have made a connection too, but she was down in Cambridge, and she and Turing were never to bond over the washing-up.

After his death, Turing's ideas never quite died, because he had talked about them enough in life. He gave a seminar to the chemists in 1951 and again the following year, during the visit of Ilya Prigogine, a Belgian chemist. Prigogine was extending the Polanyi chemical kinetics tradition into ideas which, though independent, have a similar dynamical systems flavour to Turing's biologically motivated theories. Prigogine would go on to win a Nobel Prize in Chemistry for these ideas. [254] Turing talked again in 1952 at a Manchester meeting of the Society for Experimental Biology, but for all his ambitions to explain zebra stripes, Turing made no headway in the Zoology department. [255] There Professor Graham Cannon presided over a self-consciously old-fashioned department having no truck with the new molecular biology, let alone mathematics, and which had trouble accepting Darwinism well into the 1960s. Although Cannon's perceived Darwin-denial was embarrassing to the younger members of staff, his position was a little more nuanced than this. In particular, he was set on defending Lamarck, the French evolutionary theorist held up as the opposite of

Figure 105. Two forms of the peppered moth *Biston betularia* on the same tree. The darker form, *B. b. carbonaria*, was not known before 1811, and the first live specimen was caught in Manchester in 1848. The prevalence of *carbonaria* in Manchester had risen to 98% by 1895, and then steadily fell again during the twentieth century as the air became cleaner. This literal textbook example of evolution was challenged by Graham Cannon, Manchester's Professor of Zoology until 1963, on the grounds that the darker form might well be black because it ate all the smut.

Darwin. Lamarck had been especially seized on by the Soviet geneticist Lysenko, a favourite of Stalin, and when the Soviet Union formally outlawed dissent from Lysenko's version of genetics, it was for ideological reasons rather than any peer scientific endorsement. This was a crucial criticism made by the likes of Polanyi when debating state-run science with Blackett, and the mere mention of Lamarck was highly politically charged. Cannon wrote several papers, with no mention of politics, ostensibly to distinguish what Lamarck actually wrote from what he was misunderstood to say, but to no avail, and Lamarck is simply remembered now as wrong. Cannon wasn't blind to the evidence mounting up for the twentieth century's Darwinian synthesis, but Cannon's concern was more in pointing out the substantial gaps it still had. He didn't dispute the famous shift of the peppered moth towards darker colours as a consequence of the soot of the industrial revolution. This was being fixed into school textbooks as an example of Darwinian evolution acting on genes, caused by the increased visibility and hence mortality of a light-coloured moth landing on Manchester's black tree trunks. Cannon said another hypothesis would need to be rejected first: that the soot was toxic and, well, black, and that moths that ate toxic black soot might well become black. Cannon also had little time for the statistical genetics that eventually won out in evolutionary biology, calling it *'the beginning of that invasion by mathematics which has robbed biology of so much of its charm'*.[256]

Turing did make a connection with Manchester's banana king, Claude Wardlaw. Wardlaw had made his career as a scientist in the plantations of British colonies giving practical advice on dealing with pests. He had met his artistic wife Jessie in Glasgow, and she sailed out to marry him in Jamaica and then travelled the world with him: the slim obituary volume he wrote at her death in the 1970s is touchingly tender about her, though it also inadvertently evokes some of the imperial and racist rationales of British botany.[257] By 1940 the Wardlaws came to Manchester and Claude was in charge of a department turned to wartime needs: his expertise on mould made him a consultant to ICI's penicillin plant at Trafford Park as well. Wardlaw's post-war Botany department was more progressive than Zoology,[258] and Turing's theory excited Wardlaw as one he had been waiting for *'for a long time'*: he wrote a paper that he wanted them both to put their names to, explaining the theory to biologists. In the end the paper was sent off under Wardlaw's name alone, but the ideas and their owner stayed at the front of Wardlaw's mind: in the collected essays on form in plants that he published in 1968, Turing gets more index references than any of the other giants of the field.[259] As a consequence, the Manchester botanists did attempt to engage critically with Turing's idea, at least enough to later recall that *'his knowledge of the sordid reality of plant growth was not always complete, and a seminar is remembered in which he gave an exposition on the mathematics of the arrangement of florets on a composite head, which depended on the existence of a central floret. Asked if there really was a central floret he said testily "Oh I don't know!"'*.[260]

With the authority of Professor Wardlaw's interest to reassure them that they were involved in a serious project, the botanists were genuinely trying to understand Turing rather than be amused by him, and were engaged enough to see that he had *two* projects on the go: one to say where spots came from at all, and one to say how spots, once made, came to be arranged in Fibonacci patterns. They took him seriously enough to dispute what they understood of his assumptions. But there is that defensive Mancunian use of 'sordid' as a self-description: experimentalists knew what they were talking about because they got their hands dirty while theoreticians did not: dirt, like Manchester's soot, was a badge of productive honour, even if it pushed one down the hierarchy of classical beauty. In the end, Wardlaw's interest was perhaps in the opportunity for new botanical research in testing the assumptions that went into Turing's model, rather than for testing Turing's conclusions.

Turing's Fibonacci theory would be bypassed by mathematical history. In contrast the form-creating potential of the Turing Instability made its mark on a small group of theoretically minded interdisciplinary biologists, and especially Hal Waddington. Waddington was an Edinburgh geneticist who had been a member of the Theoretical Biology group alongside Dorothy Wrinch, and part of the group consulted for both the Festival of Britain Science and the ICA Growth and Form exhibition: within a week of publication Waddington was writing to Turing about his work and he was still discussing it in the late 1960s when he ran a series of elite and delightful sounding Como conferences on Theoretical Biology amid the Italian lakes. That might have been the end; Theoretical Biology was withering under the greater attention being paid to the power and reach of the new molecular viewpoints, but just as that happened the mathematicians rediscovered the idea. Hans Meinhardt, the physicist author of the first papers of this new wave, was unaware of Turing's work, although it seems unlikely that his biological co-author Alfred Gierer was completely unaware of the ripples from Lake Como. When a British mathematician, Jim Murray, picked up the theory and established an Oxford undergraduate course in mathematical biology, the Turing Instability became a central part of the education of any applied mathematician with an interest in more than fluid mechanics. It is via this route that Turing's mathematical biology is taught in Manchester still.[261]

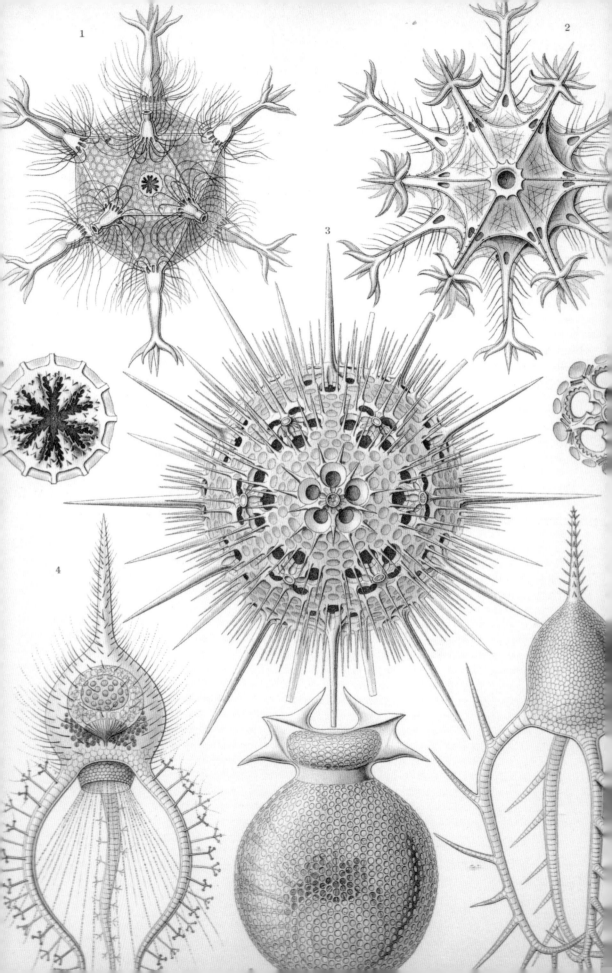

Radiolaria

Turing acquired an MSc student in 1953. MSc students, doing a year's research, should expect a supervisor to find a discrete, achievable project that is neverthe-less a worthwhile and uncertain problem: most are disappointed, but Bernard Richards struck lucky. Turing saw in the studentship the opportunity to follow up his idea, made public in 1951, that his reaction–diffusion equations on a sphere would produce solutions that looked like *Radiolaria*. In this setting, the solutions are combinations of what are known as Legendre polynomials, the analogues on a sphere of sine waves on a line. Polanyi's sparring partner Dorothy Wrinch had been publishing in the 1930s on exactly these Legendre polynomials for the generation of biological form, but even if Turing knew of her work he made no reference to it. Legendre polynomials are standard mathematical objects; ind-eed Hartree's colleague Bertha Swirles, when freed from his differential analyser, wrote a book on them without any reference to mathematical biology. Just as an acoustic sine wave can have as many peaks as we want by tuning its frequ-ency, the Legendre polynomials can be manipulated to spike a variable number of times on the sphere. Turing worked out the details and got Richards to plot the necessary solutions for two, six and twelve and spikes. Richards deserves signif-icant credit for managing to do this, but his interpretation of what he had done was inevitably limited. Richards was absolutely astonished that, when given a mathematics that had twelve spikes, the Ferranti Mark I spat out a solution that 'matched' a *Radiolaria* that had twelve spines: a more critical mathematical biol-ogist might have been rather less surprised by getting an *n* out from a model that put an *n* in. But undergraduate mathematics courses of the time couldn't produce that kind of critical biological thinker. Richards' understandable lack of experience meant he also was unable to see how it might relate to Turing's parallel Fibonacci investigations.

Almost at the end of his year, Richards arrived for a long-arranged app-ointment with his supervisor to find that Turing had died the day before. Richards hastily wrote up his material, received his MSc, and, bereft of any patron in this highly theoretical and speculative field, moved on to a career in medical informatics. A more creative thinker might have done much more, but Richards can hardly be blamed for not being a Turing. The only person formally educated about Turing's biological work wasn't shown a complete enough picture of it to be able to pass it on.[262]

Figure 106. One of Ernst Haeckel's plates from his 1904 *Kunstformen der Natur*. Haeckel's beautifully illustrated text, with careful attention given to balance and symmetry, repurposed work commissioned twenty years earlier by the British HMS *Challenger* scientific circumnavigation. The top-left hand image is of what Haeckel named *Circogonia icosahedra*. The image of this organism, with a 12-fold symmetry in its skeleton, attracted the attention of both D'Arcy Thompson and Turing, but plankton with these degrees of symmetry have never been re-identified.

Playing, Learning and Working

In a University laboratory a scientist studies a miniature representation of a draughts board on a cathode-ray tube. After careful consideration he moves one of his pieces by pressing a few switch keys. His invisible opponent makes a counter-move. After further thought the man moves, again, a typewriter crackles curtly and is silent. The man reads: 'That was a foul move; take it back at once.' The game proceeds and the man loses; he retires and is replaced by a young lady carrying a roll of punched paper tape. This she applies to a 'tape reader', which consumes it in a matter of seconds. The draughts board disappears and is replaced by a rapidly changing pattern of bright and dim dots. The typewriter rattles again and the young lady reads a love letter from an invisible suitor. The Electronic Brain is at work...or so it might appear. Actually it is only the Manchester University Electronic Digital Computer 'showing off'.

FC Williams (probably drafted by V Bowden), 1955. [263]

Ferranti chose well when they appointed **Vivian Bowden** to head their marketing effort. Memorably described as a 'master of ludicrous interpolation' by his boss, he was charged with working out who could be persuaded to pay for the new invention. [264] Electronic computing offered a faster, cheaper alternative to human computing for *numerical* processing tasks, but pre-war private sector spending on these scientific applications was tiny. By contrast *information* processing was the strand that would ultimately dominate computing, but this was invisible to the Manchester engineers because in 1948 it only existed in cryptography and in the minds of mathematicians. In a sense Kilburn's greatest technical achievement would be the Atlas of 1962, briefly the fastest computer in the world for numerical work, but for Ferranti that was a loss-making project because they only sold two and a half machines. [265]

Bowden understood that the small groups, funded by strategic defence interests, that needed numerical computation didn't really need to be persuaded, but wider market success depended ultimately on new information applications that at the time mathematicians alone could envisage but which could not exist until the machines were actually delivered and working. So while the early

Figure 107. Thermionic valves – to become the first logic technology of the electronic computer – had been widely available since their military use in the First World War. These valves for the German interwar market were advertised on a paper bag kept by Dietrich Prinz on his refugee travels.

project managers, like Newman, had rushed to disabuse the media that the new machines were electronic brains, in contrast Bowden allowed the idea of thinking machines to permeate his marketing material. He used Manchester experts to put together *Faster than Thought,* ostensibly a book explaining the new technology to the public, but including a collection of cool things that the mathematicians thought they were going to be able to do: playing chess and bridge, writing sonnets, playing music, and doing payroll (curiously, an obsession of Patrick Blackett, who spent years trying to get Ferranti to offer a system for this). No one thought that there was money in chess playing, but in the absence of anything they *could* do, it was the best way to illustrate that potentially intelligent systems were available for sale.

Wistfully, curiously, fervently

It was in this context that two very different thinkers, Christopher Strachey and Dietrich Prinz, briefly made Manchester computing playful.

Christopher Strachey was cut from a very similar British establishment cloth as Turing—in fact they had known each other slightly at King's. Strachey, nephew of arch-Bloomsburyite Lytton Strachey, was rather more socially embedded in Cambridge, but had a less stellar initial academic career, dropping out of King's for a while with depression; an experience which left him, like Turing, with a respect for Jungian psychoanalysis. [266] Like Turing he came to Manchester for the computer. This time it was not Max Newman that summoned him, but Turing himself, speaking over the airwaves on the Third Programme in 1951. Strachey already knew of the machine, but it was after he heard Turing on the radio that Strachey wrote to him and started writing programs for the Mark I. Like Turing, he wrote them without being anywhere near the machine;

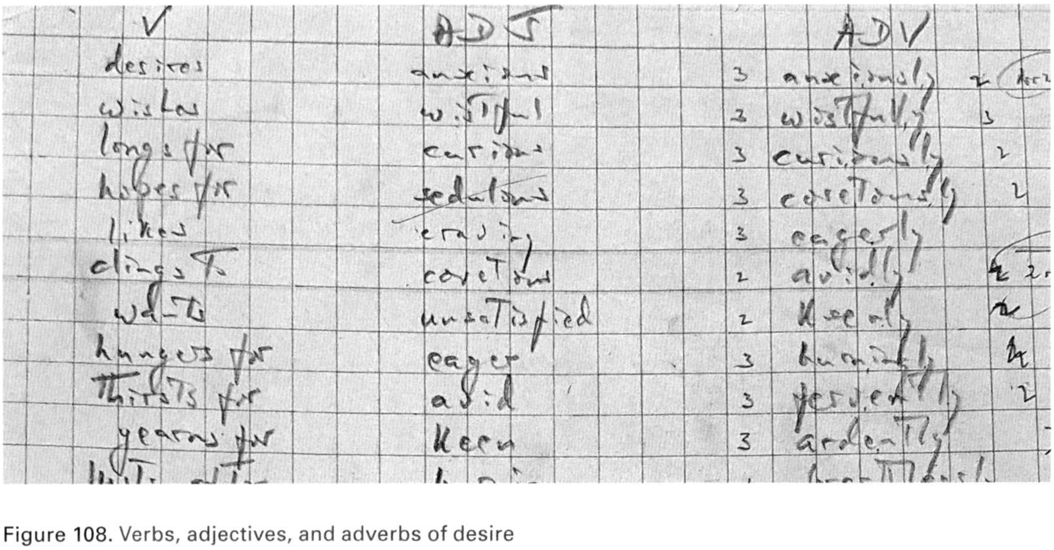

Figure 108. Verbs, adjectives, and adverbs of desire for input into Strachey's love letter program.

unlike Turing his worked first time. Like Turing, he didn't get on with Kilburn. And like Turing, Strachey was gay. Turing was not in the end a computer hacker revelling in the machine itself: for him the Ferranti Mark I was ultimately a tool to get some more interesting mathematics done, but the younger Strachey had more playful ideas. Turing had manipulated the machine's loudspeaker to make musical notes, but only used this facility to allow the user to monitor the state of the machine. By contrast one of Strachey's first programs was to join the notes together to play *God Save The King,* and soon the BBC came to record the electronic brain singing.[267] Max Newman heard the music too, and offered Strachey a job in Manchester, demonstrating in passing his continuing influence on the Computing Machine Laboratory as late as 1951. Soon the machine was heard playing tunes of its own composition. Once more the potentially displaced experts had to be reassured, and Newman told a conference of musicians that the music was 'very bad'.[268] The tunes could perhaps have been improved with help from elsewhere in the University: it so happened that Williams was Dean of the Faculty of Music as well as Professor of Engineering. But Williams held the deanship for reasons of University politics, and had absolutely no interest in classical music.[269]

Strachey wrote a program to play draughts, which has a good claim to be the first computer game in the world.[270] And then Strachey went further. He collected together the verbal forms which lovers use: they communicate *anxiously, wistfully, curiously, fervently, ardently, breathlessly, passionately*, and last of all *beautifully*. He joined the adverbs with nouns and verbs and conventional forms and soon the Ferranti Mark I was pumping out love letters. Within the year Strachey was offered a job with the funders of the machine, by now the National Research Development Corporation, and there was no attempt to keep him in Manchester. Kilburn had some difficulties with Strachey, but letting him go may have been a strategic mistake: Strachey later wrote a report for the Atomic Energy Research Establishment strongly opposed to Kilburn developing the fast but ill-fated Atlas.[271]

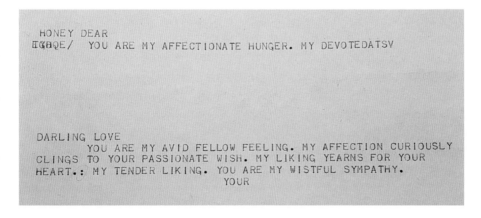

Figure 109. The resultant tender likings of the Manchester Mark 1.

If Strachey can be seen as a kind of Turing Mark II it's not too far to look for an approximate Newman Mark II. **Dietrich Prinz**, neat and tidy chess player, was full of ideas but ended up, perhaps with the insecurity of the migrant, working at the needful rather than the entertaining. He had arrived as another refugee from the Nazis, and put his electronic engineering skills to work as a valve designer for GEC, but was nevertheless interned by the British during the war. After the war he was headhunted to Ferranti specifically to develop cybernetic control systems. When first he moved to Manchester he lived close to Old Trafford, though he despised football: his gaming addiction was chess, and he had been aware of game-playing theories coming from Turing's abortive NPL project. Despite—or because of—their common German ancestry, Prinz at Ferranti and Newman at the University barely connected: this was a time when Newman was retreating into university administration and pure mathematics, where the engineer-trained Prinz couldn't follow him. Even if Prinz was, as seems likely, receptive to Turing's special wavelength there's no record of any real connection between them, though they certainly met.[272]

Prinz quickly understood Manchester's intellectual heritage. A nineteenth century University philosopher had developed the Jevons Logic Piano, a mechanical logical demonstrator. Working with Wolfe Mays in the University, Prinz designed an electronic update of the Logic Piano. Prinz had not been the designer of Nimrod, Ferranti's Nim-playing machine at the Festival of Britain, but he did accompany it when Nimrod was boxed up in the autumn and flown, of all places, to a trade fair in Berlin. A contemporary picture shows Prinz sitting next to the German Finance Minister, architect of the post-war economic miracle, who played Nimrod and lost all three games. This photo is reproduced across the internet, showing as it does the first computer game to use an electronic display, but without comment on Prinz's presence in the photograph, sitting in the city he had been forced to flee for his life 15 years earlier and where his relatives had been murdered. Though Prinz found a haven and a career working for Ferranti, it meant living an expatriate life in Rusholme. His wife, herself a post-war German economic migrant who came to the UK to work as a nurse, was still in the 1960s having to get paprika sent over from Hungary and good coffee from Germany, though by then she could find green peppers in Rusholme.[273]

Prinz made a further contribution to the playful opportunities of the computer with a program that solved chess endgames, but after this *'the number of machine users increased so much there was not enough time left for frivolities'* and he settled to the long collaborative post-war task of building an information processing industry. As well as the defence contracts that nursed the infant industry, Prinz and colleagues like Mary Lee Woods spent the next decades working on problems designed to crack open new markets, like bus timetabling.[274]

Figure 110. When *Picture Post* visited the Manchester computer in 1955, Dietrich Prinz's chess endgame program was featured as an application. Ferranti's marketers used gaming potential not as a selling point but as a way of explaining the versatility of the new machine to uncertain business and government users. Prinz sits at the console; the woman is unidentified.

VOLUME IX · NUMBER 1 · JULY 1958

THE BRITISH JOURNAL OF
DELINQUENCY

*The Official Organ of the Institute for the
Study and Treatment of Delinquency*

Published b

INSTITUTE FOR THE S   TREATMENT
OF DE

BAILLIÈRE   D COX, LTD.

SPECIAL NUMBER ON HOMOSEXUALITY

Oxford Road Show

One did not in those days...think about homosexuals and lesbians: one had heard of them, of course. There was a book called Pansies by DH Lawrence displayed...when I was an articled clerk aged about 21. 'Another boring gardening book,' I sighed ... I expect we were a little stupid.

Alan Turing's brother. [275]

What was the sexual landscape of Manchester in 1948? And how was it navigated by a Cambridge-educated boffin of a gay man, or anyone else? Turing's first impression was *'the low standard of male physique'* [276] but deeper social history is hard to come by.

Men cruising the streets for same-sex partners was not a sudden innovation of the 1940s, but the record is fragmentary. There's at least one male memory of 1920s Manchester as a *'big city scene'* affording the possibility of cruising other men at the cinema and theatre. [277] In 1952, a Methodist minister was quoted in a Sunday newspaper exposé as finding Manchester *'the worst city for homosexuality'* he had been in. There were a number of pubs, like The Rembrandt, around the city with a reputation for putting on drag shows: these were not 'gay pubs', though the performers were celebrated for their 'queer gender' identities, catering to a working-class audience or, during wartime, visiting American troops. [278] Twenty years later, the landlord of one of these pubs, The Union, was prosecuted for allowing men to dance together in a case that drew attention to the pub itself. The prosecution succeeded, but the publicity may well have contributed to changing attitudes within the City Council that ultimately created a Gay Village around the pub in Canal Street. In the 1940s, though, the centre of gay gravity may have been further west. [279] When gay clubs opened after 1967, these were located near the pre-existing main cruising areas, with two on John Dalton Street and another on Deansgate very close to Bootle Street Police Station. [280]

The most vivid and relevant descriptions of gay street culture in Turing's time and place come, not coincidentally, from Andrew Hodges' 1983 biography of Turing himself. [281] There was a *'small homosexual set'* centred on the University, the BBC, and *The Manchester Guardian*, but Turing seems not to have associated with it. [282] Turing's romantic aspirations had been centred on

Figure 111. The British Journal of Delinquency was a forum for many of the psychiatrists who were being required by the courts to mandate therapy for offenders. This 1958 special issue on the Wolfenden report on sexual behaviour and the law reflects many of the contemporary uncertainties about the role of medical intervention. The Wolfenden report would eventually lead to a 1967 act decriminalising some homosexual relationships, although not the one Turing and the under-21 Murray formed.

the King's undergraduate Neville Johnson, and Turing visited him in Cambridge every few weeks in what was, in the judgement of those who knew them, one of the most important emotional relationships of Turing's life; but, especially when Johnson graduated and moved back in with his mother in Reading, the physical connection petered out.

What was the moral atmosphere within the post-war University? The war had offered many younger people novel sexual possibilities, and the cohort of students comprised many who had spent years in the Services, and were impatient with social formalities that previous students, straight from school, had abided by.[283] Personal memories of the time recount freedom and the ability to discreetly pursue heterosexual romantic attachments, though female students showing too much affection to their boyfriends when walking home down the Oxford Road would provoke complaints from the public and reproof from those managing their halls.[284] Student attitudes in the 1950s towards homosexuality were somewhat uncertain. In October 1953 the leading Shakespearean actor of the day, John Gielgud, had been arrested for soliciting men for sex in a London

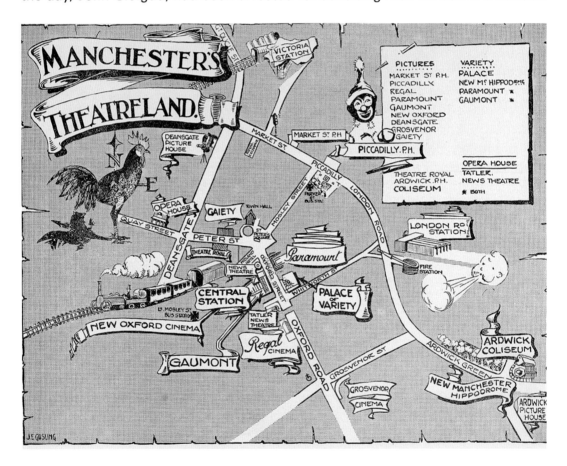

Figure 112. A pre-war map of Manchester's Theatreland, which also covers the known gay street spaces of the period.

'There were a couple of cinemas, an amusement arcade, a pub — the Union Tavern — and a very early example of the milk bar. This stretch between the urinal and the cinema was where the male homosexual eye was focussed — perhaps the same block as trodden by Ludwig Wittgenstein, such unofficial institutions lasting as long as the respectable kind. Here straggled a motley convoy of souls, and amidst them the odd independent sailing like Alan Turing. Here merged many kinds of desire — for physical excitement, for attention, for a life outside family and factory conditions, or for money. These were not sharp divisions. Money, if involved, was little but the clink of 'tipping' that was heard in any encounter between different social classes, and indeed little different from the way that women could expect to be entertained and treated by men. The most special relationship would have its quid pro quo and this kind was more likely for ten bob than a quid. This was how it was done in the ordinary England of 1930, outside privileged circles such as those of Cambridge or Oxford. For the young, in particular, without means or private space, homosexual desire meant street space.'

Figure 113. Hodges (1983) on the Oxford Road.

Figure 114. Poster for *People Will Talk*, one of the films advertised outside the Regal Cinema in December 1952. Arnold Murray remembered, many years later, that Turing had been pretending to study the film posters that day before approaching him and inviting him to a nearby café.

153

public lavatory. Gielgud had just had his first film released, and when his co-star Greer Garson promoted it at the Manchester University Students' Union, a mass-market paper reported that she was first greeted with boos when she mentioned Gielgud, then stilled the audience with a reference to Gielgud as *'the great master of Shakespearean drama'.*[285] But a student journalist covering the story for the University paper wrote *'homosexuality is far less socially destructive than adultery'* and implied that the popular newspaper reporter had exaggerated the jeering.[286]

Whatever anyone else thought, in December 1951 Alan Turing felt he had submitted a paper—the morphogenesis paper—with *'real good stuff'* in it, and had got his Christmas shopping done as well. He celebrated by catching the eye of a young man, Arnold Murray, outside the Regal cinema on Oxford Road. Murray was also in from the suburbs, although in his case from the working-class area of Wythenshawe. Turing bought him lunch, showed off a little about being the brain behind the Electronic Brain, and then offered Murray, not a quick adjournment to a railway arch, but an invitation to visit his house in Wilmslow the following week.[287]

Arrest & Trial

Six or so weeks later, in February 1952, Turing walked into Wilmslow Police Station to report a burglary, leaving Murray waiting outside. The burglar, a friend of Murray, was found and prosecuted. But during the police investigation, Turing volunteered, or admitted, that he and Murray had a physical relationship. They were charged with gross indecency, with Turing remarking incorrectly afterwards to a policeman *'Isn't there a Royal Commission to legalise it?'*[288]

Turing had no terror that his friends might know he was homosexual: indeed it was a stringent condition of close friendship to accept his sexuality.[289] But even as an unconventional member of his class, the mere public exposure

Figure 115. Wilmslow Police Station, now demolished, during the 1970s. In 1953, Turing left his lover Murray waiting outside when he went to report a burglary; he emerged the subject of a police investigation himself.

of a criminal trial could well have been catastrophic. Turing's insouciance in the face of arrest—he played the violin to visiting detectives—seems heroic, and no doubt it was. But one component of that heroism, as it often is, might well have been ignorance of the seriousness of the situation. Perhaps Turing misunderstood the geographic differences of police tolerance. What was evident and tolerated in specific, marginal zones of the industrial port city of Manchester may well have been invisible to and, when seen, unacceptable to the suburban, near rural, policing of Wilmslow. The times had changed as well as the place: there was increased intolerance following the exposure of homosexual Cambridge Apostles among traitors in 1951, and in the related American nervousness about sharing atomic and cryptographic secrets with the British. Prosecutions of gay men intensified after the flight of Burgess and Maclean in 1951.[290]

In any case, the prosecution proceeded, and Turing disclosed the charges in advance to his family and workmates. One close emotional tie for Turing was his 'father figure' Max Newman.[291] Despite their close relationship, Newman had not known of Turing's sexuality and was astonished to discover it. But now Turing made no attempt to be discreet, explaining his situation to Newman at lunch in the University refectory in a voice loud enough, Newman believed, to be deliberately heard by their colleagues. Max's response was crucially supportive. He attended the trial as a character witness and was asked by the defence whether he would receive 'such a man' in his home. He replied: *'I already have. He is a personal friend of myself and my wife'.*[292]

Turing and Murray were prosecuted on identical charges of gross indecency. Turing was sentenced to probation and to submit to unspecified 'medical' treatment, while the younger Murray was sentenced to neither. Medical treatment for homosexuality was a sub-speciality of psychiatrists with an interest in delinquency.[293]

Although the case was reported in the local papers and the northern edition of the *News of the World*, under the headline *Accused Had Powerful Brain*, it did not become a *cause célèbre* for the liberal intelligentsia of Manchester.[294] Hodges suggests that, as far as Jefferson and Polanyi were concerned, this was a private and distasteful medical matter, though in fact both of them continued to welcome him into their intellectual debates.[295] What was *not* reported was that one of the country's most senior cryptographers, Hugh Alexander, had, like Newman, spoken up for Turing at the hearing in a secret session; but the secret state either did not or could not prevent the court proceeding to judgement.[296]

The Knutsford Quarter Sessions were required to recognise homosexual acts as offences but not given guidance as to whether they were being committed by the bad or by the sad. Turing's class status, instead of protecting him, led to him being seen as a corruptor in the relationship and he was at significant risk of going to prison. Murray received an unusually lenient sentence in being bound over for a year, but Turing was put on probation with the significant condition that he *'submit for treatment by a duly qualified practitioner* at *Manchester Royal Infirmary'*. It is quite unclear why this decision was made. It might have been at the suggestion of a defence barrister as an alternative to prison. In any case, Turing's chemical castration, through the placement of oestrogen depots under his skin for a year, followed directly from this referral.[297]

The first British publication on oestrogen treatment in homosexual sex offenders had only appeared a couple of years earlier in 1949.[298] Was it understood by the Knutsford court as a standard medical treatment for a standard medical problem? In an inquiry submission very much of the time, the British Medical Association mentions oestrogen therapy as a means of suppressing sexual desire as a temporary measure *'to relieve anxiety in those who are seriously tempted'* and semi-permanently in older patients *'in whom there is no contra-indication to severe limitation of sexual life'*. And while a much more liberal submission from the Institute of Psychiatry baldly states that the law should not concern itself with the activities of private consenting adults, the Institute does agree that hormone suppression has value in *'those rather rare individuals who, though dreading imprisonment and wanting help, are truly (biologically) as opposed to neurotically highly sexed and who cannot resist their impulses'*.[299] Right across the medical submissions, to the distinctly varying extent to which homosexuality was thought to require treatment, the treatment of choice was overwhelmingly psychological. But there was also a medical consensus that

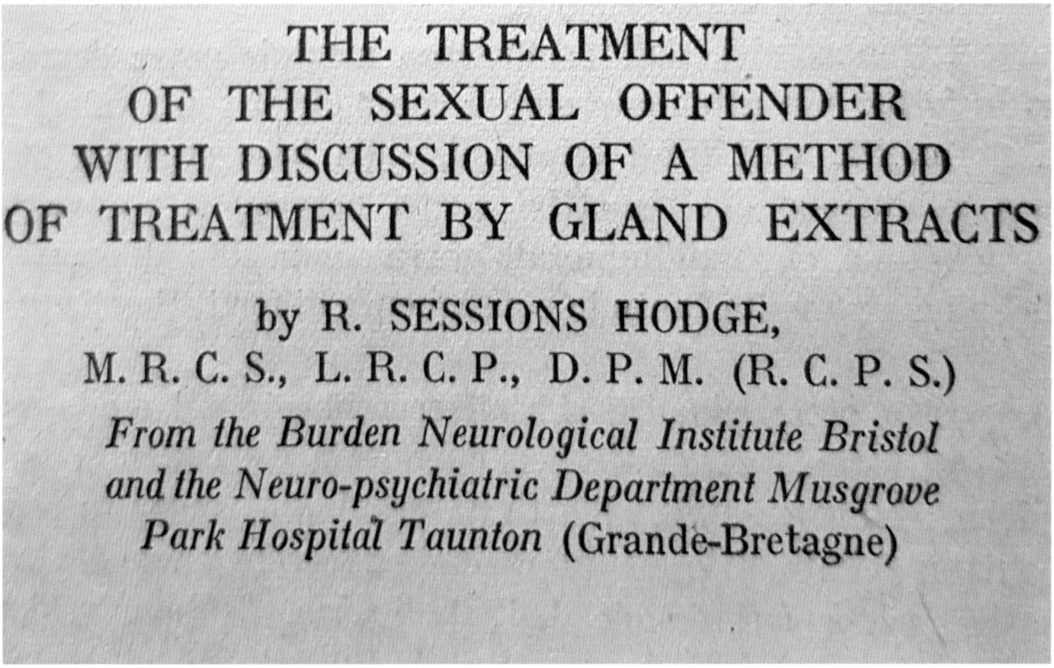

THE TREATMENT
OF THE SEXUAL OFFENDER
WITH DISCUSSION OF A METHOD
OF TREATMENT BY GLAND EXTRACTS

by R. SESSIONS HODGE,
M. R. C. S., L. R. C. P., D. P. M. (R. C. P. S.)

From the Burden Neurological Institute Bristol and the Neuro-psychiatric Department Musgrove Park Hospital Taunton (Grande-Bretagne)

Figure 116. There was little guidance available for psychiatrists presented by the courts with sexual offenders. Oestrogen therapy was seen as a way of suppressing libido for men distressed by uncontrolled and unwanted sexual urges. Centres in Bristol and London reported their work but there is no record of the practices, and the nature of consents obtained, when Turing attended the Manchester Royal Infirmary.

there was a small and specific group of men who 'wanted' help to reduce their sexual activity, in whom oestrogen therapy was useful, and that doctors could and should have the freedom to specify when this was required. It seems implausible that Turing would have identified himself in this group, but under the terms of his probation it was not up to him.

Aftermaths

Who was responsible for carrying out the sentence? We don't know which 'duly-qualified' practitioner Turing saw at the Manchester Royal Infirmary: it might even have been Geoffrey Jefferson's wife, Gertrude.[300] We don't know if the judge even had drug treatment in mind. It's most likely that the decision to prescribe oestrogen, initially as pills and then as an under-skin slow-release depot, was ultimately made by a psychiatrist.[301] If Turing had expressed a desire to change his sexuality, he could perhaps have been offered psychotherapy alone, but he told a friend that *'The psychiatrists seemed to think it useless to try and do any psychotherapy'*.[302] Oestrogen might even have been chosen because the court-mandated clinicians didn't think psychotherapy would work, but were required to prescribe some kind of 'treatment'.

But oestrogen was chosen, and though Turing talked to friends in light terms about his treatment: *'I'm growing breasts'*; *'I have just been in hospital and have had my oestrogen capsules out. It was really quite jolly there, and there was a faintly attractive nurse'*, he was nevertheless depressed by it.[303] He was more positive about a mind therapy that followed. Patrick Blackett's sister, Marion Milner, happened to be a psychoanalyst who once wrote a book *The Suppressed Madness of Sane Men,* but sane or mad the Blacketts for once stayed out of things. By the end of 1952, Turing was instead regularly seeing the therapist Franz Greenbaum. Greenbaum had fled Germany in 1939 and initially found his German medical qualifications were not recognised, His studies under Jung, though, allowed him to set up as a psychoanalyst, albeit out of the mainstream of medical psychiatric thought.[304] It was probably in this capacity, rather than through his later employment as an NHS psychiatrist, that Greenbaum treated and befriended Alan Turing. Turing came to like Greenbaum and told Lyn that he was 'making progress', but unlike Turing's mathematical biology, there was no promise that the problem, however identified, would be solved in a year's time. Given the psychoanalytic setting, and a few of Turing's own comments, it seems that the 'progress' was in part about sexual thoughts. The clinical assumption of the day was that progress meant a move towards heterosexuality, and perhaps Turing to an extent shared this assumption. But he was certainly never positive about it: in 1953 he wrote *'I have had a dream recently indicating rather clearly that I am on the way to [being] hetero, though I don't accept it with much enthusiasm either awake or in the dreams'.*[305]

There was a distinct possibility that Turing would lose his job. Patrick Blackett went to see the Vice Chancellor John Stopford, whom Lyn Irvine privately described as *'a jolly little man, who looks more like Pigling Bland than most vice-chancellors'*. Blackett was armed with statistics from that bestselling *Kinsey Report*. Stopford, an anatomist peer of Jefferson, said that it was up to Newman what happened in his department, but made sure Blackett was made aware he was trespassing on professional medical territory: the *Kinsey Report*, Stopford said, was not an authority *'I can myself respect'*. Newman, surprised to discover that it was up to him, had no doubts, and Turing kept his job. The following year Turing's Readership expired routinely, and his contract was renewed along with a pay rise. Turing's intellectual contribution was still respected: two months before Turing died he was explicitly mentioned by Geoffrey Jefferson in a public lecture, and Polanyi co-sponsored Turing's election to the Lit & Phil. [306]

Turing wrote a joke syllogism, parodying the mathematical logic that grounded his world: *'Turing believes machines think. Turing lies with men. Therefore machines do not think'.* [307] It reveals an anxiety, however jocular, about how seriously he would be taken after public exposure but perhaps like Gielgud he was protected by his specialness: he could still be a star, if not be allowed too close to state secrets.

Something to do with security definitely rattled Turing in a mysterious 1953 affair to do with Kjell Carlson. In 1952, bringing back a photo and a memory of that light Kjell kiss from Norway had caused Turing at first no more than a little gushing to everyone he knew well, but the following year something changed. There was a postcard announcing Kjell's arrival; there were police out across the North of England; there were hints of interviews with the security services;

Figure 117. Hilla and Franz Greenbaum. The couple fled Germany in the last months before the war, coming to Manchester because 'London had too many doctors'. Turing visited Franz Greenbaum for Jungian psychoanalysis and became one of a string of intellectual Manchester friends that Franz and Hilla invited into their cramped but book- and picture-filled Didsbury home.

there were worried acknowledgements to close friends of Turing's imprudence over something that was both absurd and worrying. Whatever happened, it was not a comfortable time. [308]

His next-door neighbours in Wilmslow, the Webbs, still invited him into their home. [309] At work, there were staff who *'avoided him, but then they had avoided him anyway'*. Turing's social life and deeper friendships in Manchester had never been with other gay men, and this was just as true after his exposure. Lyn had by this time escaped back to Cambridge, but they became closer friends because of her understanding some of his previous covertness; he spent time with the Polanyi and Greenbaum families. For the most part his few emotionally close, but long-distance male friendships outside Manchester continued, despite the increased risk of exposure he posed to those friends. The one definite break was with his post-war lover, Neville Johnson, whose mother in Reading stopped him seeing Turing again. [310]

The scanty evidence about Turing's state of mind in the many months between his prosecution and his death shows him outwardly defiant and flippant, privately sometimes depressed and fearful, and considering whether his sexuality was, as the state said, a problem to be addressed. He stopped going into the office so much, and he would have been unable to visit the US. He lost his security clearance to work on cryptography, the locus of one of his two greatest achievements. And the great promise of the other, the machine that could follow out your thoughts to their conclusion, was coming up against the reality of blown valves and human bugs. There's no evidence that Turing was hounded after his trial, but being publicly declared a criminal had profound emotional consequences. To some who were already friends he became a warmer, more human person to know, and for the rest he was more remote than ever. There was little prospect that Manchester would be friendlier in the future than it had been in the past. Until at least the middle of 1953, Turing maintained his engagement with those he thought worth talking to, though after that the record tails off. He was still ready to go to Cambridge to talk about 'fir cones' in December. [311]

By June 1954 Lyn's friendship with Turing was also a long-distance but not, she thought, a declining one, when she heard *'the news that Alan Turing had taken his own life ... We saw a great deal of him & were all devoted to him, for his fascinating mind— he was not only a genius but a rare kind of genius— and his very simple, humble, gentle personality. He had been with us for 5 days in April & wrote to me how very happy he had been. I never thought he would do this— no one expected it & he left no explanation at all, but everything lying about in his house as though it had been a sudden casual impulse to take the poison. Awful. He was only 41 & in the middle of a new & wonderful discovery linking biology & mathematics'*. [312]

No one knows with certainty why and how Turing died. A plausible case has been made that it was his own, long pre-meditated choice, with a method designed to avoid upsetting the mother to whom he had become increasingly close, but the evidence will never be conclusive. There has been suggestion that Turing's death was in fact accidental, or wilder and evidence-free speculations of state murder, but if Turing did commit suicide, it is not inconsistent with what we can know of a self-contained man. [313]

Turing's body was returned to the crematorium amid the colonial retirement homes of Woking and his ashes scattered there. Memorials to Turing in Manchester would have to wait for another forty years. [314] If you seek his monuments, look online. But in the physical Manchester, it was in 1994 that the city named a road the Alan Turing Way, and in 2001 a sculpture of Turing sitting on a bench was placed in Sackville Park, close to the Gay Village. [315] This was not a Council marketing effort: a local barrister raised funds privately after seeing *Breaking The Code*, the play by Hugh Whitemore closely based on Andrew Hodges' biography. The bench carries a plain and a cipher text, though as Wikipedia points out, the cipher could not have been created from the plain by an Enigma machine as at one point the letter U is coded to itself. [316] In 2004, Turing's house in Wilmslow acquired a blue plaque, and nationally the memorials have now started to multiply: there are blue plaques marking the site of his birth, his early childhood, his late childhood, his Cambridge years, his Bletchley Park service (in brass), his post-war years in London, the Manchester computer building, and the house where he met his death in Wilmslow. Only a few of Turing's years are now unaccounted for in plaques: perhaps Hale and Princeton feel they have enough famous alumni already. [317] The most meaningful Manchester memorial today is that the University has a large Turing building housing the Mathematics department. And, of course, the Alan Turing Way to the Velodrome, briefly marked by a glorious Thomas Heatherwick sculpture until the spikes started falling off.

The Course of the Bee

The men of experiment are like the ant, they only collect and use; the reasoners resemble spiders, who make cobwebs out of their own substance. But the bee takes a middle course: it gathers its material from the flowers of the garden and of the field, but transforms and digests it by a power of its own.

Francis Bacon. [318]

There are today two separate blue plaques on the same building complex off Oxford Road, but you can't see them both at the same time. There is one facing north shared by Williams and Kilburn, and after you take an inconvenient diversion around the Manchester Museum, there is one facing south for Turing, in a physical representation of a difference in viewpoint that has rumbled on ever since the events of 1948. Neither plaque says anything untrue but then again neither plaque mentions the other. They represent a history that portrays Kilburn and Williams as one type of thinker and Turing as another. In this history Kilburn and Williams are labelled as doers, as what Francis Bacon would call ants, while Turing is a reasoning spider. But both plaques decorate Manchester, the city of the bee, whose rightful reputation as a birthplace of the computer depends inextricably on all of three of those named, and on everyone going beyond stereotypes. One of the many profound consequences was that it was the child of two Manchester spiders — Tim Berners-Lee, whose parents Mary Lee and Conway had met as programmers at Ferranti — who should create the world-wide web. [319]

For most of the twentieth century, the history of Manchester computing simply started in 1948. [320] This said that Williams and Kilburn had been interested in the engineering challenge of making, rather than programming, a computer and that, it went, is what they succeeded in doing: *'Freddie Williams was not, I think, interested in the computer as a computer. What we were interested in doing was creating the computer for other people to use'*. In this account Newman's computing project had been an unsuccessful rival to Williams', an account helped by Newman's own lack of credit-seeking behaviour. [321] When a historical Turing re-emerged after 1983, it was as a National Treasure residing in Manchester at the time but with no relation to the machine, except through using it for his impenetrable biological mathematics. In 1998 the Department of Computer Science held a 50th anniversary celebration to mark the first running of the Baby: Turing, it's said, was not mentioned on the day, and in 2006 one leading local computer scientist said *'Colossus was not a machine in the direct line leading to the modern computer'*. [322] This engineer's history can't be said to be wrong, but it is partial. [323]

Figure 118. The Manchester Bee, set into the floor of Manchester Town Hall.

It wasn't until the twenty-first century that the pre-Mark I history of the Manchester computers was quarried by revisionists aiming to re-establish the role of the mathematicians. They pointed out that, even years after the event, Williams had always been generous in acknowledging the mathematicians' influence[324] and had no difficulty recalling that *Tom Kilburn and I knew nothing about computers...Professor Newman and Mr AM Turing knew a lot about computers. They took us by the hand and explained how numbers could live in houses with addresses.* In 1948, it was as electronic engineers, not as computer architects, that Williams and Kilburn led the world.[325] Kilburn, by contrast, was much more grudging: *'Between 1945 and 1947 somehow or other I knew what a digital computer was...where I got that knowledge from I've no idea'.* In fact he had got it from attending a series of lectures: the lectures given by Turing. It's unlikely that Kilburn in these later comments was deliberately obscuring credit due to Turing, and more plausible that he just didn't remember owing anything to the mathematicians. As a young PhD student, Kilburn was not interested in the past, and quite insulated from the administrative background. There is no patent on an idea, or on a funding decision, and rightly it was Kilburn listed as inventor on the computer memory patents, not Turing or Newman or Blackett.[326]

The final glimpse we have of Kilburn and Turing working together is over a long summer night in June 1950. After the somewhat fake demonstration for the BBC of doing Mersenne mathematics on the Manchester Mark I there had been a year of work by Turing on an actual research problem. Turing had developed code to explore a pure mathematical axiom known as the Riemann Hypothesis, and that, together with some work on an optical problem, may have been all that the machine did for a year.[327] Finally, in June 1950, the Riemann code ran successfully, all night: *'The calculations had been planned some time in advance but had in fact to be carried out in great haste. If it had not been for the fact that the computer remained in serviceable condition for an unusually long period from 3 p.m. one afternoon to 8 a.m. the following morning it is probable that the calculations would never have been done at all'.*[328]

An engineer had to be on standby whenever the machine ran and it was Kilburn who stayed overnight with Turing and ensured the unusually long uptime.[329] This was the first application of the Manchester computer to generate a mathematical paper, but it was also the time at which Kilburn began to realise that the aims of the Manchester logicians and (perhaps unknown to him) cryptographers were very different to those of the applied mathematicians using computing resource elsewhere in the world. Henceforth, he said, he would address the latter, and in doing this he chose a group of consumers with practical, well-funded, and plausible needs who would in fact drive the economic development of the computer for decades.[330] It meant that Manchester computers would be used to do the large repetitive calculations needed by the atom bomb projects. This was the opposite use to the automated reasoning that Newman and (perhaps) Blackett had intended. Newman seems to have accepted this, though

Figure 119. Two plaques on the same building between Coupland Street and Bridgeford Street, one facing to the south, the other to the north.

Figure 120. The Turing building, opened in 2008. Mainly housing the Mathematics department, it contains seminar rooms memorialising Phyllis Nicolson among others.

Figure 121. The Kilburn building, half a minute's walk away from the Turing building, was built to house the School of Computer Science in 1972. Like the department's 1955 building, it was designed around two large rooms, each housing one monolithic computer: one for service and one to do research.

it took Manchester off a path pointing to intelligent machines. Blackett, on the other hand, was unhappy, perhaps because of his opposition to atomic weapons themselves. [331] But Blackett no longer had any leverage over the project.

Though Kilburn and Turing worked together in the early days, they never collaborated in any intellectually meaningful way. Had they done so, the potential for an early breakthrough in artificial intelligence would have been enormous. They were two people of creativity and achievement, with much knowledge and background in common, and with different and complementary skills in a field ripe for innovation. But something about those differences kept them apart. They were both productive bees, but one looked like an ant and one a spider. This is a story where it is very tempting to align two men on opposite sides of an apparently intuitive divide. Asked to assign one member of each pair from: North/South, Manchester/Cambridge, grammar school/public school, engineer/mathematician, applied/pure, doer/thinker, hardware/software, trade/gentry, earned/entitled, patent holder/private thinker, the labels that apply to Kilburn/Turing might seem at first obvious and factual. [332] Binary reductions are as addictive as they are misleading, so that adding into the list masculine/effeminate, straight/gay, legal/illegal might give hardly more pause for thought. It is a short step, then, to a conclusion that manly Manchester's judgement of Turing as an effeminate Cambridge criminal led to ostracism and Turing's depression and suicide. But it is a simplistic step without direct evidence.

There is clear evidence that there was coldness. Perhaps it was the engineers that felt looked down on: some of the mathematicians considered Williams and Kilburn as not *'ideas men'*. [333] Williams later gave a lecture, *Engineering Must Not Degenerate Into Mathematics,* which under cover of a successfully jocular tone revealed a distinct bitterness about the class distinctions in the *'traditional aristocratic attitude: to be really tops two things are required: (a) one must be supremely good at something. (b) The something at which one is supremely good must be absolutely useless'.* [334]

It was more than class, though. Kilburn and Turing are recorded by multiple sources as not getting on, and Geoff Tootill, in long hindsight, speculated that this was because Kilburn knew of Turing's sexuality. But after this the binaries start to fray. Tootill also thought there may have been disapproval of Turing's general untidiness and tendency for his underpants to show above his trousers, and another programmer thought Kilburn in general liberal and broadminded. [335] The dichotomies don't always survive inspection: Kilburn had had a Cambridge mathematics education too, and Turing also came to Manchester through choice and with hands-on electronic expertise. And though to begin with Turing was paid more than Kilburn, by 1954 Kilburn's career prospects and consulting fees were rapidly improving.[336] There may have been a 'jagged rift' between the engineers and the mathematicians, but it was perhaps more a silence of incomprehension than anything more destructive.[337] One heir on the programming side wrote: *'Turing, Kilburn, and Williams, were all three quite different people... stars of the scientific establishment to my mind...good, kind people'*.[338]

Whatever the reasons, Manchester's Electrical Engineering department, and the Computer Science department that succeeded it on Oxford Road, became a place where people made computers more than one where they used them. The place of the Manchester Mark I in the history of computer development is secured far more by its hardware than by its software.[339] The histories of the 1950s and '60s are histories of ground-breaking machines more than of programs. In hindsight, that may have been a poor long-term bet. For a few decades Moston and then Gorton were the sites of factories that made mainframe computers; meetings of the Lit & Phil can still attract the men and women who made them. But the engineers who can say they have built computers in Manchester are all now retired. Although the Ferranti Mark I had the largest share of the new market and British hardware would continue to compete on speed, they started to lose out to American machines on reliability and cost. Within a few years of the delivery of the Ferranti Mark I to AWRE, the British atom bomb designers were demanding an IBM replacement, not a British one, and certainly not Kilburn's Atlas. Large, centralised computing facilities based around IBM hardware did evolve locally, and in the 1950s and '60s Shell, Barclays and the TSB all set up large new centres in Wythenshawe.[340] Today computing power has become a commodity, provided by huge server farms who choose not to advertise their physical location, and if Manchester is still a significant provider of information processing capacity to the UK we have no accurate way of knowing: in any case, the industrial estates of Manchester no longer make computers, or even disk drives.[341]

But Manchester is still visibly home to a thriving, if small, software industry, though the Kilburn building still, to the surprise of some newcomers, makes little of the connection between the Computer Science Department and Turing as local hero and founder of Computer Science. The red-brick building, glazed with narrow slits in a 1970s version of housing for machine acolytes, sits across a bare plaza from a more transparent glass and steel Mathematics building which *is* named after Alan Turing. When the mathematicians planning that twenty-first century development had warily enquired if Computer Science had any major developments *they* wanted to name after Turing, the mathematicians were emphatically told that if Turing had lived longer he would have set back computer science by decades and that the mathematicians were welcome to him. And so they are.[342]

Appendix: Turing's Biomathematics

Nobody who heard Turing talk about his theory —and he spoke to mathematicians, chemists, physiologists, zoologists and botanists—had much idea of what his mathematics was. It contained an idea of genius, simple enough to explain to an applied mathematician in a few lines today.[343] But Turing never gave a lay account of his mathematics, so here is mine.[344]

Giving the missionaries bicycles

Imagine a tropical island, with an impenetrable mountainous interior and a lush ring of habitable sea-fringed forest. This paradise is at first inhabited by a group of noble savages, whose specific lack of civilisation is that they are competent hunter-gatherers but occasional cannibals. Despite the occasional feast, for the most part the population is constrained by the amount of food they can sustainably extract from their habitat. They move around, and when they 'happen to pass by' each other enough births happen to balance the inevitable deaths. Because the supply of plant food is evenly spread, so is the population: even if a particularly big feast on one side of the island requires a few extra sacrifices or encourages the survivors to seize the moment and pass by each other a little more, emigration and birth and malnutrition eventually smooth out the temporary local blip. Then the missionaries arrive. A sub-mission of theirs is to do Science and they plot the population density around the island. This shows an uninteresting flat graph; the savages are unable to organise themselves. A constant small re-supply of missionaries keeps arriving, but with guns, germs and steel they also convert a fraction of the population. Since it is a condition of being a missionary to be celibate, the population falls a little. But the underlying food supply is uniform, and so wherever you go you find the same number of cannibals and a few missionaries, in what the scientific reports back to the sponsoring Academy call a uniform distribution.

Now we can see Turing's stroke of genius: *he gave the missionaries bicycles*.[345] Because the missionaries can move around more quickly, something new happens. Now, when there is a local blip that changes the balance between missionaries and cannibals, it doesn't get smoothed out. For if there is a temporary local excess of missionaries, the short term will see relatively more missionaries than cannibals arrive from the rest of the island, so even more conversion than normal occurs. This instability becomes magnified, stopping only later when the cannibals belatedly turn up for the feast. This effect relies on a balance of speed and time, so it has a characteristic distance: for each local peak of missionaries there will be a trough a particular distance away, which in turn induces a further peak so on all the way around the island. When the report to the Academy is due, the graph is no longer flat. The cannibals have arranged themselves into civilised groups.

Returning from these Western fantasies to Turing's actual paper, he showed that, starting from a blank canvas, he could generate a characteristic length-scale. Given that, spots and stripes and all things math-biological can emerge. Turing simply presents this as a model with no discussion of why it has been chosen over rivals. I have long puzzled about how Turing came to discover the Turing Instability. He acknowledged Waddington's idea of 'evocators' as an example of his own morphogens, a word Turing invented for unnamed biochemicals that could react and diffuse across his canvas, but did he deliberately construct a system of equations for them that would have the right property or did he discover it when analysing what he thought a plausible model? The technology for this analysis is, in the jargon of applied mathematics, a linearization into Fourier modes, which had been around for decades and well known to any mathematician. Turing was familiar from electronics with the possibility that instability could be encoded in a system, as was FC Williams.[346] And in Turing's role as an applications consultant he might have had to think about how to design crystallographic algorithms in Fourier space.

The majority of the mathematics in Turing's paper is concerned with what happens on the thin outer ring of the island, keeping track of the number of missionaries per mile as we go around the beach. Some calculations, such as working out how fast the bicycles need to go to generate instability, can be calculated by hand, perhaps with a few turns on a mechanical calculator: he had a Brunsviga machine at home to do just this. But others are more complicated. To cope with this, the beach can to be broken up into little sub-beaches, each of which is approximately constant in its missionary load. Take too few sub-beaches and you can't have a pattern; take too many and the calculations become overwhelming to a human. So Turing compromised on 20 sub-beaches, multiplying his computing load by 20, and thus produced a Figure in which a random starter pattern evolves to a series of three stripes. This is one of four separate runs he reports under different conditions, and, he says, 'some' of these results were with the aid of the computer. Given a first chance on the Ferranti Mark I at the beginning of September and the submission of his paper on the 9th of November, he must have worked remarkably fast and accurately in programming the machine.[347]

In a Year or Two: Turing's Fibonacci strategy

The second remarkable attack Turing made on developmental biology was to develop a theory of the appearance of Fibonacci structure. Turing had created a mechanism for making spots appear, and the spots were separated by a typical length-scale, which depended on a complicated but tractable way on the numbers put into the model. The number of spots one might see developing in a narrow ring of tissue, as he used in his 1952 paper, would depend not only on that length-scale but the circumference of the ring. But now suppose the ring is no longer narrow, so that patterns can develop across as well along it, in a way where the placement of new spots depends on where the older ones went. What Turing saw was that this dynamic model could allow the pattern to get more and more complicated as the inter-spot distance got smaller. What emerges is a lattice of points, gently stretched as the geometry of the underlying biological ring where spot-formation is happening changes. Lattices are regular objects, amenable to mathematics, and in this case they can be usefully described by pairs of integers; simple lattices at the beginning of development have small pairs like (0,1) and (1,1) and (1,2); more complicated lattices, evolving from these as the lattices stretched to fit the new geometry of the growing plan, might be described as (1,3), or (2,3). And this is where Turing quickly isolated a problem to prove. Independently of the model assumptions, it turns out to be an unavoidable feature of geometry that a (1,2) pattern can only evolve to either a (1,3) or a (2,3): more generally that if there are two numbers, then the sum of the two will appear in the more complicated lattice paired with either the smaller

or the larger of the two. The latter choice — in this case going from a (1,2) not to a (1,3) but to a (2,3) — preserves the property that the pairs of numbers involved will always be Fibonacci numbers, for then the next pair will be (3,5) and then (5,8) and so on. Turing called this the 'H of GP': the Hypothesis of Geometrical Phyllotaxis, and it is this hypothesis he was using the Ferranti Mark I to test. He was right: the 'H of GP' does hold for a wide family of mathematical models of spot formation in growing tissue. But Turing never managed to prove it in his lifetime and the mathematicians and physicists — not botanists — who carried out that proof many decades later did so in ignorance of Turing's work.

The framing of the 'H of GP' must have been the reason why Turing was confident in 1951 that he could get himself a good theory in 'a year or two'.[348]

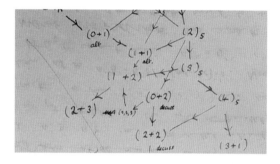

Figure 122. Turing's 'tree' classifying possible shifts between patterns.

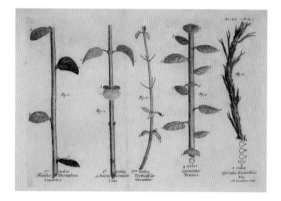

Figure 123. Classifications of leaf placement on plant stems from Bonnet's eighteenth-century text on plant growth. In the fourth example, the leaves are arranged in a spiral and if the bottom leaf is labelled as leaf 0 and numbering is continued upwards, then leaf 0 is closest to leaves 1 and 2: this is why this pattern can be described as a (1,2) spiral.

Acknowledgements

We like to identify with our heroes. My own first identification with Turing's story came, not from through his work on the *Entscheidungsproblem* or the Enigma or the Knutsford Quarter Sessions, or even that he had more-or-less singlehandedly created the discipline of mathematical biology that I was to follow as my career, but because he had, like me, disappointed his Cambridge tutors by failing to get a First in his end of first year mathematics exam. Perhaps I, like he, could go on from this to become an FRS at the age of 41. Sadly, my correspondence with Turing in achievement ended with that exam result. No one will ever name an Instability after me. I was though proud to become a Fellow of Turing's old college, later discovering that is a distinction that only matters to those to whom it applies, but which did give me a privileged push that started this book off two decades ago, and I'm grateful to King's College and the wider intellectual world it opinionatedly introduced me to.

The second identification came when I followed Turing in moving from what I thought a romantic Cambridge to a hard-headed Manchester. In 1953 Francis Crick was so thrilled to work out the structure of DNA that he went across the road to Cambridge's Eagle pub, burst in and announced he had discovered the secret of life. It is a story that the Cambridge tour guides love to mention, although often neglecting to mention that he was reputed to say this *every* night. Two decades ago I arrived in a Manchester that I wrongly thought did not have such storied places. I needed to find remarkable tales in the stones of Manchester too: and I eventually realised what I should have done before: that virtue is not located in the pub. It was in this sometimes ugly, sometimes thrilling, always self-boosting city, that I found the most productive work of my life, with rewarding colleagues and supportive friends, and indeed quite good pubs. Manchester became my city, and a home in which to negotiate love and grief and love again, and my thanks are due to the many Mancunians who helped me on that path.

Almost all of the archivists I have needed help from have provided it with grace. But I am particularly grateful to those who have taken the trouble to find out about my enquiry and to offer extra suggestions: these include Fiona Colbert, Elizabeth Ennion-Smith, Patricia McGuire, Kathryn McKee, Lizette Royer Barton, James Peters, Lewis Pollard, Jan Shearsmith and Catherine Twilley.

Unitemizable thanks are due to Janet Allen, David Anderson, Emma Jane Caroline Anderson, Paul Bernal, Giovanna Blackett Bloor, Margaret Boden, Christopher Brett, Robert Brunner, Dorothy Clayton, Jonathan Dawes, Daniella Derbyshire, Catherine Dewar, Martin Dodge, Fay Dowker, Charlotte Fischer, Julia Gog, Pete Goodeve, Len Grant, Paul Glendinning, Andrew Hodges, Ken Howarth, George Hill, Glyn Hughes, Allan Jones, Aoife Larkin, David Link, Shelley Lockwood, Eva Navarro López, Henry McGhie, the Modernists, the Newman family, Don Nicolson, Erinma Ochu, Elaine O'Hanrahan, John Pickstone, Michael Proctor, Peter and Frances Readman, Marjorie Senechal, Maria Summerscale, James Sumner, Julian Skyrme, Adam Swinton, Alexander Swinton, the late and beloved Dorothy Trump, George Turnbull, Georgina Young, Alan Cameron Wells, Hannah Williamson, Nicolette Zeeman and many others.

This second printing has a number of minor corrections from the March 2019 printing, as listed at manturing.net/oops. I'm grateful to all my readers and listeners (and especially Simon Lavington), for all their post-publication comments on the book and will continue to collect them by email to jonathan@swintons.net.

Notes

The standard, and best, biography of Alan Turing is still Andrew Hodges' extraordinary achievement of the 1980s (Hodges 1983). Page references to *Alan Turing The Enigma* (ATTE) are to the 2014 paperback edition (Hodges 2014).

The computer that ran from June 1948 was called the Small-Scale Experimental Machine, or Baby or sometimes the Mark I. The subsequent prototype machines, also built by Williams' team in the University, were sometimes called MADM, but more usually also the 'Mark I'; the team called the Mark I which ran from April 1949 to October 1949 'the improved machine' and another which ran from then until August 1950 'the large-scale machine': the machine that Ferranti built based on these is called here the 'Ferranti Mark I'. Ferranti built nine of these, the first two going to Manchester and Toronto universities. The following seven were of an improved design named the Mark I* (Campbell-Kelly 1980). I am mindful that I use the words 'mind' and 'brain' synonymously. 'The war' means the worldwide war that started in 1939; 'GCHQ' and Bletchley Park are used interchangeably, although the former was called GC&CS until after it left Bletchley Park, first for Eastcote soon after the end of that war and then finally Cheltenham. Piccadilly Station was once London Road. Housing statistics are for the City of Manchester itself but I have used 'here' for a Manchester which includes Salford, Moston and Hyde, Wilmslow and Altrincham and, just about, Glossop. 'The University' is that of Manchester, which encompasses Owen's College, the Victoria University and even UMIST, but not what is now Manchester Metropolitan University. 'Computing' means stored-program electronic general-purpose machine computing. I use 'gay' to refer to male homosexuality: female sexual practice beyond monogamous heterosexuality barely appears, but not for want of looking. In terms of attention, I never expected this University-centred history to say much about working-class life, but only reflecting on my text am I aware of its imbalance in the representation of race. There were black faces on Oxford Road in 1949, even in the University Staff House in the person of Arthur Lewis, Nobel winning Professor of Economics, but the accounts of academic and engineering life I quarried recall only an ethnically homogeneous world.

Lyn Lloyd Irvine retained her maiden name in her writing, but called herself Mrs Newman throughout her life as a married woman. (Mr) Pat Blackett was perhaps referred to on occasion as Professor Patrick Maynard Stuart Blackett, Baron Blackett OM CH PRS.

The quotation on the flyleaf from Peck and Ward (2002) uses 'perverse' to mean taking a pleasurable interest in the signs of industrial decay; the quote from *The Guardian* is via Read (1964).

Primary Sources

AMT: Papers of Alan Turing at King's College, Cambridge.

LP: Papers of Dorothy Emmet at Lucy Cavendish College, Cambridge.

MMC, NAHC, TUR, UCS, VCA: University of Manchester. Some online catalogue entry numbers have changed from the printed version that I used, but there is no systematic guide to the changes. This may affect NAHC/MUC5 to 9 in particular.

MSI: Archives of The Science Museum Group, held at the Museum of Science and Industry, Manchester.

JEFFREYS, NEWMANL, NEWMANM: St John's College, Cambridge. One of Lyn's richest correspondences is with Lady Antoinette Esher. Her letters to Esher are in NEWMANL/A/3, here abbreviated as ESHER.

STRACHEY: Papers of Christopher Strachey in the Bodleian Library Oxford.

TGA: Tate Gallery archives.

TNA: The National Archives, London.

Endnotes

1 'If he is to stay...' (ATTE p34).

2 On Manchester science at the time see Sumner (2016). The undergraduate intake was small, but mathematics was no backwater in 1930: the Professor was Mordell, a pure mathematician of some significance, who was appointed to Cambridge after the war and thus made a Manchester vacancy for Max Newman.

3 Turing was not at first outstanding academically. He did win a scholarship to King's, worth £80 a year, which Sherborne supplemented with an additional £30. But he only went to King's because he failed to get into Trinity College, which considered itself the natural location for the most high-flying mathematicians, and he failed to achieve a First in his first-year exams. Turing's prestigious later Fellowship paid £300 per year, with free meals and subsidised accommodation in the College, simultaneously grand and spartan.

4 Dermot Turing (Turing 2015) has more on the Apostles in relation to Turing. On the Heretics see Howarth (1978) and (Sargant Florence 1968).

5 Russell, with his co-worker Whitehead, was the most significant British thinker — until Turing — in this field of mathematical logic, but at the time it was largely a German field, dominated by Frege, Gödel, and Hilbert. Another disciple was a young Hungarian, John von Neumann, who exported the school to Princeton in the US, and there played a comparable theoretical and practical role to Turing in the development of the computer.

6 'the first-rank' from Newman's 1976 audio interview with Christopher Evans (Newman 1976). There have been a number of attempts to understand how Turing arrived at the Turing Machine: one intriguing hypothesis is that he was influenced by the data-processing duties of his India Office father (Agar 2003).

7 'men of the Professor type': (Erskine 1986).

8 Turing went to the NPL in October 1945. On the plans, problems and heritage of the ACE see (Copeland 2005).

9 One unnamed Oxford professor is said to have estimated around 10^6 neurons in the human brain; Turing couldn't find anyone to give him a direct answer in 1948, but made his own estimate a thousand times larger at 10^9. By the time his speculations on machine intelligence were causing him to be taken more seriously by biologists in 1951, Turing was in correspondence with leading physiologist JZ Young about the implications of there being around 10^{10} (ATTE p486 and 548). Current estimates are around 10^{12}.

10 Historian AJP Taylor (Taylor 1957). Taylor's view of Manchester has been critiqued by subsequent historians (Savage and Wolff 2015).

11 Noel Hush arrived from Australia as a 25-year-old chemist in 1949 (Hush 2011).

12 Post-war Manchester: (Kidd and Wyke 2016). The industrial base of the region: (Timmins 1998) and the history of the University: (Pullan and Abendstern 2000).

13 Pre-war industry and the growth of Trafford Park: (Kidd 2006).

14 Women had been permanently employed by Ferranti since the 1914–18 war; pre-war Ferranti had employed only single women but during the war the percentage of married women had risen to over 40%. The supervisor of women workers, Miss CM Forbes, reported their outlook was 'rather different from that of men. Most of them are not only happy on repetition work, but some, particularly housewives, prefer it "because we don't have to think". Although the majority belong to trade unions, the women tend to be less union-minded than the men, and the closed shop-principle is not as rigid' (Gwyer 1949). Forbes had worked for the firm since 1915 and was awarded an MBE in 1950 (Gwyer 1950).

15 'Everything they've got' was the proposal of a Brunner, Mond chemist called Francis Freeth (Kennedy 1993).

16 The Department for Scientific and Industrial Research was set up in 1916 as a way of organising science into producing commodities of importance for war; funds to Universities were channelled through the University Grants Council from 1919. (Reader 1975) is a corporate history of ICI during this period.

17 'Blackley': the original factory was set up in 1864 by Ivan Levinstein. The Pharmaceutical Division was set up in 1938. Paludrine:

(Kennedy 1993). One of its developers, Garnet Davy, who had been drafted to Blackley from the University of Cardiff by the Ministry of Supply, said he would otherwise never have gone into industry, 'being cursed with academic snobbery like so many people in this country'.

18 'You couldn't open the window': Frank Rose recalled in (Kennedy 1993). The Stockport victim was his colleague Frank Curd (Hill 2016).

19 Alderley Park: it was a Bury-born dye chemist with a Manchester BSc, Cecil Cronshaw, who overruled Bogue (Hill 2016).

20 The Bogues lived at 28 Hartley Road, Altrincham.

21 The Simons: (Duxbury-Neumann 2017).

22 Collapse in defence orders: (Gandy 2013).

23 Wartime bombing in Manchester: (Anonymous 1995).

24 Bernard Lovell's lament: (Lovell 1990). Lovell was yet another of Blackett's recruits to Manchester.

25 Houses falling down in 1944: City Surveyor Rowland Nicholas, 1962, cited in (Parkinson-Bailey 2000). 'Dismal': compare (Sumner 2013). Ernest Simon: (Manchester Luncheon Club 1947).

26 London Road Fire Station: (Thomas 2003).

27 First impressions: Shapley: (Shapley 1996), Taylor (Taylor 1983), Bethe (Schweber 2012), Peierls: (Peierls 1985) quoted in (Froese Fischer 2003), Kermode (Kermode 1997), Tootill (2009), Barbirolli: (Rigby 1948), Lovell: (Lovell 1990) Hush:(Hush 2011); Woods: (Berners-Lee 2011) and (Berners-Lee 2001); John Polanyi: (Wigner and Hodgkin 1977). Kellermann: (Kellermann 2010). The attitude that air pollution was inextricably linked to affluence was certainly present in Victorian Manchester: (Mosley 2004).

28 Smoke control in post-war Manchester: (Dodge 2018, Mosley 2013).

29 The visual richness and counterfactual nature of the City Plan is discussed in (Perkins and Dodge 2012). On slum clearance: (Shapely 2016). One of the delays in slum clearance was the reluctance of suburban and rural communities outside Manchester to accept relocated working-class migration.

30 Wythenshawe: (Kidd and Wyke 2016).

31 Water history (Manchester Corporation 1974; City Treasurer's Department 1946). Water had been drawn from Longdendale since 1848, and then via a long aqueduct from Thirlmere in the Lake District from 1898. Lyn Newman records the threats to cut water off in (ESHER 29 Oct 1947 & 10 Nov 1947).

32 'The climate' (The Manchester Joint Research Council 1954). 'snooty' (Streat 1987).

33 Kermode (Kermode 1997).

34 'career train south': (Wilson 2008). 'special opportunities': (VCA/7/708). Peppered moth: Note 332.

35 'Only man' (Lovell 1990). See also (Kellermann 2010).

36 On Pat Blackett, see the articles by Anderson (Anderson 2013b, 2007c), Lovell (Lovell 1988) and the full-length study by Nye (Nye 2004). Oppenheimer undoubtedly told friends that he had left a poisoned apple—the cyanide detail seems to be a later addition—but biographers disagree on how serious his intention was. See (Monk 2012) or (Bird and Sherwin 2006).

37 'handsomest…' is from (Zichichi 2016).

38 On the Half Moon Club see (Pattenden 2006). Teulon Porter's autobiography (Teulon Porter 1962) is unreliable.

39 'Didsbury' see Chapter 6 of (Nye 2011). The Blacketts at first lived in a modest house at 238 Wilmslow Road, Didsbury, but by 1949 had moved to a flat in a grand villa, The Oaks, close by on Oak Drive, and adjacent to the home from where CP Scott had daily cycled to edit The Manchester Guardian (TNA KV/2/3217/84).

40 'rare language' (Lovell 1990); Nobel party (Nye 2004).

41 Guernica: (Schofield 2017; Nye 2004), (Desmarais 2010).

42 Blackett's security file is in the National Archives (TNA/PF/44137). See also (Agar 2016).

43 AJP Taylor on Blackett: (Taylor 1983: 227).

44 There is no full-length biography of Max Newman but there is a short memoir by his son (Newman 2006) and a Royal Society biography (Adams 1985); I draw heavily on rival articles by Anderson (Anderson 2007b, 2009b, 2010, 2013a) and Copeland (Copeland 2011b, 2011a). On Newman the logician, and the influence of Penrose see (Grattan-

Guiness 2012). Newman is mentioned in a number of memoirs of Cambridge in the 1920s and 1930s by Stevie Smith, (Spalding 2002), Frances Partridge (Partridge 2001) and especially Margaret Gardiner (Gardiner 1988) at the Heretics; a complex portrait of him over the decades emerges in his wife's unpublished letters now in St John's College Cambridge at NEWMANL. His own papers are at NEWMANM.

45 Not on the list: (Turing 2015). The Blackett letter: (NEWMANM/3/1 Blackett 26 Jul 1942). Newman unhappy at Bletchley: (Good 2006).

46 On Bletchley Park, there are many historical accounts including ATTE. The film *The Imitation Game* is best treated as fiction (von Tunzelmann 2014).

47 Newman's knowledge of the use of electronics for radioactivity counts at the Cavendish is stated in (Copeland 2017c); that it was via Blackett is my speculation.

48 'overlooked' (Good 1982).

49 Lyn's letters are held in St John's College Cambridge. 'Pride': (ESHER 5 May 1948); utterly appalled: (NEWMANL/A/2/Weyl/64 12 Mar 1945).

50 The appointment file is (VCA/7/10/1/2).

51 Newman and GCHQ (TNA/HW/64/59). Chassis from a Colossus (Anderson 2004); (Copeland 2017a).

52 'hundred times': The junior staff, Rees and Good, that Newman first recruited to the laboratory, were initially on salaries of £350 and £450 respectively.

53 'urgent appeals': (VCA/7/318/2 Newman to Vice-Chancellor 9 Jun 1946).

54 'Calculating machine laboratory'. By the time of its first official report in March 1948, the name had changed to *Computing* Machine Laboratory but there is no explicit record of the reason (VCA/7/318 and VCA/7/71).

55 Discarded cloud chamber: from the Manchester 60 website (Thomas 2017).

56 Max Newman's diary 6 Dec 1948 (NEWMANM/4/19).

57 Layby: (NAHC/SHL/FA1).

58 There is only one brief biographical sketch in print of Lyn Irvine (Newman 2002).

59 In 1929, years before Max, the Woolfs had set Lyn up on a dinner date with Max's close friend Richard Braithwaite, recently widowed. It doesn't seem to have been a romantic success, perhaps because Braithwaite nearly burst into tears when the Woolfs turned the conversation to sodomy (Woolf 1978). Braithwaite did finally have romantic success with Margaret Masterman, who had been one of Wittgenstein's disciples; many years later in retirement Dorothy Emmet set up home in Cambridge with the couple.

60 Lyn 'string and struggle' was a family phrase created by William aged 5 (ESHER 3 Nov 1948); Costanza's visit in 1947 (ESHER 17 Jun 1947). 'Complicated and angular' (ESHER 1 Nov 1950). 'Kink' (ESHER 1 Apr 1957): she added later that 'The material seems to me of the greatest interest but should have been digested over a considerable period by someone with literary talent' (ESHER 3 Dec 1957).

61 Some non-stop trains from Altrincham to Manchester Central (now the Exhibition Centre) took 14 minutes (Knight 1999).

62 Poorer in Manchester (NEWMANL/A/2/Weyl/70 4 Oct 1946); she desires pigeonholes: (ESHER 19 Mar 1947); 'BORING': (ESHER 23 Jul 1949); the Cartwright slight: (ESHER 6 May 1948); the lack of good bookshops: (ESHER 12 Apr 1947); desires pigeonholes: (ESHER 19 Mar 1947).

63 'chickens': the migrant refugee Mathematics lecturer Walter Lederman was grateful to be asked to stay in the Newmans' house while they were in Criccieth, but first he had to learn how to feed the chickens (Ledermann 2009b).

64 These included Garrett Birkhoff, Mary Cartwright, Haskell Curry (NEWMANM/2/3/17), Max Born (NEWMANM/2/4/2), and Brouwer (NEWMANM/2/7/5).

65 Growth of Cheadle Hulme: (Parkinson-Bailey 2000).

66 The Bogues: (ESHER/17 Jan 1949). Epilepsy: (ESHER/20 Jul 1951).

67 'Nash': (ESHER 26 Feb 1950).

68 'Daily Mail': (ESHER/1 Jun 1954). Irvine had written to *The Times* on 22 Apr 1954.

69 Max not getting Rouse-Ball Chair: (ESHER/26 Feb 1950). Bowdon views: (ESHER 19 Mar 1955). The appointment would probably have been determined by a judgement on the quality of Max Newman's mathematics, which was unlikely to be as high as Lyn thought. Though a creative mathematician,

today he is considered influential through his able leadership of a strong department (Hoffmann 1984) rather than through his own contributions. I'm grateful to Martin Hyland for discussion on this point.

70 'mathematical logic': (McGuinness 1988). Kite-flying may have had a profound influence: Sterrett has argued that it was Wittgenstein's Manchester applied mathematical experience of representing the world through simplified models that gave birth to his first philosophy (Sterrett 2006).

71 Newman 'drowned at birth': (Partridge 1981). At one stage Newman took over as the supervisor of Wittgenstein's PhD student, Alice Ambrose, because she and Wittgenstein had rowed over her lack of meek discipleship. (McGuinness 2008).

72 A modern opinion is that Wittgenstein's thesis would fail a PhD because of its lack of scholarly apparatus (Goldstein 1999).

73 Floyd (Floyd 2017) has recently argued that Turing and Wittgenstein had more intellectual common ground and more influence on each other than this more standard account.

74 ''odd fish' and 'special train': (McGuinness 1988) and (Flowers 1999). The friend was William Eccles, whom Wittgenstein met while staying at the Grouse Inn in Glossop for his kite experiments; Eccles spent the rest of his career working for Metropolitan Vickers. When Wittgenstein returned to Manchester he lived at what is now 154 Palatine Road.

75 I rely largely on a biography of Hartree by his last student (Froese Fischer 2003).

76 (Froese Fischer 2003).

77 Uranium separation: (Howlett 1993).

78 '1000-times' is Hartree's own estimation from *The Daily Telegraph* 7 Nov 1947 reproduced in (Copeland 2005).

79 The fate of the differential analyser: (VCA/7/71).

80 On the need for four machines, the Hartree quote is, unlike most, remembered as a direct statement, specific in time and place, albeit two decades later (Swann 1975). On the lack of applications for the new machines, see (McGregor Ross 2005).

81 'Nazism' from *The Daily Telegraph* 7 Nov 1947 reproduced in (Copeland 2005).

82 '£5,000' is an oral memory of Tony Brooker (p626 of ATTE) and seems implausibly, but not impossibly, high. For comparison, at the end of the war Newman was earning £950 at GCHQ. Turing was offered £1,200 as the Deputy Director in Manchester (ATTE p496).

83 MIT invitation: (TUR Add/35). 'Nancy' ATTE p497. The Nancy job seems to have been via Norbert Wiener. The 1938 Princeton Institute of Advanced Studies job had offered $1,500 a year.

84 See the Notes for the different machine names.

85 'World's first': I have already described the wartime Colossus as a world's first. With suitable definitions, the medals in this race can be awarded elsewhere in the world, or multiple times to Manchester. The Manchester Baby of Williams is the first computer to run a program stored in a practical electronic memory; its successor Ferranti Mark I of 1951 marks the first commercial purchase of an electronic computer. Williams (Williams 1997) is a good general introduction to the history of computing technology.

86 Flowers as first choice is implicit in the note of Womersley cited in (Turing 2015).

87 Manchester's Professor of electromechanical engineering, Willis Jackson, had just moved to Imperial College London, and Williams was installed as the replacement Professor of Electro-technics. Williams himself and Lovell, Blackett's Royal Society biographer, both thought it likely that Blackett was primarily responsible for Williams' appointment (Lovell 1975). By contrast, Kilburn told Simon Lavington that Blackett could not have been responsible, on the grounds that Williams was third choice for the post (MAN/MUC/9/44). It is true that initially, Williams was not the front-runner, and was more or less unknown to Willis Jackson, despite being acknowledged as one of the most brilliant circuit designers in the country. The appointment file is VCA/7/46.

88 Williams was born in Romiley, about 10 miles south-east of Manchester (Anderson 2007a).

89 On William's avoidance of Turing, Anderson writes plausibly, albeit without a source, that 'Turing's weltanschauung was so at odds with his own that working together might have been problematic' (Anderson 2007a).

90 'Williams moved on' (Anderson 2007a).

91 'Boddingtons': it's not clear from the context if this is a direct quote from Williams (Copeland 2012). Freddie vs FC: Simon Lavington. 'Timperley': Williams lived at Oakacre, 113 Park Road, Timperley. Oakacre was a little further south than where James Joule had lived in Sale a lifetime earlier, but not as far south as the Newmans in Bowdon. Nevertheless it is a house of some scale.

92 Kilburn's holidays not too far from Manchester (Wilkes and Kahn 2003) and (NAHC/MUC/8/1); Manchester United season ticket holder (NAHC/MUC/7/18).

93 Kilburn and chemistry: (University of Manchester Department of Computer Science 1998).

94 'Applied mathematics camp': (Bowker and Giordano 1993). At the time Imperial College was shortening its mathematics courses to two years with the explicit goal of generating trained staff for the engineering war effort (Brooker 2010); the Cambridge course was also shortened for two years and may well have had the same intention.

95 Kilburn 'more of an engineer' from (Howarth 1982).

96 Dewsbury: (Edwards 2010). The train detail is Kilburn's memory (Howarth 1982); much closer in time, Turing said Newman had made up the routine and that Kilburn had 'put them through on the machine' (TUR Add/28). From 1951 to 1959 the Kilburns lived at 13 Tewkesbury Avenue, Davyhulme, moving to 11 Carlton Crescent, Urmston around the time he was appointed to a Professorship.

97 'great loyalty': (Anderson 2009a)

98 It's sometimes said that there was never a Director, but Kilburn, with William's knowledge, was describing himself as exactly this to Ferranti in 1951 in a side consulting agreement: (NAHC/MUC/5/156).

99 'standardised'. CRTs were already being made in Manchester for radar work. The CRTs for the first prototypes were supplied by GEC in London, but Ferranti did later produce customised CRTs for the machines (Edwards 2010).

100 (ATTE p491). The resulting Williams memory consisted of a CRT tube with a detection head covering it, and sometimes with a second tube electronically duplicating the first so the memory could be inspected. Kilburn had an increasing role: all the patents except the very first were jointly held by the two men and Lavington suggests the memory device is most fairly called the Williams-Kilburn tube (Lavington 2012); Kilburn gave a lay explanation of the basic principle in (Howarth 1982).

101 'instructions from Newman' (Williams 1976) as transcribed in (NAHC/MUC/9/33).

102 'Out of the creative process': the later revisionist histories have argued that the instruction sets were designed with much input from mathematicians, especially Jack Good (Copeland 2017a): but what there was not was a formal design process under the control of the mathematicians.

103 The Lockspeiser visit: (Wilson 2000) and (Streat 1987).

104 Lockspeiser had just moved from being Chief Scientist at the Ministry of Supply and was technically the Secretary of the Department of Scientific and Industrial Research (Edwards 1994).

105 Compulsory Purchase Inquiry: *The Manchester Guardian* 30 Mar 1950.

106 The Mathematics department was located on the top floor.

107 Glazed tiling: (Schuster 1900). A 1912 plan shows the room intended as a 'Magnetism Test' room.

108 Hartree's Differential Analyser, in a different room of the 1909 physics building, was also described as in a 'lavatory-tiled basement' (Howlett 1996).

109 The plans for the 1951 building show first-floor offices, with one each for Mr Kilburn, Mr Turing, Engineers and Mathematicians, Typist, and Machine Operators.

110 'like an oracle' (Pullan and Abendstern 2000). The building was planned in 1951 to be finished by the summer of 1953 but was delayed, partly by an electricians' strike, until the summer of 1954 (NAHC/MUC/1/C/1).

111 'dinner at the Blacketts' (NAHC/MUC/1/B/8): the same file records 'regret' that the $1,000 could not be disguised as something that was not a fee.

112 Turing's consultancy with Ferranti was confirmed in July 1951: (MAN/Tur_Add/22).

113 'consultancy': (NAHC/MUC/1/B/4) and (TUR Add/135).

114 'unapproachable and rude': (Edwards 2010)

115 'excellent tutorial': (Sumner 1994).

116 Manchester rain: (ATTE p503).

117 'not trying to be funny' is a comment of Maurice Wilkes, who was the leader of the Cambridge computer project (Wilkes 1968).

118 'shabby ...' (ATTE p559). April 1951: (NAHC/MUC/5/102).

119 (ATTE p506).

120 (ATTE p515). GCHQ had been developing their own random number generator (Donald Duck) for some years and Simon Lavington suggests they would be unlikely to have used the Ferranti Mark I's facility for production purposes, but it may have been important for research.

121 The successor machine was the 'Colorob': (Lavington 2006).

122 This sentence is mainly here for the internal rhymes, but in the minds of the 1945 funders was the plan that Cambridge computing would be stronger at numerical problems and Manchester at logical ones.

123 'violin': (ATTE p521). Turing lodged at 25 Nursery Road (AMT/A/35).

124 William Newman & the rhododendron leaf: (Turing 2015).

125 'mucky': (ATTE p497).

126 running to work: (ATTE p497); see also (Bennett 1996).

127 'Democratic': (Scott and Bent 1984; Hill and Shuttleworth 2003).

128 Turing and Garner: (ATTE pxxv: this is not in earlier editions). Garner did not know of Turing's conviction and was later warned by the police to stay away from him (Hodges 2016a).

129 A confirmation that Turing was a consultant to GCHQ at one time is in (Murray 1975).

130 Roy Webb: (ATTE p537). It is possible that Turing chose Wilmslow simply because of this connection.

131 'We had built a network of railways...': (Jha 1998).

132 Emanuel Freud had emigrated from Vienna to run a business at 61 Bloom Street, now the Musicians Union office. The postcard is in (Freud 2002).

133 Lyn on Turing from her preface to (Turing 1959); they had rented the house from a Manchester solicitor Niel Pearson and his wife Ruth; Pearson would later be the chair of the '51 Society.

134 Russell was living more or less permanently at Penrallt Goch, Llan Ffestiniog, Merioneth (NewmanM/2/15/9); 'senile': (NewmanM/2/3/5). Hartree also holidayed at Portmadoc (VCA/7/71/3). The Polanyis had been to visit the Blacketts at their cottage at Penparc, Llanfrothern, Penrhyndeudrath in 1939 (Nye 2007). 'Manchester gang' was the Blacketts, Pearsons and Newmans in 1948 (ESHER 23 Jun 1948); 'chores' (ESHER 2 Aug 1949); Hobsbawm: (Hobsbawm 2002) cited in (Nye 2004).

135 (ESHER 17 Jun 1947) and around 8 Jun 1952 or 25 Nov 1952. The Newmans replaced their Morris with a Daimler in 1955 (ESHER/19 Mar 1955). The Red Witch: (Nye 2004).

136 Emmet's travels: (LP/17/6/4/1). Turing and Clarke: (ATTE p272).

137 Norway and Kjell (ATTE p599). Norwegian grammar (ATT p604).

138 AMT/F to PN Furbank 12 Jul 1953.

139 (TUR Add/100). Hodges suggests that Turing may have belatedly realised that his importance to the state meant a loss of privacy and that he would find it increasingly difficult to slip unnoticed into different worlds on these trips.

140 Audrey Bates was headhunted to Toronto in 1953 (DTIC 1979, Pedwell, 2017 #1166); Popplewell was giving lectures in Argentina in the 1960s (Impagliazzo 2006). 'I detest America': (TUR Add/107 20 Feb 1953) to Donald Mackay about a Macy conference.

141 'wildly innocent': (ESHER 24 Jun 1949).

142 '1946' The Times, 1 Nov 1946, and The Manchester Guardian of 2 Nov 1946. The Nature report was drawn on in a presidential address to the British Institution of Radio Engineers, which was in turn reported in The Times, perhaps because it had been given by Lord Mountbatten: (Sumner 2014) and (Martin 1995). It attracted the attention of Ferranti, who paid particular attention to the ACE at a June 1947 Open Day at the NPL (Lunt 1947).

143 On Wiener see (Conway and Siegelman 2005).

144 News Review, 11 Feb 1949.

145 The first publishable response at least; in a letter to Turing, W Ross Ashby had called it *'good radar but...pretty poor physiology'* (TUR Add/2).

146 For a biography of Jefferson in Manchester see (Butler 2005); a longer but over-dutiful biography is (Schurr 1997).

147 Jefferson's tax return from 1945 shows income of £3,500 and the majority of this was taxed at a rate of 50% (JEF/1/7/2). This may have been temporarily low; his surgical colleague Harry Platt was earning over £5,000 a year pre-war (Butler 2005). In 1954 the Jeffersons lived at High Bank, Stenner Lane, Didsbury. (Manchester Literary and Philosophical Society 2018). The Lake District story is MMC/2/Jefferson/1/8.

148 The Oration was published in (Jefferson 1949a).

149 'petulant': (Brockbank 1965).

150 'draw the line at sonnets': *The Times*, 11 Jun 1949.

151 'wildly innocent': (ESHER 24 Jun 1949).

152 Newman's letter: *The Times* 14 Jun 1949. From this date the Vice-Chancellor's cuttings book starts to monitor coverage of the Manchester Computer (VCA/1).

153 'good brownie': (NewmanL/A3/2/23 Jul 1949).

154 *Illustrated London News* 25 Jun 1949; the 1949 BBC film clip was included in the computer50 celebration CD (Napper 1998). The date of 1948 sometimes attached to the clip is wrong.

155 'chaired': at any rate the seminar was organised under her aegis, and in the transcript it is Emmet who outlines the questions to be addressed (albeit unsuccessfully).

156 'strike break': Blackett (Nye 2007).

157 'undogmatic' from Emmet DNB entry (O'Neill 2018). 'inure her': (Emmet 1996).

158 Whitehead photograph: (LP/17/6/4/1).

159 'civilise the scientists': (VCA/7/71). The scheme seems to have come to nothing.

160 Newman went for dinner at Emmet's house in the year they arrived (NewmanM/4/13/1 18 May 1948 and 12 Oct 1948). The following year she and Newman were sharing discussions on Brouwer's philosophy of consciousness (NEWMANM/2/7/7).

161 Polanyi's economics: (Nye 2011).

162 'Social Studies' p82 of (Emmet 1996); Mansfield Cooper, who was later to become Vice Chancellor, recalled that it was obvious that Polanyi had to be kept but that there was no chance he could persuade the University to create a new chair in Philosophy: (Wigner and Hodgkin 1977).

163 'Social Science' seminar: (Pullan 2007).

164 'a Higher obscurantist' cited in (Jha 1998). Emmet was probably the 'other philosopher' who is cited as warning the Vice Chancellor in (Wigner and Hodgkin 1977).

165 'the penumbra' (Emmet 1996).

166 'meat ration' (Emmet 1996).

167 'Blue Pilgrims: (LP/17/8/5). In retirement, Emmet left Manchester to move to Cambridge, partly to be near her aged mother, but also to move in with Richard Braithwaite and his wife Margaret with whom she shared an interest in philosophical thinking about religion (Emmet 1996). This was the same Braithwaite who had invited the undergraduate Turing to give a paper on mathematics and logic to the Cambridge University philosophy society.

168 'second attempt': a selection committee recommended leaving the chair unfilled but instead promoting Emmet to the post of Reader; it's unclear why the decision was reconsidered a year later (VCA 7/227). The outgoing Professor Ritchie, who rated Emmet very highly, was like Polanyi trained as a chemist and not as a philosopher.

169 'only woman' from (Pullan and Abendstern 2000). Violet Cane became the Professor of Statistics: in 1952 she had written, in collaboration with psychologist Richard Gregory, to Turing about the possibility of constructing a model electronic brain to study: (AMT/D/16). Emmet's house at 21 Yew Tree Lane, Northenden cost £500 in 1939: (LP/17/11/5) and (LP/17/6/4/1).

170 'violent attack'; 'un-tenured and mediocre' and Manchester's response to refugees in general: (Williams 2013). The technician was Martin Schmalz (Nye 2011).

171 Magda's application: (USC/4/1); Lyn's acquaintance: (NEWMANL/A/2/Pearson). On the other hand the Polanyis plural seem to have put the Blacketts up at one point in 1945 (Nye 2007), and the families holidayed together. By the late 1950s Magda and Michael were travelling together and Magda followed her husband's move to London and

then the United States. Before the war the Polanyis were at 30 Sandileigh Avenue. In 1947–1950 Michael was living at 10 Gilbert Road in Hale and after that gave his address as the University.

172 Polanyi protest against Nazism: (Jha 1998); 'headhunted' is (Hush 2011).

173 Polanyi extended this belief to his students who recall notable freedom to choose what to work on (Calvin 1991).

174 'Blackett the great theoretical planner': Mansfield Cooper cited in (Wigner and Hodgkin 1977).

175 'rational scientific planning': (Agar 2016); 'banned as subversives': Polanyi's banning may have been by mistake: (Jha 1998; Nye 2007). Blackett's ban: (Nye 2011). Respect and affection: (Wigner and Hodgkin 1977).

176 Polanyi's notes are published in (Blum 2010); the prepared remarks also prompted a brief last-minute paper from the new Professor of Statistics, Maurice Bartlett, on the statistical nature of learning: (LP/17/6/6/14). Emmet is remembered by Margaret Boden as more sympathetic to Polanyi's position than to Turing's (Boden 2008b). Newman's surprise that he was expected to prepare for the seminar is Newman to Polanyi, 19 Sep 1949, MPP/B5/F6 in the Michael Polanyi Archive, University of Chicago.

177 The discussion was summarised in a typescript of unknown authorship which was published in (Blum 2010); Emmet's original copy is in (LP/17/6/6/14), which also contains the response by Meier. Emmet's copy appears identical to the copy owned by Wolfe Mays, of which scans are available online. The author may have been Desmond Paul Henry, a junior member of the Philosophy Department (O'Hanrahan 2018). The ICI representative is described as 'HEWELL (?) (ICI Research)' and makes comments which suggest knowledge of electro-neurology and of epilepsy, subjects under investigation by Yule Bogue at ICI at the time. It's most likely the speaker was Dr LB (Ben) Wevill, an anaesthetist who was head of the medical department of ICI Pharmaceuticals (I'm grateful to George B Hill for this suggestion), or just conceivably a surgeon called Christopher Hewer who had worked with ICI in the 1940s developing trichlorethylene as an anaesthetic in London (Kennedy 1993). Also present was the London-based physiologist JZ Young, whom Jefferson

had recently consulted on his Lister Oration. Also contributing were a young Mathematics lecturer, Bernhard Neuman, and Maurice Bartlett. Wolfe Mays was a young philosophy lecturer, who preserved the transcription and later published a version of it (Mays 2000). Ferranti were not present, although they were also developing an EEG machine (Heaton 1950).

178 'Unimpressed': recollections of the then just-graduated and new member of the department Desmond Henry in about 1998, as further recounted by JB Kennedy to Elaine O'Hanrahan in 2018. I'm grateful to the latter for passing this on. Piaget: (ATTE p604).

179 Turing had an earlier, restricted version of the Test in a 1948 manuscript (AMT/C/11), which was only narrowly circulated (Copeland 2004); this only conceived of telling the difference between a machine and a human when they played chess. The *Mind* paper was published as (Turing 1950); Wolfe Mays published his own response later (Mays 1952), revised much later as (Mays 2001).

180 Jefferson covered the idea of mechanical minds in the third of three public lectures in 1952; the note was taken by Michael Polanyi (Blum 2010).

181 *The Manchester Guardian* 7 Jul and 15 Nov 1951.

182 The five 1951 broadcasts: (Jones 2004).

183 The talk, *Intelligent Machines, a Heretical Theory* was published by Copeland (Copeland 2004), who says Turing gave this talk to the '51 Society. The typescripts are in AMT/B/20 and AMT/B/4. Neither typescript makes any reference to the '51 Society and both are undated; and I've been unable to find any reference to a suitable meeting in the apparently complete record of the '51 Society meetings held in the BBC Archives (at N8/62/1).

184 'little old ladies': (ATTE p526), though Max Newman recalls a slightly different version (Newman 1955) and it is not in the typed transcripts in KCC of Turing's talk.

185 More details of the Third Programme recording are in Proudfoot (Proudfoot 2015), which seems to be largely drawn from BBC archive material. 'trying to listen to': (ATTE p572). Lyn: (ESHER 13 Nov 1951).

186 (ESHER 13 Mar 1949).

187 Turing discussed *Le Rouge et Le Noir* with Nick Furbank (Turing 2015); *Finistère* and *The Cloven Pine* with Fred Clayton and *The Heart in Exile* and *Hemlock and After* with Robin Gandy (ATTE p613). 'Though they had little in common': (Furbank 1979) 'when he launched': (ESHER 13 Mar 1949). 'Without gifts': (ESHER 13 Nov 1957).

188 The Annual Report: (Anonymous 1955). The Lit & Phil's membership is online at (Anonymous 2018b). Hartree, Polanyi and Jefferson, but none of the women, each took a turn as President; Dorothy Emmet made it to Vice Chair of the Social Philosophy section in 1948. Turing is not listed in any of the Memoirs as a member but he is recorded in the Council Minutes of 12 Oct 1953 as being proposed as one by Michael Polanyi and Niel Pearson. I'm grateful to Kathryn Slater of the Lit & Phil for this information.

189 'The Luncheon Club': (Manchester Luncheon Club 1947).

190 The '51 Society: (Coles and Smith 2006). *The Manchester Guardian*, 12 Nov 1951.

191 'say nowt': (ESHER 12 Feb 1957). 100th meeting: (ESHER 19 Mar 1955).

192 'Atoms and whimsy': (Atkinson 2012).

193 The logbooks are at NAHC/MUC/2/C/6. There is a difference between these dates and when Ferranti Mark I is generally accepted to have arrived in February 1951. There is no logbook before April, and August is more compatible with Turing's November statement that 'we have had the machine for a few months' (TUR ADD/45).

194 The sodomy risk is recounted in Turner (Turner 2011).

195 'Lions and unicorns' (Conekin 2003).

196 'July 1950': (Duffy 1951). Ferranti told the Festival organisers on 30 Nov 1950 that they wouldn't supply a computer on the grounds of 'cost', although they did not have anything to show; Nimrod was designed in December 1950 (Stuart-Williams and Byrd 1951). 'gawk' and the Nimrod account is from the Australian John Bennett. Bennett was newly arrived at Ferranti as a programmer (Bennett 1994) and was the designer of the machine, which was built by Ferranti engineer Raymond Stuart-Williams (Smith 2014, Stuart-Williams 1951). Bennett may have been inspired by the Nimatron, an a electro-mechanical Nim machine at the 1940 New York World's Fair (Smith 2014), but the team would also have been aware of 'Bertie the Brain', a fully electronic noughts and crosses game shown in Toronto in 1950 by the team behind the computer project that was in the end replaced by FERUT. Smith suggests that Bertie has priority over Nimrod as the first known computer game. Turing at the Festival: (ATTE p562); he went with Cambridge friends Robin Gandy and Nick Furbank.

197 'ICI': Megaw received crystallography images from Charles William Bunn and his colleague Myra Bailey (Jackson 2008). Farid Ahmed: (Ahmed 2009).

198 Barlow and Jones cloth was based on a haemoglobin structure drawn by Max Perutz and was used in the South Bank's Regatta Restaurant (Jackson 2008).

199 ICI Trafford Park applied their expertise in scaling up production to an American-developed fermentation process in Trafford Park. (Quirke 2013; Kennedy 1993). On penicillin as the emblem of a New Elizabethan era, see (Bud 1998, 2007).

200 'largest ever': it had 3,000 exhibits (Taylor 1951).

201 'Searchlights' from (Conekin 2003).

202 The Shrapnel article was in *The Manchester Guardian* of 4 May 1951 and has been edited here but the full text is online (Shrapnel 1951).

203 Fiore de Henriquez: (Marsh 2004). Her Festival piece, *The Skill of the British People,* was made of plaster and was probably destroyed afterwards.

204 Unlike Liverpool and many other cities, Manchester held no independent Arts Festival. Perhaps relatedly, the Hyde mural, reproduced by (England 2015), is *way* too ugly to show here. Its painter, Harry Rutherford, was also an early BBC TV star from 1936, sketching variety acts as they performed. According to a Tameside Council history, the producer insisted he remain silent and would not allow a Lancashire accent on the air (Tameside Borough Council 2018).

205 'wirewoman' (Tootill 2009).

206 Ida Fitzgerald: (Lavington 1975). Pankhurst and pre-war women engineers: (Pursell 1993).

207 On a similar transition in the US: (Light 1999).

208 'Bedales' The Hartrees lived at 1 Didsbury Park, with five family bedrooms and rooms for two maids (Froese Fischer 2003); during the war they put up several academic families including the Blacketts.

209 'Chubby': (Froese Fischer 2003)

210 Hartree's biography is (Froese Fischer 2003).

211 Croarken in Hartree's group: (Lindsey 2010); Croarken's history: (Croarken 1993, 1990).

212 Two pianos: (Williams 2006).

213 Harold Jeffreys and psychoanalysis: (Forrester 2018).

214 Some time after moving in and naming all its seminar rooms after men, in 2016 the Manchester Mathematics department named two spaces in its Turing building after Phyllis Nicolson and Hanna Neumann. Neumann arrived in Manchester as a mathematics lecturer at UMIST in 1958, but her husband Bernhard had been a lecturer in the University since 1948: he attended Dorothy Emmet's 1949 seminar on the brain as a computer.

215 On the costs to the British of not valuing female computing labour: (Hicks 2017).

216 The files of Turing's secretary were rediscovered in 2017 and are now catalogued at NAHC/TUR_Add. Simon Lavington has identified her as SJ Wagstaff.

217 'not really' (ATTE p505 and p555). 'Shockable': (ATTE p 587). Popplewell's account was written in 1979: (ATTE p506) and (Campbell-Kelly 1980).

218 The programming manual was rewritten with contributions from Popplewell and Tony Brooker. Popplewell was giving coding courses in 1959: (NAHC/MUC/1/B/4). Popplewell is remembered in the 1960s by Mike Wyld (Lavington 2013), and as teaching users in Argentina how to use a new Ferranti Mercury in the 1960s (Impagliazzo 2006). Popplewell writing *exp* and *sin* routines is attested by Strachey (STRACHEY/C/3/4).

219 Popplewell was born in Stockport in October 1919. Simon Lavington recalls that she retired from the Computing Service in around 1965 when it was decoupled from the academic department. She married in September 1969.

220 Audrey Bates' First: (Lavington 2012). The second machine had been due to go to AWRE for £100,000 (Swann 1975). There is no direct evidence of national security need: FERUT was said to be needed for calculations for the St Lawrence Seaway (Swann 1975) and there was an existing domestic computer project which was failing, but the speed and size of the contract seems suggestive. Canada had no atomic weapons project but was pooling some cryptographic resources with the UK. The machine arrived in Toronto in April 1952; it was Calvin Gottlieb who headhunted Bates to Toronto. The photograph of Bates is in (Pedwell 2017).

221 Popplewell is remembered by her step-family as visiting Canada in 1952, but transatlantic passenger records suggest she instead spent much of 1953 there.

222 This biographical information comes from (DTIC 1979): by 1979 she had changed her name to Audrey Clayton.

223 The equal pay dispute is remembered in (Berners-Lee 2011) and can usefully be read alongside (Hicks 2017).

224 Woods' memory is in (Berners-Lee 2011).

225 Worsley and Turing: (TUR/Add 13 and 92). On Worsley: (Campbell 2003).

226. On the lack of written information about sex: (Bullough 1994).

227 (Brewster 1913).

228 'Mashed potato': (ESHER 26 Feb 1950). Mahler: (Ledermann 2009b).

229 (ATTE p538). Hodges writes that some people were annoyed by this role challenging. Mrs Clayton was presumably working class; she came from a street of terraced houses, Mount Pleasant, a few minutes' cycle away in Lacey Green.

230 Mary Lee Woods' memories (Berners-Lee 2011); John Bennett's: (Bennett 1994).

231 'tin hut': (Berners-Lee 2011). It was in fact a pre-fabricated nursery school largely made of asbestos.

232 'Attractive young ladies': (Sumner 1994). Vera and Tony Brooker were one of the Ferranti marriages.

233 Staff common rooms: (Taylor 1983). Students' Union: (University of Manchester 2017).

234 Burgess: two of the losses were reported in (Burgess 1987) and a third in a Granada TV interview. I'm grateful to Andrew Biswell and Anna Edwards at the the International Anthony Burgess Foundation for this.

235 On the turn to Greek culture as a response to the Wilde trial see (Hall 2012).

236 'Exhibition catalogue': (Bronowski 1951).

237 *On Growth and Form* was circulating in art schools prior to Richard Hamilton's 1951 ICA exhibition (Jacobi 2014). The exhibition ran from 3 Jul to 1 Sep at ICA's first home in Dover St: (Moffat 2000, 2002) and (TGA 955.1.12.26). There was a book produced too, *Aspects of Form* (Whyte 1951), with chapters by Waddington and Grey Walter, which must have been discussed at the Ratio Club. The exhibition catalogue records photographs of various plankton but does not name the organisms used for glass models; some of the contemporary photographs appear to show a *Radiolaria*-like structure.

238 On D'Arcy Thompson's legacy: (Boden 2008a). In the 1930s, Thomson met pure mathematician Lederman in the St Andrew's University Library and, with the words 'Here is a good boy. Come along with me to my house and tell me all about it', got Lederman to write out the answer to his question about differential equations (Ledermann 2009a).

239 Dorothy Wrinch: (Senechal 2013).

240 The Theoretical Biology group (Senechal 2013) had at its centre, as well as Dorothy Wrinch: JD Bernal, who slept with his student Dorothy Hodgkin among many others; Joseph Needham, who would have a lifelong relationship with his student Lu Gwei-djen; Dorothy Needham, who would share her house with both her husband Joseph and with Lu Gwei-djen; Hal Waddington, just going through a divorce; and Joseph Woodger, who seems to have lived an entirely conventional family life in London. One of Joseph Woodger's four children was Mike Woodger, who would become close platonic friend of Turing's in the post-war period after working with him at NPL.

241 'You and I': Polanyi to Wrinch, 1948. Dorothy Wrinch Papers, Sophia Smith Collection, Smith College, Northampton, Mass.

242 Wrinch wrote to D'Arcy Thompson in 1931 that she had at last got her 'biological hypothesis. I am so thrilled. Without your wonderful book I should never have got it. Enclosed is first draft of cytology paper...I do think morphology is electrostatic, don't you?' (Senechal 2013). I've not been able to identify such a paper; at the time Wrinch did publish a number of papers on harmonics on spheroids which could lead to such a theory.

243 'Best cryptanalyst': a personal remark about Joan Clarke by a senior GCHQ figure of the 2000s who gave me a lift after a talk in Cheltenham and whose name I have forgotten. The same figure said that his peers did not consider Turing should receive a retrospective pardon for breaking the law of a democratic state; (ATTE p245).

244 There had been some attempts to explore the mystery. The Fibonacci numbers are very closely related to the Golden Ratio, = 0.61803..., and there had been a few books, more number mystical than mathematical, putting the Golden Ratio at the centre of a harmonious universe. D'Arcy Thomson is dismissive of Fibonacci structure, but his argument for this dismissal is hard to follow.

245 When combined with a mid-distance focus and facial expressions denoting passionate mental effort, discussing Fibonacci numbers is a surprisingly effective courtship strategy.

246 'influential': The 1931 paper, as a text, had no impact on emerging computer engineering, though as the academic discipline of computer science emerged, it became necessary to retrofit Turing indirectly as the 'Father of Computer Science' through this work of mathematical logic (Daylight 2015). Through the 1951 paper Turing was a direct, but distant, founder of a mathematical biology that currently supports a handful of Professorships in the UK alone (Fox Keller 2002).

247 There is no definitive record of Turing's path to the Turing Instability. Gandy remembered being told that Turing wanted to 'defeat the argument from design' (ATTE p543), and Schrodinger's 1941 lecture *What Is Life?* was well known to Turing. Hodges records that Polanyi had explicit objections to the principle of being able to explain embryonic form, and perhaps this goaded Turing into explicit mathematics just as Jefferson had goaded him about machine intelligence. More positively, Polanyi had more or less invented the systematic theory of reaction kinetics, and Polanyi's protégé Meredith Evans pushed his student Noel Hush and Turing together to talk kinetics (Hush 2011); but whatever influence the Manchester chemists had, it has left no formal acknowledgement. There were biologists involved too, outside of Manchester, notably the London neuroscientist John Zachary Young, who had known Turing at least since the 1949 seminar and had a series

of discussions with him during 1949–1951; Young recalled Turing's 'frightening attention to everything one said' (ATTE p548). With the Ferranti Mark I on the way, it was Young whom Turing told that his theory was 'yielding to treatment' (AMT/K/1/78 8 Feb 1951), and Mike Woodger that he was hoping to make progress with the 'new machine' on 12 Feb 1951 (ATTE p551). Another source of ideas was the 'Ratio Club', the London-based group which Turing attended in 1950 and 1951 (Turing 2015). Highly interested in theoretical ideas, this was primarily a biological group, and of all the talks John Pringle's on 'Noise in the nervous system' may have been the closest to Turing's emerging thinking.

248 On the posthumous influence of the Turing Instability, see (Nanjundiah 2003). Both the 1952 paper and the substantial unpublished later material contain a much wider exploration of reaction–diffusion behaviour than the Turing Instability: see (Dawes 2016) and (Allaerts 2003).

249 Bonnet: (Bonnet 1754). ·

250 Memories of John Bennett in (Bennett 1996).

251 'I doubt': (NEWMANM/4/5/1).

252 A more mathematical account of Turing's programme is in my (Swinton 2013).

253 Turing spoke at a Henley conference organised by the Nuffield Foundation (Anonymous 1952).

254 On the Prigogine seminar: (ATTE p586).

255 SEB: (TUR Add/38). Turing also talked 'on fir cones' in Cambridge on 14 Nov 1951 (TUR Add/184).

256 Cannon on Lamarck: (Cannon 1959, 2017, 1960). Cannon on statistical genetics, especially Galton, is (Cannon 1958) cited in (Kraft 2000).

257 Wardlaw's memoir of his wife is (Wardlaw 1971).

258 On the development of biology in Manchester see (Wilson 2008).

259 'A long time' is from Wardlaw's essays collected in (Wardlaw 1968). They include two papers written at the time of the collaboration: the one that Wardlaw had invited Turing to co-author with him as an account of the reaction–diffusion theory (Wardlaw 1953), and another that describes experimental support for the theory (Wardlaw 1954).

260 Botany memories of Turing from (Charlton and Cutter 1986). It's very unlikely that Turing did ever claim 'the existence of a central floret'. Turing was always well aware that the centre of the sunflower is developmentally the youngest and has no influence on the form already laid down in the rest of the plant.

261 Fox Keller (Fox Keller 2002) is perceptive on the biological reception and rejection of Turing's reaction–diffusion theories and the challenges to Theoretical Biology at the time.

262 Bernard Richard's account of his MSc: (Richards, 1998, 2013).

263 'In a University Laboratory': *The Manchester Guardian,* 15 Mar 1955. The byline on the article is Williams, but the language is much closer to Bowden's, and the accompanying photograph is probably one commissioned by Ferranti and still held in the Ferranti archive. The article incorrectly says that the 1948 designs were intended only for 'lengthy calculations of an ordinary kind': other intended uses may have been invisible to Williams.

264 'Ludicrous interpolation': Lord Halsbury in (Bowden 1953); Bowden's strategy and Blackett and PAYE: (Tweedale 1993). Bowden lived in Bowdon (and grew sunflowers there): (Bowdon History Society 1999).

265 Commercial failure of the Atlas: (Gandy 2013). The 'half' machine was a full machine sold to Manchester University well below a commercial price.

266 Strachey's Jungian analysis: (Campbell-Kelly 1985).

267 The use of the Ferranti Mark I for music is described in (Copeland and Long 2017a).

268 'Very bad': *The Manchester Guardian* 4 Jun 1952.

269 Dean of the Faculty of Music: (Kilburn and Piggott 1978).

270 Strachey's draughts as computer game: (Smith 2014).

271 Brief biographies of Christopher Strachey include (Campbell-Kelly 1985) and (Gaboury 2013). Not getting on with Kilburn: (Hendry 1990); (ATTE p557). Music on the Mark I: (Copeland and Long 2017b).

272 Prinz's recruitment to Ferranti was via Eric Grundy, head of the Instrument Department, on the recommendation of the Royal Military

College of Science: (Gandy 2013). Other biographical statements about Prinz are from his daughter Dani Prinz.

273 Logical machines: (Mays and Prinz 1950). Prinz is photographed between the British General in charge of the Sector and Ludwig Erhard, the West German finance minister. The Federal Chancellor Adenauer was also present but declined to play (HNF 2015; Stuart-Williams and Byrd 1951).

274 Turing had earlier developed an algorithm — but not a program — for playing chess; Prinz's work was quite independent and limited to endgame problems: (Copeland and Prinz 2017). 'frivolities': (Copeland and Prinz 2017). Bus timetabling: (NAHC/PRI/C).

275 John Turing's memoir of his brother printed in the Second Edition of their mother's biography (Turing 2012). John Turing was perhaps doubly ignorant: *Pansies* had had struggles with the censor over 'obscene phraseology' (Anonymous 2017) but though the title, a corruption of the French *Pensées,* consciously alluded to homosexuality, most of the subject matter is pretty standard DH Lawrence in the vigour of its heterosexuality.

276 (ATTE p496).

277 'big city scene' from (Weeks and Porter 1998) as cited in Tebbutt (Tebbutt 2006).

278 'worst city' *Sunday Pictorial* 25 May, 1 Jun and 8 Jun 1955, cited in ATTE p580. Drag shows at the Union pub were popular with American troops during the war. (Cook et al. 2007); 'queer gender' identities (Tebbutt 2006): it's noticeable that Tebbutt's principal reference for gay culture in Manchester is Hodges (Hodges 2014, 1983).

279 The Rembrandt and the Union: (Taylor, Evans, and Fraser 1996) p183 and (Cook et al. 2007) p155.

280 'Openly gay clubs' from Whittle and Jones (1994) cited in (Taylor, Evans, and Fraser 1996) p183.

281 (ATTE p540). Hodges interviewed Arnold Murray around 1980 and the account in his book is primarily based on Murray's memory. The encounter between Turing and Murray was remembered as being outside the Regal Cinema, now the Dancehouse, and half a mile south of a more widely remembered cruising area around the Gaumont. Tebbutt (Tebbutt 2006) writes that

the Trafford Bar, within the Gaumont Cinema at the corner of Oxford Street and Portland Street, was popular with gay men and that the adjacent urinal at the corner of Bridgewater Street and Oxford Street was popular for cottaging. Whittle (Whittle and Jones 1994) seems to be referring to the same cinema, but puts the meeting place in the Long Bar of the Odeon, a different cinema 100m further north. The Union Pub that Hodges names is five minutes' walk east from this stretch of cinemas.

282 'small homosexual set': (ATTE p499). This seems to have left no historical record.

283 A brief description of the University's post-war mood is in (Rowley and Lees 2001); wartime licence is recorded for example in (Cook et al. 2007).

284 Personal memories as recounted to me. Reproof for Oxford Road affection: (Pullan and Abendstern 2000).

285 'Gielgud' in (Pullan and Abendstern 2000). Gielgud appeared in court on 22 Oct 1953. When he next appeared in public it was in Liverpool at the premiere of a new play. Thanks in part to his co-star Sybil Thorndike, he received a standing ovation, and the play came to Manchester two weeks later without incident. Although Gielgud's film career was undamaged by the affair, he was personally affected and briefly suffered a nervous breakdown.

286 (Pullan and Abendstern 2000). Anthony Burgess' pre-war observation on homosexuality in student life was that he only felt its 'full blast in the thespian form' (p201) and that 'how the homosexuals got on we did not know. There did not seem to be many of them about' (Burgess 1987).

287 Turing and Murray's meeting: (ATTE p565) from Arnold Murray's memories of a quarter of a century earlier. 'real good stuff' is Turing's description of his fictional counterpart Alec Pryce's achievement.

288 The arrest and trial were reported in the local *Alderley and Wilmslow Advertiser* on 29 Feb and 4 Apr 1952.

289 Stringent condition: (ATTE p582).

290 Shortly after the event Turing wrote that he had estimated the chances of getting into trouble with the law at about 10:1 against: (AMT/D/14a Feb 1952). Hodges rightly emphasises the difference between the tolerance of King's and the intolerance

of Manchester, but I've been unable to find any evidence on my more local speculation one way or the other. US-driven security tightening and increasing prosecutions after 1951: (Hyde 1970).

291 'father-figure' and the account that follows (ATTE p584) is from an interview Hodges had with Max Newman.

292 Cited in passive voice in (ATTE p594).

293 Special number on homosexuality: (Glover, Mannheim, and Miller 1958).

294 From start to finish, the *News of the World* had a contemptible element, but you have to admire the occasional headline (ATTE p597). The northern edition of the *NotW* is not archived anywhere except by News International, who did not make a copy available to Hodges.

295 Hodges has clarified that he was referring to the overall social climate at the time rather than any specific comment of Jefferson or Polanyi.

296 Alexander: (ATTE p594).

297 In 1952, England and Wales saw over 600 men found guilty for 'gross indecency', with 65% being sent to prison. Probation was ordered in most of the remaining cases (HMSO 1956). 'Gross indecency' more or less meant consensual sexual activity between men, whether in public or private. Dermot Turing (Turing 2015) is strong on the medico-legal background to Turing's case. Class status and the trial: ATTE.

298 The specific drugs administered to Turing were probably two different oestrogens – first oestrone by mouth, and later oestradiol benzoate injected under the skin as an oily depot. This latter drug was most likely obtained as Dimenforman from the Dutch company Organon, who may have used the urine of pregnant women as a source. These were the drugs used in the only British publication on male libido suppression at the time. This came from a Bristol hospital (Golla and Sessions Hodge 1949) and was presented as a more desirable alternative to physical castration in cases where a sexual criminal continued to be a social nuisance. Similar treatment was also in use at the Portman Clinic in London, and in the rest of Europe. There are no published reports of experience with the treatment in Manchester; though in the late 1950s the Medical Faculty

of the University were offering a course in 'homosexuality and other perversions' (Pullan and Abendstern 2000).

299 The Wolfenden Report was published in 1957 (HMSO 1957). The submissions, mainly dating from 1954 and 1955, are preserved in the National Archives and were published with a commentary by Lewis (Lewis 2016). The Report is primarily remembered as enabling the 1967 Act which decriminalised male homosexuality, but it was also concerned with (female) prostitution, for which the streets of Manchester had been, for some, notorious. In 1930, AJP Taylor asked himself 'where were the prostitutes who my father said used to line Oxford Street? In all my walks in the city I identified only one...maybe she, like me, just liked walking and was not a prostitute at all'. The Methodist preacher Bill Gowland, who came to the Albert Hall in 1948, though, had no difficulty and spent his Saturday evenings in Piccadilly Gardens 'conversing with prostitutes' (Connolly 2013).

300 Gertrude Jefferson was an assistant psychiatrist at the MRI: *The Manchester Guardian* 13 Feb 1961.

301 In London, similar referrals were being made to a psychiatrist, Dr Mary Woodward, who gave almost all of her patients psychotherapy alone, though a handful were also treated 'with the hormone method'. (Woodward 1958) cited in (Turing 2015).

302 (ATTE p595): 17 Apr 1952 to Philip Hall.

303 'I'm growing breasts' recounted by Norman Routledge to Hodges; 'attractive nurse' Turing to Nick Furbank (AMT/F). The evidence for clinical depression is weak: there are no medical records, and depression is not a word used by Turing's emotionally close friend Robin Gandy. Noel Hush did explicitly use the word depression, but though Hush worked productively with Turing he was not an intimate and this memory was recorded long afterwards, and in particular after Hodges' book had been published (Hush 2011). Moreover, Turing was productive and engaged with colleagues throughout the period of his probation.

304 Hodges interviewed Franz Greenbaum's wife Hilla, and reports that Greenbaum was not considered as very respectable in the Manchester intellectual community because of his Jungian leanings (ATTE p611). Some

say that Lyn Newman prompted Turing to see Greenbaum (Turing 2015), others that it was Ruthi, wife of mathematician Walter Lederman (Ledermann 2009b), but it could also have been a referral via the probation service. Greenbaum was also an NHS psychiatrist at Salford Royal Hospital but the Hall letter (Note 387) suggests his was not the court-ordered referral.

305 'I have had a dream': (AMT/F 10 Dec 1953 to PN Furbank). Greenbaum was also an NHS psychiatrist at Salford Royal Hospital but a letter from Turing to Philip Hall suggests the court-ordered referral was not to Greenbaum.

306 The conversation between Blackett and Stopford is (ATTE p586) and probably a memory of Newman's. Turing's new contract was confirmed at the beginning of 1953 (ATTE p612). Jefferson gave his talk at the Lit & Phil on 5 Apr 1954 (Jefferson 1954). 'Pigling Bland': (ESHER 13 Dec 1948). Lit & Phil election: the co-sponsor was Niel Pearson of the '51 Society (Lit & Phil Council Minutes for 12 Oct 1953). I thank Kathryn Slater of the Lit & Phil for this information.

307 'Turing lies with men': (AMT/D/14a Feb 1952 to Norman Routledge).

308 The significance of the Kjell affair is unclear, and the facts likely to remain mysterious unless made sense of from the Norwegian end or with the release of files from the Security Service. This account is from ATTE (p609, p617); see especially note 8.21, which refers to a loss of a list of names and addresses from within Turing's morphogenesis papers at the time held at AWRE. I believe Hodges is referring here to Nick Hoskin, who was generous with me in discussing the morphogenesis papers he had helped to publish after Turing's death.

309 The Webbs: (ATTE p586).

310 Turing with the Greenbaums: (ATTE p612); 'avoided him' is an unsourced statement (ATTE p585), perhaps from Dai Edwards.

311 Turing agreed to give a talk to the student mathematical society on 15 Jan 1954 and probably stayed with the Newmans afterwards (TUR Add/136).

312 'the news' (ESHER 18 Jul 1954).

313 Hodges has long made a strong and clear case for pre-meditation (Hodges 2016b); Copeland has suggested an accident on slimmer but not dismissable grounds (Copeland 2017b).

314 In 2012 I was delighted to take part in a mass science experiment based in Manchester called Turing's Sunflowers (Swinton, Ochu, and The MSI Turing's Sunflower Consortium 2016).

315 Alan Turing Way: (Kelner 2014).

316 The cipher text is IEKYF ROMSI ADXUO KVKZC GUBJ and Hughes has said it encodes 'Founder of Computer Science': (Wyke and Cocks 2004). A small amount of support came from Manchester City Council but the majority came from individuals. See also (Hejhal 2007).

317 Bowdon *does* have a blue plaque for children's writer Alison Uttley, who additionally gets a second plaque just near Turing in the University as she was also an early female physics undergraduate there.

318 Aphorism 95 of Book I of Bacon's 1620 work The New Organon, or True Directions Concerning the Interpretation of Nature: *Empirici, formicae more, congerunt tantum, et utuntur: rationales, aranearum more, telas ex se conficiunt: apis vero ratio media est, quae materiam ex floribus horti et agri elicit sed tamen eam propria facultate vertit et digerit.*

319 Though both plaques are in essence correct, their brevity means they can mislead in more ways than ignoring each other. The Baby was the first running demonstration of a practical computer memory, but is not universally considered the 'first stored-program computer'. Many computer scientists, most notably the local department, might challenge the idea that Turing is a 'creator' of their discipline. And calling Kilburn a graduate of Manchester is artfully accurate, but his first degree was from Cambridge. His PhD was from Manchester, while Williams's BSc was from Manchester and his DPhil from Oxford.

320 Turing and Newman do have roles, albeit supporting ones, in the historical webpages compiled to support the 50th celebrations by Brian Napper (Napper 1998).

321 Newman was careful, when interviewed in the 1970s, to distinguish what he thought his part contribution to the Colossus had been, but despite his modesty a sense of pride is present. (Newman 1976).

322 'Colossus': (NAHC/MUC/7/18).

323 The engineers are still prominent in (Lavington 2012), although Lavington has recently expanded on the role of Newman's

mathematicians, especially Jack Good, in the initial design and even naming of the Baby. I'm grateful to Lavington for sharing this from his forthcoming book.

324 Williams generous with credit: (Edwards 2010). Kilburn's 'Where I've got the knowledge from, I've no idea' is transcribed in (Bowker and Giordano 1993); Williams 'when we arrived' is from (Williams 1976) as cited in (Copeland 2011b). Kilburn's irritability when asked about the source of the idea of the computer is cited in (Copeland and Long 2017b).

325 'It was as electrical engineers' (Copeland 2017a).

326 Williams and Kilburn split the income on all of the memory patents, which Kilburn was sensitively keen to explain as Williams' generosity. Kilburn's also wrote that Williams had 'handed over his patents to the University allowing it to freely determine how the benefits should be distributed' (Kilburn and Piggott 1978). Lavington's notes of a conversation with Kilburn, available at NAHC/MUC/9/44, suggest that there were substantial sums involved in the patent income, through arrangements which were confidential and are still unclear, and it's a speculation that some defensiveness about these arrangements may have emerged as prickliness about credit allocation.

327 Lavington (2012) places the ray tracing work as occurring in autumn 1949. He suggests the application was probably to lens design for spy plane photography.

328 'The calculations': (Turing 1953).

329 'all night': (ATTE p515).

330 Addressing numerical computation: (Napper 2010, 1998).

331 Newman's and Blackett's response to the use for atomic weapons calculations were recalled by Newman to Hodges, who recalled this orally to me.

332 Hodges suggested some of these dichotomies — without merely simplifying to them — in a talk I saw in Manchester in 2004 which was profoundly influential in the writing of this book. His account of them is at (Hodges 2003). Hodges also points out a further tension arising from a perception in TRE staff like Kilburn, who were not indoctrinated into the Enigma secret, that

wartime Bletchley Park had been a waste of time in comparison with the triumph of radar.

333 'ideas men': recalled by Hilton in (Copeland 2017a).

334 'Engineering research must not be allowed to degenerate into mathematics', typescript for a talk by Williams to the National Physical Laboratory on 5 May 1965 (NAHC/MUC/1).

335 'no time for Turing': (Tootill 2009). At the time Tootill was puzzled by the coldness and he only speculated about this as the motivation in hindsight. Tootill remembers Turing as pleasant and was invited to his house, though he did not know of Turing's sexuality until after his death. 'Broadminded': (Brooker 2010).

336 In 1948 Turing was paid £1,350/year as a Reader and Kilburn £800 as a Lecturer: (NAHC/MUC/2); Kilburn was made a Reader in 1955: (NAHC/MUC/7/1). Kilburn's Ferranti consultancy rose from £200/year in 1951 to £500/year in 1959: (NAHC/MUC/5).

337 'jagged rift': and the mathematician/engineer divide more generally (Sumner 2012).

338 (Brooker 2010).

339 'machines more than programs': (Campbell-Kelly, 1980).

340 'IBM replacement': In 1956 The Board of Trade were acknowledging the view that the US Univac was faster than any British computer for business purposes, and an IBM machine for scientific ones (NAHC/MUC/1/B/1). On Wythenshawe developing large computing centres: (Martin 2013).

341 'Industrial estates': Ferranti later moved some computer production to a subsidiary at Gem Mill in Chadderton. Though Gem Mill is now demolished, and the subsidiary American owned, it still manufactures semiconductors nearby under the name Diodes Zetec.

342 The 'set back by decades' story is second-hand personal information. The computer scientists believed (incorrectly) that Turing had an indifference to programming convenience. Lack of Turing's representation in the Kilburn building: (Sumner 2013).

343 Here are those lines: Turing constructed a pair of coupled nonlinear partial differential equations in a two-dimensional plane. These described the concentrations of two reacting and diffusing chemicals. With the ratio of

diffusion constants as a bifurcation parameter, the system can move from having a globally stable spatially constant state to a variety of patterned solutions. Linearisation of the equation at the spatially constant state yields a dispersion relation, between the wave-number of Fourier modes and their growth-rate, which allows analysis of the emergent pattern. Turing's contribution was not so much this analysis, but the construction of a model that could yield an instability when analysed this way.

344   The colonial worldview of this analogy is based on one that Turing might have possessed as the son of an Indian Civil Servant (cf (Agar 2003)), but greatly exaggerated for effect. Turing mainly used the language of 'growth' and 'poison' but in his own private notes he did once describe a related system he was looking at as 'cannibals and missionaries': it is the missionaries who are the poison here.

345   He didn't, and never used the bicycle bit of the analogy at all: I did. In the talks I started giving in the 1990s, and in print in 2003 (Swinton 2003), I never said that Turing had said anything about bicycles, but it has turned out too good an image not to attach to Turing's name instead of mine (Leppänen 2004; Woolley 2014; Yong 2010; Leppanen et al. 2003; Huw Jones, McWilliam, and Purvis 2011). I am pleased to find my invention thought in good company with Turing's 'comical but brilliantly apt analogies' (Newman 1955), even if a leading textbook (Maini et al. 2016) doesn't credit me. But there is no copyright in a joke analogy and I can be grateful some of these authors at least included unchanged my disclaimer about its imperialist nature.

One of Turing's major followers into mathematical biology, Meinhardt (2013), while sharing my admiration for the 1952 paper, disagrees that Turing consciously used what I call a bicycle mechanism to create an instability at all. He might be right, but this doesn't account for how Turing could have stumbled upon a specific numerical example with exactly this property.

346   Turing had also been thinking about a system extended in space, such as the problem of chain reactions between barrels of gunpowder on a grid. It was this that made Jack Good suspect Turing had had some indoctrination into the atomic bomb programme. Berestykic (2013) suggests the possibility that Turing was aware of Hodgkin-Huxley's reaction–diffusion models for nerve propagation coming out of Cambridge, of which the first was submitted five months after Turing's was. This is quite possible, though neither paper mentions the other while Turing *was* perfectly happy to cite the contemporary biologist Waddington.

347   The first entry by Turing in the logbooks is on 4 Sep 1951 (NAHC/MUC/2C6). As far as I know, no one has tried to check Turing's calculations in Table 1 of his paper; the fact that only some of them were done by computer suggests he may have had hand calculations completed as a way of checking. By 'Manchester university computer' Turing *might* not have been referring to the Ferranti Mark I owned by the University from 1951, but the University-built machine, which had been disassembled in June 1950 and was even harder to program, though this is unlikely given his comment to JZ Young in February 1951 that the model was yielding to treatment but that he hoped to do more when the new computer arrived. Either way it was a remarkable feat: a solution of a nonlinear partial differential equation with minimal development time and in tiny memory.

348   For more mathematical details see (Swinton 2013) and references in (Swinton, Ochu, and The MSI Turing's Sunflower Consortium 2016).

Figure Notes

The author has made reasonable efforts to contact the copyright owner of every image not reproduced under a fair-use exemption. ©HU denotes that the most likely copyright holder has been unidentifiable, or unresponsive at their self-advertised contact details. The absence of a © denotes that the author believes either that the work is in the public domain because of the expiry of copyright, or that it is a work in which any author (JS) copyright is hereby shared under a Creative Common Attribution 4.0 International License. KCC denotes King's College Cambridge. Author and publisher alike are grateful to all those who supplied images and will amend any incorrect copyright statements in subsequent editions.

The front- and end-papers are from the Manchester Chamber of Commerce *1931–1932 Handbook.* ©HU. The city map is signed by Norah Simcock (1907–1960); a version of it appeared in a 1926 *Manchester Guardian* Civic Week supplement, there signed with the initials HM (Wyke, Robson and Dodge, 2018).

Figure 1. (Nicholas and Hellier, 1947).

Figure 2. JS.

Figure 3. Raphael Tuck 'Oilette' series c1905 held in KCC.

Figure 4. Crown ©; TNA FO 366/1059, first published in (Erskine 1986).

Figure 5. ©HU; (HMSO 1951).

Figure 6. (Metropolitan Vickers 1946).

Figure 7. (Dummelow 1949).

Figure 8. ©Estate of Ethel Gabain; Manchester Art Gallery.

Figure 9. Imperial War Museum.

Figure 10. ©HU; JS.

Figure 11. ©HU; (Textile Recorder Annual 1954).

Figure 12. ©HU; (Manchester Chamber of Commerce 1937)

Figure 13. ©Greater Manchester Fire Service Museum. Details of the wash from Bob Bonner of GMFSM.

Figure 14. Manchester Central Reference Library.

Figure 15. Manchester City Art Gallery.

Figure 16. Chetham's Library.

Figure 17. (City Treasurer's Department 1946).

Figure 18. ©University of Manchester Student's Union. Still from Technological Education in Britain, 1961, North West Film Archive.

Figure 19. ©Antonia Cunliffe Davis; English Heritage.

Figure 20. ©The Museum of Transport, Greater Manchester.

Figure 21. (Rowland and Hellier, 1947).

Figure 22. ©DACS; National Portrait Gallery.

Figure 23. ©Estate of Noel Teulon-Porter; p31 of Volume 6 of (Teulon-Porter 1962).

Figure 24. Crown ©; TNA KV/3219.

Figure 25. ©RAF Museum, released under CC-by-SA Creative Commons license; RAF Museum Object 85/I/726

Figure 26. ©St John's College Cambridge.

Figure 27. ©Newman family; NEWMANM/4/13

Figure 28. Crown ©TNA HW 64/59/22. The feet that tripped are memories of Tom Kilburn and Dai Edwards reported by Simon Lavington.

Figure 29. ©Newman family; Cambridge University Library.

Figure 30. NS Roberts, Manchester Local Image Collection.

Figure 31. From Virginia Woolf's photograph album MH3, Harvard University Widener Library.

Figure 32. JS.

Figure 33. ©Newman family; ESHER.

Figure 34. Wittgenstein Archive Cambridge. Via (Sterrett 2006).

Figure 35. JS; The Science Museum Group Y1994.145.2.

Figure 36. ©Graham Floyd.

Figure 37. ©*Illustrated London News,* 25 Jun 1949.

Figure 38. ©The University of Manchester; (MUC/9/62). Lavington dates this to 1952. Norway: (MUC/9/85).

Figure 39. JS.

Figure 40. JS. Based on (University of Manchester 1926) with the 1951 building added. The offices of the Pure Mathematics Professor were on the top floor of the 1872 main building, but their location there is speculative. The applied mathematics Professor,

Goldstein, and his (human) computer were on the ground floor of the Christie Building, not marked (VCA/7/318). The Philosophy Seminar room was planned in 1926 on the ground floor of the Arts Building. I'm grateful to Martin Dodge for supplying a plan of this building.

Figure 41. ©HU; reproduced in (Wainwright 2011).

Figure 42. ©The University of Manchester; provided to me by Martin Dodge.

Figure 43. ©HU. NAHC/FER/C/13b, January 1954.

Figure 44. ©HU; MSI 1996/10/6/15.

Figure 45. ©HU.

Figure 46. ©KCC; TUR/C.

Figure 47. (Nicholas and Hellier, 1947). Relative rainfall from (British Association, 1962).

Figure 48. JS.

Figure 49. JS. The Hollymeade plaque was organised by Andrew Crompton, a University of Manchester lecturer in architecture.

Figure 50. ©KCC; the letter was sold at auction in 2016 but its location is unknown.

Figure 51. ©Ken Howarth; heritagephotoarchive.co.uk.

Figure 52. ©HU.

Figure 53. ©HU.

Figure 54. Freud Museum London.

Figure 55. ©KCC; AMT C/27.

Figure 56. ©HU; NAHC/MUC/5/64

Figure 57. TNA WORK 25/75/B3/D4. Much more detail on the tortoises and the British cybernetics activity they sprang from is in (Boden 2008b).

Figure 58. Crown ©; TNA BW 150/1. Walter also co-published studies of the EEGs of delinquent youth with R Sessions-Hodge, the second author on Golla's chemical castration paper.

Figure 59. Alberto Magnus's *Philosophia naturalis* in (Jefferson 1949b). Jefferson and Emmet are known to have discussed Descartes (LP 19/9/1).

Figure 60. ©The British Society of Neurological Surgeons; Hunterian Museum.

Figure 61. ©HU; LP/17/2. Whitehead: (Emmet 1996); Whitehead's daughter Jessie is on the left.

Figure 62. JS.

Figure 63. ©HU; LP 17/2.

Figure 64. JS. Wittgenstein said, probably unreliably, that when in Manchester he had considered discussing philosophy with Alexander but decided 'no good would come of it' (Emmet 1967, Mitchison 1979, Drury 2003).

Figure 65. ©HU; ancestry.co.uk.

Figure 66. JS.

Figure 67. ©HU; LP/17/6/6/14.

Figure 68. ©HU; LP/17/2.

Figure 69. ©HU; Portico Library.

Figure 70. ©HU; around 1934.

Figure 71. ©Getty.

Figure 72. ©HU; *Discovery*, March 1951.

Figure 73. ©Getty.

Figure 74. ©HU; From *Applications of Ferranti Computers,* January 1957, MOSI 1996.10/6/15/4; the Ferranti marketing article this is drawn from is signed by Ahmed's supervisor, DJC Cruickshank, who did not work on the Manchester machines (Ahmed 2009).

Figure 75. ©IUCr released under CC-SA; IUCr website. Ahmed's estimate: (Ahmed and Cruickshank 1953) cited in (Cranwick 2008).

Figure 76. Crown ©; TNA WORK 25/72.

Figure 77. ©KCC; AMT/K/4; see (Swinton 2013).

Figure 78. ©HU; Midwinter Pottery: (Jenkins 1997); Festival Pattern Group: (Jackson 2008). The plate is from the collection of the late Professor Dorothy Trump. On the atomic bomb underneath Festival imagery: (Jolivette 2014).

Figure 79. ©Antonia Cunliffe Davis. Terylene was developed, under the noses of a much larger research effort by both ICI and foreign companies, by a small group in the Calico Printers' Association, now St James' Building (Kennedy 1993). Cunliffe's childcare advice is at NEWMANL/A/2/Cunliffe.

Figure 80. ©Antonia Cunliffe Davis

Figure 81. Wellcome Collection.

Figure 82. Venereal Disease Visual History Archive.

Figure 83. ©Popperfoto/Getty.

Figure 84. Crown ©; TNA WORK 25/210.

Figure 85. ©HU.

Figure 86. ©HU; MSI Ferranti archive. The knitting shot was used in Ferranti's December 1952 brochure. Neither operator is named. Although knitting was a common private skill for men, Joan Clarke recalled that Turing was unusual in being happy to knit in front of his junior staff during air raids at Bletchley Park (Clarke 1993).

Figure 87. ©Kleboe/Picture Post/Getty; Picture Post 26 Feb 1955.

Figure 88. ©Cambridge University Press (Jeffreys and Swirles 1999).

Figure 89. ©ancestry.co.uk; Sydney Morning Herald, 2 Aug 1959.

Figure 90. Portrait ©Nicolson family; Differential analyser ©British Council. Radioactive basement: (Todd 2008). Computer history mythology for some time wrongly had it that the figure on the top left was atom spy Klaus Fuchs (Lindsey 2010), although Fuchs did recruit Howlett (Howlett 1979) to the numerical computing group at Harwell's atomic bomb programme. Howlett recalls that when he joined the group 'consisted of about eight young people, mostly girls'.

Figure 91. ©University of Toronto Archives.

Figure 92. 1939 ©Stearn and Sons/Archives Lafayette; Girton College Cambridge. 1970 ©HU; Peter Readman.

Figure 93. ©HU; (Berners-Lee 2011).

Figure 94. ©HU; (Campbell 2003).

Figure 95. ©HU; (Wainwright 2001).

Figure 96. ©Cambridge University Press; (Wardlaw 1968).

Figure 97. (HMSO 1951).

Figure 98. ©HU; reconstruction by Museo Reina Sofía, Madrid.

Figure 99. ©St John's College Cambridge; JEFFREYS/H108.

Figure 100. JS.

Figure 101. (Church 1904). Sunflower patterns as investigated by Manchester: (Swinton, Ochu, and The MSI Turing's Sunflower Consortium 2016).

Figure 102. ©KCC; AMT/K3/5.

Figure 103. ©KCC; TUR/C.

Figure 104. ©KCC; TUR/C.

Figure 105. Cannon was wrong and Darwinism was right: (Cook et al. 2012).

Figure 106. Plate 1 of (Haeckel 1914); *Circogonia icosohedra* is redrawn from the type report in (Haeckel 1887) and no taxonomic databases has further reports on it.

Figure 107. NAHC PRINZ/A.

Figure 108. ©Camphill Village Trust; STRACHEY.

Figure 109. ©Camphill Village Trust; STRACHEY.

Figure 110. ©Kleboe/Picture Post/Getty; Picture Post 26 Feb 1955.

Figure 111. JS.

Figure 112. (Manchester City News, 1938); Martin Dodge

Figure 113. ©Hodges; (Hodges 1983).

Figure 114. ©HU. This was one of a dozen films showing at the Regal in December 1952: it is pure speculation that this poster for this film was visible to Turing on the unknown day of the meeting.

Figure 115. @HU.

Figure 116. ©HU; (Sessions-Hodge 1950).

Figure 117. ©Maria Summerscale.

Figure 118. ©Adobe Stock.

Figure 119. JS.

Figure 120. JS.

Figure 121. JS.

Figure 122. ©KCC; TUR/C.

Figure 123. Bonnet: (Bonnet 1754).

References

Adams, JF. 1985. 'Maxwell Herman Alexander Newman. 7 February 1897–22 February 1984', *Biographical Memoirs of Fellows of the Royal Society*, 31:436-52.

Agar, J. 2003. *The Government Machine: A Revolutionary History of the Computer* (MIT Press). 2016. 'Britain's Oppenheimer?', STS Observatory 25 Feb. www.blogs.ucl.ac.uk/sts-observatory/2016/02/25/britains-oppenheimer.

Ahmed, FR. 2009. 'For the love of computers in the 1950s', *Canadian National Committee for Crystallography Newsletter*, 1.

Ahmed, FR, and Cruickshank, DWJ. 1953. 'Crystallographic calculations on the Manchester University electronic digital computer (Mark II)', *Acta Crystallographica*, 6:765-69.

Allaerts, W. 2003. 'Fifty years after Alan M Turing. An extraordinary theory of morphogenesis', *Belgian Journal of Zoology*, 133:3-14.

Anderson, DP. 2004. 'Was the Manchester Baby conceived at Bletchley Park?' *Alan Mathison Turing 2004: A celebration of his life and achievements*, University of Manchester. British Computer Society. 2007a. 'Frederic Calland Williams: The Manchester Baby's Chief Engineer', *IEEE Annals of the History of Computing*:90-102. 2007b. 'Max Newman: Topologist, Codebreaker, and Pioneer of Computing', *IEEE Annals of the History of Computing*:76-81. 2007c. 'Patrick Blackett: Physicist, Radical, and Chief Architect of the Manchester Computing Phenomenon', *IEEE Annals of the History of Computing*:82-85. 2009a. 'Biographies: Tom Kilburn: A Pioneer of Computer Design', *IEEE Annals of the History of Computing*, 31:82-86. 2009b. 'The contribution of MHA Newman and his mathematicians to the creation of the Manchester 'Baby'', *BSHM Bulletin: Journal of the British Society for the History of Mathematics*, 24:27-39. 2010. 'Contested Histories: De-mythologising the early history of modern British computing' in A Tatnall (ed.), *History of Computing: Learning from the Past.* (Springer). 2013a. 'Max Newman: Forgotten Man of Early British Computing', *Communications of the ACM*, 56:29-29. 2013b. 'Patrick Blackett: Providing 'White Heat' to the British Computing Revolution', *Communications of the ACM*, 56.

Anonymous. 'Biological conference at Henley-on-Thames 21st–23rd March 1952'. Nuffield Foundation. 1955. 'Annual Report of Council', *Memoirs and Proceedings of the Manchester Literary and Philosophical Society*, 97. 1962. *Manchester and Its Region* (Manchester University Press). 1995. *Our blitz: red skies over Manchester, a wartime facsimile* (Aurora). 2017. 'DH Lawrence work shows censor battle', BBC News. www.bbc.co.uk/news/uk-england-nottinghamshire-34647492. 2018a. 'Ferranti'. www.gracesguide.co.uk/Ferranti. 2018b. 'Lit and Phil Card Index'. www.cardindex.manlitphil.ac.uk.

Atkinson, H. 2012. *The Festival of Britain: a land and its people* (IB Tauris).

Bennett, JM. 1994. 'Autobiographical Snippets' in JM Bennett (ed.), *Computing in Australia: The development of a profession* (Hale and Iremonger).

Bennett, JM. 1996. 'Ferranti recollections (1950–1965)', *IEEE Annals of the History of Computing*, 18.

Berdichevsky, C. 2006. 'The Beginning of Computer Science in Argentina: Clementina 1961–1966.' in J Impagliazzo (ed.), *History of Computing and Education 2* (Springer)

Berestykic, H. 2013. 'Alan Turing and Reaction–Diffusion Equations' in SB Cooper and others (eds.), *Alan Turing: His Work and Impact* (Elsevier).

Berners-Lee, ML. 2001. 'Mary Lee Berners-Lee, an interview.' Interview by J Abbate. IEEE History Center. 2011. 'Conway and Mary Lee Berners-Lee: Voices of Science.' Interview by T Lean. An Oral History of British Science, The British Library.

Bird, K, and Sherwin, M. 2006. *American Prometheus: the triumph and tragedy of J. Robert Oppenheimer* (Knopf).

Blum, PR. 2010. 'Michael Polanyi: Can the Mind be represented by a Machine?', *Polanyiana*, 19:35-60.

Boden, MA. 2008a. 'D'Arcy Thompson: A grandfather of A-Life' in P Husbands (ed.), *The Mechanical Mind in History* (MIT Press). 2008b. *Mind as Machine: A History of Cognitive Science* (Clarendon Press).

Bonnet, C. 1754. *Recherches sur l'usage des feuilles dans les plantes* (Luzac).

Bowden, RV. 1953. *Faster Than Thought: A Symposium on Digital Computing Machines* (Pitman).

Bowdon History Society. 1999. *Bowdon and Dunham Massey* (Tempus).

Bowker, G, and Giordano, R. 1993. 'Interview with Tom Kilburn', *IEEE Annals of the History of Computing*, 15:17-32.

Brewster, ET. 1913. *A Guide To Living Things* (Doubleday, Page).

British Association, 1962. *Manchester and its region* (British Association for the Advancement of Science)

Brockbank, W. 1965. *The honorary medical staff of the Manchester Royal Infirmary, 1830–1948* (Manchester University Press).

Brooker, T. 2010. 'Tony Brooker interviewed by Thomas Lean.' An Oral History of British Science, British Library.

Bud, R. 1998. 'Penicillin and the new Elizabethans', *The British Journal for the History of Science*, 31:305-33. 2007. *Penicillin: Triumph and Tragedy* (Oxford University Press).

Bullough, VL. 1994. *Science in the Bedroom: A History of Sex Research* (Basic Books).

Burgess, A. 1987. *Little Wilson and Big God* (Heinemann).

Butler, S. 2005. 'Academic Medicine in Manchester: the careers of Geoffrey Jefferson, Harry Platt and John Stopford 1914-1939', *Bulletin of the John Rylands University Library of Manchester*, 87:133-54.

Calvin, M. 1991. 'Memories of Michael Polanyi in Manchester', *Tradition and Discovery*, 18:40-42.

Campbell-Kelly, M. 1980. 'Programming the Mark I: Early Programming Activity at the University of Manchester', *IEEE Annals of the History of Computing*, 2:130-68. 1985. 'Christopher Strachey, 1916-1975: A Biographical Note', *IEEE Annals of the History of Computing*, 7:19-42.

Campbell, SM. 2003. 'Beatrice Helen Worsley: Canada's female computer pioneer', *IEEE Annals of the History of Computing*, 25:51-62.

Cannon, HG. 1958. *The Evolution of Living Things* (Manchester University Press). 1959. *Lamarck and Modern Genetics* (Manchester University Press). 1960. 'The myth of the inheritance of acquired characters', *New Scientist*:798. 2017. 'An essay on evolution and modern genetics'., *Zoological Journal of the Linnean Society*, 43:1-17.

Charlton, WA, and Cutter, EG. 1986. *135 Years of Botany at Manchester* (University of Manchester).

Church, AH. 1904. *On the Relation of Phyllotaxis to Mechanical Laws* (Williams and Norgate).

City Treasurer's Department. 1946. *The City's Finances: a pictorial summary* (Manchester Corporation).

Clarke, J. 1993. 'Letters from Joan Clarke to Professor Tropp, published by Kerry Howard of Bletchley Park Research'.

Coles, J, and Smith, D. 2006. 'The Fifty-One Society: A case study of BBC radio and the education of adults', *Studies in the Education of Adults*.

Conekin, B. 2003. *The autobiography of a nation: The 1951 Festival of Britain* (Manchester University Press).

Connolly, A. 2013. '"He saw the city and wept": the Manchester and Salford Methodist mission 1910-60' in J Wolff and others (eds.), *Culture in Manchester: institutions and urban change since 1850* (Manchester University Press).

Conway, F, and Siegelman, J. 2005. *Dark Hero of the Information Age: In search of Norbert Wiener, the Father of Cybernetics* (Basic Books).

Cook, LM, Grant, BS, Saccheri, IJ, and Mallet, J. 2012. 'Selective bird predation on the peppered moth: the last experiment of Michael Majerus', *Biology Letters*.

Cook, M, Mills, R, Trumbach, R, and Cocks, H. 2007. *A gay history of Britain* (Greenwood World).

Copeland, BJ (ed.). 2004. *The Essential Turing* (Oxford University Press). 2005. *Alan Turing's Automatic Computing Engine* (Oxford University Press). 2011a. 'The Manchester computer: A revised history. Part 1: The memory', *IEEE Annals of the History of Computing*, 33:4-21. 2011b. 'The Manchester computer: A revised history. Part 2: The Baby computer', *IEEE Annals of the History of Computing*, 33:22-37. 2012. *Turing: Pioneer of the Information Age* (Oxford University Press). 2017a. 'Baby' in BJ Copeland and others (eds.), *The Turing Guide* (Oxford University Press). 2017b. 'Life and work' in BJ Copeland and others (eds.), *The Turing Guide* (Oxford University Press). 2017c. 'Tunny: Hitler's biggest fish' in BJ Copeland and others (eds.), *The Turing Guide* (Oxford University Press).

Copeland, BJ, and Long, J. 2017a. 'Computer Music' in BJ Copeland and others (eds.), *The*

Turing Guide (Oxford University Press). 2017b. 'Turing and the History of Computer Music' in J Floyd and others (eds.), *Philosophical Explorations of the Legacy of Alan Turing* (Springer).

Copeland, BJ, and Prinz, D. 2017. 'Computer chess: the first moments' in BJ Copeland and others (eds.), *The Turing Guide* (Oxford University Press).

Cranwick, LMDC. 2008. 'Busting out of crystallography's Sisyphean prison', *Acta crystallographica A*, 64:65-87.

Croarken, M. 1990. *Early Scientific Computing in Britain* (Oxford University Press). 1993. 'The Beginnings of the Manchester Computer Phenomenon: People and Influences', *IEEE Annals of the History of Computing*, 15:9-16.

Dawes, JHP. 2016. 'After 1952: The later development of Alan Turing's ideas on the mathematics of pattern formation', *Historia Mathematica*, 43:49-64.

Daylight, EG. 2015. 'Towards a Historical Notion of "Turing—the Father of Computer Science"', *History and Philosophy of Logic*, 36:205-28.

Desmarais, RJ. 2010. 'Science, Scientific Intellectuals and British Culture in The Early Atomic Age, 1945–1956: A Case Study of George Orwell, Jacob Bronowski, JG Crowther and PMS Blackett', PhD thesis, Imperial College London.

Dodge, M. 2018. 'Healthier modern cities: cleaning the air', *The Modernist*.

Drury, MOC. 2003. *The Danger of Words and Writings on Wittgenstein* (Thoemmes Continuum).

DTIC. 1979. *ADA083756: An Assessment of the Influence of Emerging Social and Economic Trends on the People and Management of the Coast Guard. Volume II.* (Defense Technical Information Center).

Dummelow, J. 1949. *1899-1949*. Metropolitan-Vickers Electrical Company Ltd, Manchester.

Duffy, WN. 1951. 'Ferranti Ltd & The Festival of Britain', *The Ferranti Journal*, 9.

Duxbury-Neumann, S. 2017. *What have the Germans ever done for us? A history of the German population of Great Britain* (Amberley).

Edwards, APJ. 1994. 'Ben Lockspeiser', *Biographical Memoirs of Fellows of the Royal Society*, 39:246-61.

Edwards, D. 2010. 'National Life Stories: An Oral History of British Science.' Interview by T Lean. British Library.

Emmet, DM. 1967. 'Alexander, Samuel' *The Encyclopaedia of Philosophy*. Macmillan. 1996. *Philosophers and Friends: Reminiscences of Seventy Years in Philosophy* (Macmillan).

England, G. 2015. 'Harry Rutherford's Festival of Britain Mural'. www.hydedaily.blogspot.co.uk/2015/01/harry-rutherfords-festival-of-britain.html.

Erskine, R. 1986. 'GC and CS Mobilizes "Men of the Professor Type"', *Cryptologia*, 10:50-59.

Flowers, FA. 1999. *Portraits of Wittgenstein* (Thoemmes).

Floyd, J. 2017. 'Turing on "Common Sense": Cambridge Resonances' in J Floyd and others (eds.), *Philosophical Explorations of the Legacy of Alan Turing* (Springer).

Forrester, J. 2018. *Freud in Cambridge* (Cambridge University Press).

Fox Keller, E. 2002. *Making Sense of Life* (Harvard University Press).

Freud, S. 2002. *Unser Herz zeigt nach dem Süden: Reisebriefe 1895–1923* (Aufbau-Verlag).

Froese Fischer, C. 2003. *Douglas Rayner Hartree* (World Scientific).

Furbank, PN. 1979. *EM Forster: A life* (Secker and Warburg).

Gaboury, J. 2013. 'A Queer History of Computing: Part Three – Rhizome'. www.rhizome.org/editorial/2013/apr/9/queer-history-computing-part-three.

Gandy, A. 2013. *The Early Computer Industry - Limitations of Scale and Scope* (Palgrave Macmillan).

Gardiner, M. 1988. *A Scatter of Memories* (Free Association Books).

Glover, E, Mannheim, H, and Miller, E. 1958. 'Special Number on Homosexuality', *The British Journal of Delinquency*, 9.

Goldstein, L. 1999. 'Wittgenstein's PhD Viva: A Re-creation', *Philosophy*, 74 499-513.

Golla, FL, and Sessions Hodge, R. 1949. 'Hormone treatment of the sexual offender', *The Lancet*, 11 Jun.

Good, IJ. 1982. 'A Report on TH Flowers's Lectures on Colossus', *Annals of the History of Computing*, 4:55-59. 2006. 'From Hut 8 to the Newmanry' in BJ Copeland (ed.), *Colossus* (Oxford University Press).

Goodeve, P. 2011. 'Nimrod'. www.goodeveca.net/nimrod.

Grattan-Guiness, I. 2012. 'On Mathematicians Who Liked Logic: The Case of Max Newman'. In BS Cooper and others (eds.), *How the World Computes*. Springer.

Gwyer, RGB. 1949. 'Editorial', *The Ferranti Journal*, 7. 1950. 'Personal Notes', *The Ferranti Journal*, 8.

Haeckel, E. 1887. *Zoology, Volume XVIII: Report on the Radiolaria collected by HMS Challenger* (HMSO). 1914. *Kunstformen der Natur* (Bibliographisches Institut Leipzig).

Hall, LA. 2012. *Sex, Gender and Social Change in Britain since 1880* (Macmillan).

Heaton, W. 1950. 'The Ferranti Electroencephalograph: what it is and what it does', *The Ferranti Journal*, 8.

Hejhal, DA. 2007. 'Turing: a Bit Off the Beaten Path', *Mathematical Intelligencer*, 29(1).

Hendry, J. 1990. *Innovating for Failure: Government Policy and the Early British Computer Industry* (MIT Press).

Hicks, M. 2017. *Programmed Inequality: How Britain Discarded Women Technologists and Lost its Edge in Computing* (MIT Press).

Hill, GB. 2016. *Alderley Park discovered* (Carnegie Publishing).

Hill, R, and Shuttleworth, N. 2003. *Manchester Marathons, 1908–2002* (Ron Hill Running Enterprises).

HMSO. 1951. *Exhibition of Science, Festival of Britain South Kensington*. 1957 *Report of the Committee on Homosexual Offences and Prostitution*.

HNF. 2015. 'Das Elektronengehirn kommt'. www.blog.hnf.de/das-elektronengehirn-kommt.

Hobsbawm, EJ. 2002. *Interesting Times: A Twentieth-Century Life* (Allen Lane).

Hodges, A. 1983. *Alan Turing: The Enigma* (Hutchinson). 2003. 'Website: Alan Turing Home Page'. www.www.turing.org.uk. 2014. *Alan Turing: The Enigma* (Vintage). 2016a. 'Alan Garner and Alan Turing: On the Road' in E Wagner (ed.), *First Light* (Random House). 2016b. 'University of Oxford Strachey Lecture: The Once and Future Turing'.

Hoffmann, B. 1984. 'The Princeton Mathematics Community in the 1930s. Transcript Number 20.' Interview by A Tucker. Princeton University.

Howarth, K. 1982. 'The "Birth" of the Computer: Tom Kilburn interview at the North West Sound Archive.'

Howarth, TEB. 1978. *Cambridge Between Two Wars* (Collins).

Howlett, J. 1979. 'Computing at Harwell'. www.www.chilton-computing.org.uk/acl/literature/reports/p009.htm. 1993. 'Differential Analysers'. www.chilton-computing.org.uk/acl/associates/permanent/howlett/croaken.htm. 1996. 'Foreword', *Advances in Computational Mathematics*, 6.

Hush, N. 2011. 'Professor Noel Hush, theoretical chemist.' Interview by R Williams. Australian Academy of Science

Huw Jones, D, McWilliam, R, and Purvis, A. 2011. 'Design of Self-Assembling, Self-Repairing 3D Irregular Cellular Automata' in A Salcido (ed.), *Cellular Automata* (InTech).

Hyde, HM. 1970. *The Other Love* (Heinemann).

Jackson, L. 2008. *From Atoms to Patterns: Crystal Structure Designs from the 1951 Festival of Britain*. (Richard Dennis).

Jacobi, C. 2014. 'Kind of cold war feeling' in C Jolivette (ed.), *British Art in the Nuclear Age* (Routledge).

Jefferson, G. 1949a. 'The Mind of Mechanical Man', *British Medical Journal*, 1:1105-10. 1949b. 'Rene Descartes on the Localisation of the Soul', *Irish Journal of Medical Science*, 285. 1954. 'The Search For The Mechanisms Involved in Thinking and Talking', *Memoirs and Proceedings of the Manchester Literary and Philosophical Society*, 95:69-84.

Jeffreys H and Swirles B. 1999. *Methods of Mathematical Physics*. (Cambridge University Press)

Jenkins, S. 1997. *Midwinter Pottery: A Revolution in British Tableware* (Richard Dennis).

Jha, SR. 1998. 'On the Duties of Intellectuals to Truth: The Life and Work of Chemist-Philosopher Michael Polanyi', *Science in Context*, 11.

Jolivette, C. 2014. 'Representations of Atomic Power at the Festival of Britain' in C Jolivette (ed.), *Representations of Atomic Power at the Festival of Britain* (Routledge).

Jones, A. 2004. 'Five 1951 BBC Broadcasts on Automatic Calculating Machines', *IEEE Annals of the History of Computing*, 26:3-15.

Kellermann, EW. 2010. *A Physicists Labour in War & Peace* (Stamford House).

Kelner, S. 2014. 'Manchester was ahead of the pack in honouring Alan Turing', *The Independent*, 28 Nov.

Kennedy, C. 1993. *ICI: The Company That Changed Our Lives* (SAGE Publications Ltd). 2nd edition.

Kermode, F. 1997. *Not Entitled* (Flamingo).

Kidd, A, and Wyke, T. 2016. *Manchester: Making the Modern City* (Liverpool University Press).

Kidd, AJ. 2006. *Manchester: a history* (Carnegie Publishing). 4th edition.

Kilburn, T, and Piggott, L. 1978. 'Frederic Calland Williams', *Biographical Memoirs of Fellows of the Royal Society*, 24:583-604.

Knight, NR. 1999. *Altrincham to Manchester before Metrolink* (Foxline).

Kraft, A. 2000. 'Building Manchester biology 1851–1963: National agendas, provincial strategies', PhD thesis, University of Manchester.

Lavington, SH. 1975. *A history of Manchester computers* (NCC Publications). 2006. 'In the Footsteps of Colossus: A Description of Oedipus', *IEEE Annals of the History of Computing*, 28:44-55. 2012. *Alan Turing and his contemporaries: building the world's first computers* (BCS). 2013. 'Audio Interview: David Howarth and Mike Wylde'. www.chilton-computing.org.uk/acl/technology/atlas50th/p009.htm.

Ledermann, W. 2009a. 'Ledermann on D'Arcy Thompson'. www-history.mcs.st-andrews.ac.uk/Extras/Ledermann_DArcy_Thompson.html#Thompson_DArcy. 2009b. 'Manchester: 1946–62'. www-history.mcs.st-and.ac.uk/Ledermann/Ch8.html.

Leppänen, T. 2004. 'Computational studies of pattern formation in Turing systems', Helsinki University of Technology.

Leppanen, T, Karttunen, M, Kaski, K, and Barrio, RA. 2003. 'Dimensionality effects in Turing pattern formation', *International Journal of Modern Physics B*, 17:5541-53.

Lewis, B. 2016. *Wolfenden's Witnesses, Homosexuality in Postwar Britain* (Springer).

Light, JS. 1999. 'When computers were women', *Technology and Culture* 40(3):455-483.

Lindsey, C. 2010. 'The Hartree Differential Analyser', *Computer Resurrection*.

Lovell, B. 1975. 'Patrick Maynard Stuart Blackett, Baron Blackett, of Chelsea', *Biographical Memoirs of Fellows of the Royal Society*, 21:1-115. 1988. 'Blackett in War and Peace', *The Journal of the Operational Research Society,*, 39:221-33. 1990. *Astronomer by Chance* (Macmillan).

Lunt, TJ. 1947. 'Open Day at the National Physical Laboratory', *The Ferranti Journal*, 5.

Manchester Chamber of Commerce. 1931. *Handbook 1931–1932* (Manchester Chamber of Commerce).

Manchester City News. 1938. A Pictorial and Descriptive Guide to Manchester.

Manchester Corporation. 1974. *Water for the Millions: Manchester Corporation Waterworks 1847–1974* (Manchester Corporation)

Manchester Literary and Philosophical Society. 2018. 'Lit and Phil Card Index'. www.cardindex.manlitphil.ac.uk.

Manchester Luncheon Club. 1947. *Silver Jubilee Commemorative volume* (Privately printed).

Marsh, J. 2004. *Art & Androgyny: The Life of Sculptor Fiore de Henriquez* (Elliott & Thompson).

Martin, CD. 1995. 'ENIAC: The Press Conference That Shook the World', *IEEE Technology and Society Magazine*, December.

Martin, I. 2013. 'Private Places in Public Space: Commerce, Community and Computers in Wythenshawe's Civic Centre'. https://postwarmcr.wordpress.com/2013/04/27/95.

Mays, W. 1952. 'Can Machines Think?', *Philosophy*:148-62. 2000. 'Turing and Polanyi on Minds and Machines', *Appraisal*, 3. 2001. 'My Reply to Turing: Fiftieth Anniversary', *Journal of the British Society for Phenomenology*, 32:4-23.

Mays, W, and Prinz, DG. 1950. 'A Relay Machine for the Demonstration of Symbolic Logic', *Nature*, 165:197–98.

McGregor Ross, H. 2005. 'Finding the Necessity for Invention', *Computer Resurrection.*

McGuinness, B. 1988. *Wittgenstein: A Life. Volume 1: Young Ludwig, 1889–1921,* (Duckworth). (ed.). 2008. *Wittgenstein in Cambridge: Letters and Documents 1911–1951* (Blackwell).

Meinhardt, H. 2013. 'Traveling waves and oscillations out of phase: an almost forgotten part of Turing's paper' in SB Cooper and others (eds.), *Alan Turing: His Work and Impact* (Elsevier).

Metropolitan Vickers. 1946. 'Now for reconstruction'. *The British Trade Journal and Export World.*

Mitchison, N. 1979. *You May Well Ask* (Flamingo).

Moffat, I. 2000. 'A Horror of Abstract Thought': Postwar Britain and Hamilton's 1951 'Growth and Form' Exhibition', *October,* 94. 2002. 'The Independent Group's encounters with logical positivism and searches for unity in the 1951 Growth and Form Exhibition', PhD thesis, MIT.

Monk, R. 2012. *Inside The Centre: The Life of J. Robert Oppenheimer* (Random House).

Moran, J. 2006. 'Milk bars, Starbucks and the uses of literacy', *Cultural Studies*, 20:552–73.

Mosley, S. 2004. 'Public Perceptions of Smoke Pollution in Victorian Manchester.' in EM Dupuis (ed.), *Smoke and Mirrors: The Politics and Culture of Air Pollution* (New York University Press.). 2013. 'Clearing the Skies: Air Pollution Problems in Post-war Manchester'. https://postwarmcr. wordpress.com/2013/04/27/clearing-the-skies-air-pollution-problems-in-post-war-manchester.

Murray, J. 1975. 'A personal contribution to the bombe story', *NSA Technical Journal*, 20:41–6.

Nanjundiah, V. 2003. 'Alan Turing and "The Chemical basis of Morphogenesis"' in T Sekimura (ed.), *Morphogenesis and Pattern Formation in Biological Systems* (Springer-Verlag).

Napper, B. 1998. '50th Anniversary of the Manchester Baby computer'. www.curation.cs. manchester.ac.uk/computer50/www.computer50. org.

Newman, MHA. 1955. 'Alan Mathison Turing', *Biographical Memoirs of Fellows of the Royal Society*, 1:253-66. 1976. "Pioneers of Computing 15." Interview by CR Evans. Science Museum.

Newman, W. 2002. 'Married to a Mathematician: Lyn Newman's Life in Letters', *The Eagle*: 2-7. 2006. 'Max Newman: Mathematician,

Codebreaker and Computer Pioneer' in BJ Copeland (ed.), *Colossus* (Oxford University Press).

Nicholas, R, and Hellier MJ 1947. *An Advisory Plan* (South Lancashire and North Cheshire Advisory Planning Committee).

Nye, MJ. 2004. *Blackett: Physics, War, and Politics in the Twentieth Century* (Harvard University Press). 2007. 'Manchester friends at odds: Michael Polanyi, P. M. S. Blackett and the scientist as political speaker' in JV Pickstone (ed.), *The History of Science and Technology in the North West/Manchester Region History Review* (Carnegie Publishing). 2011. *Michael Polanyi and His Generation: Origins of the Social Construction of Science* (University of Chicago Press).

O'Hanrahan, E. 2018. 'Philosophy at Manchester and Alan Turing'. Unpublished notes.

O'Neill, O. 2018. 'Emmet, Dorothy Mary (1904–2000)' *Dictionary of National Biography* (Oxford University Press).

Parkinson-Bailey, JJ. 2000. *Manchester: An Architectural History* (Manchester University Press).

Partridge, F. 1981. *Love in Bloomsbury* (IN Tauris). 2001. *Ups and Downs* (Weidenfeld & Nicolson).

Pattenden, P. 2006. *Peterhouse Annual Record* (Peterhouse College Cambridge).

Peck, J, and Ward, K. 2002. *City of revolution: Restructuring Manchester* (Manchester University Press).

Peierls, RE. 1985. *Bird of Passage: Recollections of a Physicist* (Princeton University Press).

Perkins, C, and Dodge, M. 2012. 'Mapping the Imagined Future: The Roles of Visual Representation in the 1945 City of Manchester Plan', *Bulletin of the John Rylands University Library of Manchester, 89.*

Proudfoot, D. 2015. 'What Turing Himself Said About the Imitation Game' *IEEE Spectrum.*

Pullan, B. 2007. *A Portrait of The University of Manchester* (Third Millennium).

Pullan, B, and Abendstern, M. 2000. *A History of the University of Manchester, 1951–73* (Manchester University Press).

Pursell, C. 1993. '"Am I a Lady or an Engineer?" The Origins of the Women's Engineering Society in Britain, 1918–1940', *Technology and Culture*, 34.

Quirke, V. 2013. 'The Material Culture of British Pharmaceutical Laboratories in the Golden Age of Drug Discovery (c. 1935–75)', *The International Journal for the History of Engineering & Technology* 79:280-99.

Read, D. 1964. *The English Provinces* (Edward Arnold).

Reader, WJ. 1975. *Imperial Chemical Industries: A History. Volume II 1926–1952.* (Oxford University Press).

Rigby, C. 1948. *John Barbirolli: A Biographical Sketch* (Sherratt).

Rowley, EE, and Lees, C. 2001. *The University of Manchester at War 1939–1946* (Development & Alumni Office, Manchester University).

Rowlinson, F. 1947. *Contribution to Victory* (Metropolitan Vickers).

Salveson, P. 1996. 'Loving Comrades: Lancashire's Links to Walt Whitman', *Quarterly Review,* 14:57-84.

Sargant Florence, P. 1968. 'The Cambridge Heretics 1909–1932' in AJ Ayer (ed.), *The Humanist Outlook* (Pemberton).

Savage, M, and Wolff, J. 2015. 'Manchester: City of Culture' in J Wolff and others (eds.), *Culture in Manchester* (Manchester University Press).

Schofield, J. 2017. *Illusion and Change: Manchester* (MCR Books).

Schurr, PH. 1997. *So That Was Life: A Biography of Sir Geoffrey Jefferson* (Royal Society of Medicine Press).

Schuster, A. 1900. 'The new physical laboratory', *Manchester Guardian,* 29 June.

Schweber, SS. 2012. *Nuclear Forces: The Making of the Physicist Hans Bethe* (Harvard University Press).

Scott, D, and Bent, C. 1984. *Borrowed Time: A Social History of Salford Harriers. 1884–1984* (Salford Harriers).

Senechal, M. 2013. *I died for beauty: Dorothy Wrinch and the cultures of science* (Oxford University Press).

Sessions-Hodge, R. 1950. 'The Treatment of the Sexual Offender with Discussion of a Method of Treatment by Gland Extracts', *Actes du IIe Congrès international de criminologie,* 306-317.

Shapely, P. 2016. 'Post-war housing in Manchester: making the same mistakes?' in R Brook and others (eds.), *Making Post-War Manchester: Visions of an Unmade City* (Modernist Society).

Shapley, O. 1996. *Broadcasting a Life* (Scarlet Press).

Shrapnel, N. 1951. 'Britain as it might be', *The Guardian,* 4 May (republished 2015).

Smith, A. 2014. 'The Priesthood At Play: Computer Games In The 1950s'. https://videogamehistorian. wordpress.com/tag/nimrod.

Spalding, F. 2002. *Stevie Smith: A Biography* (Sutton).

Sterrett, SG. 2006. *Wittgenstein Flies a Kite: A Story of Models of Wings and Models of the World* (Pi Press).

Streat, R. 1987. *Lancashire and Whitehall: The Diary of Sir Raymond Streat* (Manchester University Press).

Stuart-Williams, R, and Byrd, DJP. 1951. 'Das Fliegende Gehirn or "A Bird Grows Wings"', *The Ferranti Journal,* 9:104.

Stuart-Williams, RS. 1951. 'Ferranti Nimrod Computer', *Electronic Engineering.*

Sumner, F. 1994. 'Memories of the Manchester Mark 1', *Computer Resurrection.*

Sumner, J. 2012. 'Turing today', *Notes and Records of the Royal Society,* 66:295-300. 2013. 'Walls of resonance: Institutional history and the buildings of the University of Manchester', *Studies in History and Philosophy of Science Part A,* 44:700-15. 2014. 'Defiance to compliance: Visions of the computer in postwar Britain', *History and Technology,* 30:309-33.

2016. 'Science, technology and medicine' in A Kidd and others (eds.), *Manchester: Making the Modern City* (Liverpool University Press).

Swann, BB. 1975. 'An informal history of the Ferranti computer department'. www.chilton-computing.org.uk/acl/pdfs/swann.htm.

Swinton, J. 2003. 'Watching the daisies grow: Turing and Fibonacci phyllotaxis' in CA Teuscher (ed.), *Alan Turing: Life and Legacy of a Great Thinker* (Springer).

2013. 'Turing, morphogenesis, and Fibonacci phyllotaxis: Life in Pictures' in SB Cooper and others (eds.), *Alan Turing: His Work and Impact* (Elsevier).

Swinton, J, Ochu, E, and The MSI Turing's Sunflower Consortium. 2016. 'Novel Fibonacci and non- Fibonacci structure in the sunflower: results of a citizen science experiment', *Royal Society Open Science,* 3:160091-91.

Tameside Borough Council. 2018. 'Blue Plaque: Harry Rutherford'. https://www.tameside.gov.uk/blueplaque/harryrutherford.

Taylor, AJP. 1957. 'The World's Cities (1): Manchester', *Encounter*.

1983. *A Personal History* (Atheneum).

Taylor, B. 1951. *The Official Book of The Festival of Britain (Advance programme)* (HMSO).

Taylor, I, Evans, K, and Fraser, P. 1996. *A Tale of Two Cities: Global change, Local Feeling and Everday Life*

in the North of England (Routledge).

Textile Recorder Annual (1954) (Harlequin Press).

Tebbutt, C. 2006. 'Beyond the Village', MA thesis, University of Manchester.

Teulon Porter, N. 1962. 'As I seem to Remember'. Cambridge University Library.

The Manchester Joint Research Council. 1954. *Industry and Science* (Manchester University Press).

The Pauling Blog. 2013. 'Dorothy Wrinch'. https://paulingblog.wordpress.com/tag/dorothy-wrinch.

Thomas, D. 2003. *Around Manchester in the 50s & 60s* (Manchester Evening News).

Thomas, T. 2017. 'Recollections of "Magnetic drum" storage for the Mark I'. www.curation.cs.manchester.ac.uk/digital60/www.digital60.org/about/biographies/tommythomas/manchester_drums.html.

Timmins. 1998. *Made in Lancashire: A History of Regional Industrialisation* (Manchester University Press).

Todd, N. 2008. 'Historical And Radio-Archaeological Perspectives On The Use Of Radioactive Substances By Ernest Rutherford.' (University of Manchester).

Tootill, G. 2009. 'National Life Stories: An Oral History of British Science.' Interview by T Lean. British Library.

Turing, AM. 1950. 'Computing Machinery and Intelligence', *Mind*, 59:433-60.

1953. 'Some Calculations of the Riemann Zeta Function', *Proceedings of the London Mathematical Society*, S3-3.

Turing, D. 2015. *Prof: Alan Turing Decoded* (The History Press).

Turing, SS. 1959. *Alan M. Turing* (W. Heffer).

2012. *Alan M. Turing* (Cambridge University Press). Second edition.

Turner, B. 2011. *Beacon for change: how the 1951 Festival of Britain helped to shape a new age* (Aurum).

Tweedale, G. 1993. 'A Manchester computer pioneer: Ferranti in retrospect', *IEEE Annals of the History of Computing*.

University of Manchester. 1926. *The Victoria University of Manchester: a short historical and descriptive account* (Manchester University Press).

2017. 'The old Students' Union'. www.manchester.ac.uk/discover/history-heritage/history/buildings/students-union.

University of Manchester Department of Computer Science. 1998. *The Computer That Changed The World*, *CD-ROM* (Europress)

von Tunzelmann, A. 2014. 'The Imitation Game: inventing a new slander to insult Alan Turing', *The Guardian*, 20 Nov.

Wainwright, M. 2001. *Looking Back: The University of Manchester* (Manchester University Press).

Wardlaw, CW. 1953. 'A commentary on Turing's diffusion-reaction theory of morphogenesis', *New Phytologist*, 52:40-47.

1954. 'Evidence relating to the diffusion-reaction theory of morphogenesis', *New Phytologist*, 54:3949.

1968. *Essays on Form in Plants* (Manchester University Press).

1971. *A quiet talent: Jessie Wardlaw, 1903–1971* (Privately published).

Weeks, J, and Porter, K. 1998. *Between the acts: lives of homosexual men 1885–1967* (Rivers Oram).

Whittle, S, and Jones, A. 1994. *Consuming Differences: the collaboration of the gay body with the cultural state* (Arena).

Whyte, LL. 1951. *Aspects of Form: A Symposium on Form in Nature and Art* (Lund Humphries).

Wigner, EP, and Hodgkin, RA. 1977. 'Michael Polanyi', *Biographical Memoirs of Fellows of the Royal Society*, 23:437-45.

Wilkes, MV. 1968. 'Computers Then and Now', *Journal of the ACM*, 15:1-7.

Wilkes, MV, and Kahn, HJ. 2003. 'Tom Kilburn CBE FREng. 11 August 1921– 17 January 2001', *Biographical Memoirs of Fellows of the Royal Society*, 49:283-97.

Williams, B. 2013. *Jews and other Foreigners* (Manchester University Press).

Williams, FC. 1976. 'Pioneers of Computing 7.' Interview by CR Evans. Science Museum.

Williams, MR. 1997. *A History of Computing Technology* (Wiley).

Williams, RM. 2006. 'Bertha Swirles Jeffreys (1903–1999)' in G Williams and others (eds.), *Out of the Shadows: Contributions of Twentieth-Century women to physics* (Cambridge University Press).

Wilson, D. 2008. *Reconfiguring biological sciences in the late twentieth century: a study of the University of Manchester* (Faculty of Life Sciences, University of Manchester).

Wilson, JF. 2000. *Ferranti: A History* (Manchester University Press).

Woodward, M. 1958. 'The Diagnosis and Treatment of the Sexual Offender', *British Journal of Delinquency*, 9:44-59.

Woolf, V. 1978. *A Reflection of the Other Person: The Letters of Virginia Woolf 1929–1931* (Hogarth Press).

Woolley, TE. 2014. 'Mighty morphogenesis' in S Parc (ed.), *50 Visions of Mathematics* (Oxford University Press).

Wyke, T, and Cocks, H. 2004. *Public Sculpture of Greater Manchester* (Liverpool University Press).

Wyke, T, Robson, B, and Dodge, M. 2018. *Manchester: Mapping the City* (Birlinn).

Yong, E. 2010. 'Spots plus spots equals maze: how animals create living patterns', National Geographic 7 Sep.

Zichichi, A. 2016. *A Lesson for the Future of Our Science* (World Scientific).

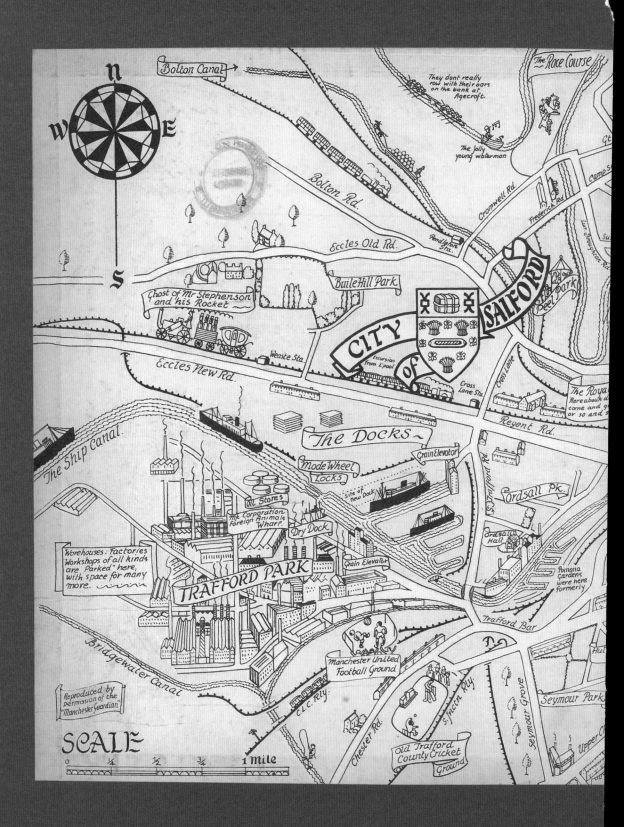

City of Salford and City of Manchester, from the Manchester Chamber of Commerce *Handbook 1931–1932.* See p191.